ICK FACTOR

SEASON OF REVENGE
BOOK 4

MORGAN ELIZABETH

To everyone with the power of the ick.
Listen to your gut: it's always right.

PLAYLIST

Blank Space - Taylor Swift
Nervous - Maren Morris
Glitch - Taylor Swift
I could use a love song - Maren Morris
Run - Maisie Peters
Hits Different - Taylor Swift
False Confidence - Noah Kahan
Shake It Off - Florence and the Machine
Get Busy Living or Get Busy Dying - Fall Out Boy
Caves - Noah Kahan
Guy on a Horse - Maisie Peters
Breakfast - Dove Cameron
bad idea right? - Olivia Rodrigo
Karma - Taylor Swift
What If I Love You - Gatlin
Background Music - Maren Morris
Missing Piece - Vance Joy

A NOTE FROM MORGAN

Hello, my friends!

This book is so utterly bittersweet for me. Tis the Season for Revenge was originally intended to be a standalone novel that with all of your love and adoration, turned into my rom-com inspired series of revenge books.

That book and this series changed my life and helped me meet so many of you. I'll forever be thankful for that. I'm also so excited for you all to finally meet Kat and Theo, the final couple in the Season of Revenge series.

It's also important to note that Katrina is Mexican-American and I had a few sensitivity readers and consultants work with me to make sure I was portraying her and her culture as sensitively as possible.

A few notes: this book stars Theo, who has two parents who have passed away. While this isn't addressed on page, it is mentioned! Ick Factor also features anxiety, cheating (not my MMC), bullying, ADHD rep, death of parents and divorced parents. There is also adult language and explicit sex, including inappropriate use of office space.

Remember to always put yourself and your mental health first. Reading is meant to be our happy place.

I love you to the moon and to Saturn.

-Morgan Elizabeth

ONE

THEO

"Janie had her baby, sign this," my executive assistant, Katrina, orders, shoving a piece of paper into my face within three seconds of me walking into my office.

"Can I sit first?" I ask before taking a sip of the to-go coffee I grabbed on my way to work this morning.

She shakes her head, one hand on her hip as she glares at me.

"No. Sign it. You're already late."

I shrug off my jacket, which barely keeps the East Coast February chill at bay despite the thick wool, and hang it on the coat rack before putting my briefcase on the chair beside the door. When I turn back to face Katrina, her arms are now crossed on her chest and her face is pinched to show irritation I know she doesn't actually mean. She's tapping the toe of her black, patent leather heels and glaring at me.

"I wasn't late; I had a breakfast meeting with an artist," I inform her as if she doesn't already know this. She just rolls her big brown eyes, liberally flecked with gold.

I don't normally notice that kind of thing, the undertones in the eyes of the women I work with, but I'm with Katrina Delgado more than I'm alone. You tend to notice the tiniest things when you spend that much time with anyone.

"And now," she says, her signature sass laced in each word. "We have eighteen million things to do to catch up."

"I always find it so interesting how you say we as if you're going to execute any of these tasks we have to do," I say as I sit down, knowing her response will be entertaining.

She doesn't disappoint.

"Are you fucking joking me?"

Katrina has been working for me for nearly a year, and it only took two weeks for her cordial professionalism to wear off and for what I assume is the real version of her to break through. Polite requests turned into mouthy demands; sweet smiles morphed into her poking fun at me.

I've never had an assistant like Katrina, and I mean that in all the best ways possible.

While it took her little to no time to get accustomed to me, it took me about a month to start poking her back, finding the buttons that would make her nose flare or her eyes roll just for a bit of entertainment in my long, boring days.

It's a strange working relationship we have, but it works all the same.

I smile and shrug at her. "I'm just saying, you always come to me with all of these tasks, giving me shit about deadlines and due dates, but who's the one actually doing the work?" She stares at me with venom in her eyes, and I wonder if this is the moment she snaps.

The moment I take it too far, when she realizes I am way too much work and she doesn't get paid nearly enough to deal with me, despite her healthy salary.

Instead, she says what she always does.

"You would crumble without me, Theo Carter." Her face moves from irritation to smugness.

She's right, of course. I would absolutely crumble without Katrina keeping things here at Catalyst Records organized, and I have no idea how I managed before she came to work for me.

"You're right," I agree, sitting behind my desk and putting my hand out. "Boy or girl?" She hands me the green card with *Congrats!* written in swirling letters.

"Girl. Six pounds, four ounces, cute as can be. I forwarded the announcement to your inbox, in case you want to see." I write a quick note wishing my employee and her new baby all the best before handing it back to Katrina, who is now sitting at the chair across from me, one sleek leg crossed over the other and her iPad in her hand, waiting to give me the next task on her list.

Her job is technically the basics: answering emails, managing my calendar, making sure no one comes into my office to bother me, and other organizational tasks, but somehow, over the past year, she's taken it upon herself to do more.

According to her, she finishes her tasks too quickly, gets bored, and then starts digging, resulting in—

"Blacknote is looking into Monika Devlin," she says. Blacknote Records is our closest competitor and the absolute bane of my existence.

We're both in the business of music, of finding raw talent, polishing it up, and presenting it to the masses to create the next big star. While Catalyst strives to do so in a way that makes the relationship stronger and ensures the artists always retain control of their art, Blacknote doesn't care what happens once they get their end of the check, often signing new, desperate acts into ludicrous contracts exploiting their talent for little to no return.

They also, more often than not lately, get wind of which artist we're looking into, forcing us into a bidding battle that benefits absolutely no one.

Because of that, when I can, I love to return the favor.

"Pull a report on her and have it on my desk by the end of the day, please. Genre, audience, social media reach, and social reaction. Current streams, sales. Anything you can find. Have Garden State

Security run a check, make sure there aren't any skeletons in the closet that could come to light if she gains notoriety," I say, rifling mentally through why Blacknote could want that artist.

From what I remember, she's an indie folk singer, not the easiest to get onto top 40 stations where the bulk of both Catalyst and Blacknote's artists tend to live. It's nothing exciting, but maybe there's something there I don't understand, something Travis, the owner, knows that I don't.

"Already done," Katrina says with a small smile. "It's in your email." See? A godsend. "I'm just waiting on the background check from Zander Davidson. Still think you're the only one who does shit around here?" I smile, and she rolls her eyes before continuing on her early morning check-in.

"Okay, next up, I found out that Steven is accepting PTO donations on behalf of Micheal Shackford." My head moves back in confusion.

"What?" She gives me an *I know* look and shrugs.

"It seems he ran out of PTO days, and his treatment is expected to take another few weeks at least." I blink at her, thoroughly confused. Michael has been out for nearly two weeks, getting chemotherapy and recovering from the rough treatments, but still, this makes no sense.

"What do you mean he's getting PTO donations?"

"Steven set up some kind of program where people can gift one of their PTO days so he can have them. He's collected . . ." She taps something on her screen before looking at me again. "Two weeks so far." I shake my head, irritated by this.

"Put him on paid leave, for the love of God. Indefinitely. Not sure why he isn't already. And make sure the insurance is covering everything he needs. If not, set up a fund for him."

"I thought you'd say that," she says, looking down at the tablet again and tapping a few more times before looking up at me and smiling. "I already was processing the leave. You just need to approve it. I'll call HR today and make sure that's goes through, but Sara is the one who told me what we'd need from you to get it rolling, so it should be fine." I nod and sigh, irritated anyone who works for me would think instead of talking to his manager, he would need to take donations.

But still, it's a testament to the people we've collected here that they're willing to help out a coworker that way.

My father and Jeffrey Banks started Catalyst Records with little more than an idea and a couple of demos, and even though the company rapidly grew with its very first client going multiplatinum in a year, we've always valued the community of employees helping the business to grow. We consider everyone here to be family and treat them as such.

At least, most of the company does.

"And everyone who was donating PTO, match it so they have double. Anyone willing to step up deserves to know we appreciate it." Katrina smiles, as if she approves of my decision, then scribbles something on the screen with a digital pen.

"Got it. You have a call in," She looks at the ever-present watch on her wrist and then at me. "Thirty minutes with Meg Wilson about her next record—she wants to go a new direction but development is giving her a hard time, so we might need to step in and have a conversation with them—and the monthly board meeting is at one. The meeting agenda is in your inbox, and a printed copy is on your desk."

It's sitting next to me with a hot pink sticky note on it, with a few sections highlighted. Clipped behind the printout will be any numbers, charts, and information I need to speak on at the meeting, neatly matched up and color-coordinated with the agenda so I can easily find anything I need. I sigh and lean back in my chair.

"You're invaluable, Katrina," I say, my tone serious.

"I know," she says with a smile and a wink before leaving my office and walking toward her desk, a bouncer allowing only the right people in throughout the day. I stand and lean on the doorframe, looking at her, and she pulls open the drawer of her desk where she stores all of her snacks.

The woman rarely stops long enough to have a meal, instead pulling from her drawer all day long. When she first started here, I was worried she had too much on her plate and was unable to find time. I confronted her about it, but she just laughed, telling me she would rather snack all day than sit still for that long.

"Keeps things exciting," she said with a smile.

Now, she grabs a mini bag of pretzels, the packaging squeaking as she pulls the sides open and pops one in her mouth before turning to me, somehow knowing I'm staring at her.

"You know, one day, you're going to get a much better job and leave me, and I'll be fucking stuck trying to figure this out myself."

"Not likely," she says. "I'm drowning in student loans, and no one pays nearly as well as you do."

"Why do you bring that up all the time?" Her smile goes wider.

"I just need you to know my true motivation for being here, since it's not your glowing personality." I smile in return and shake my head as Warren Michaels walks into the building, waving at everyone like he owns the place.

I force my face to remain neutral as I always have to do around him, but Katrina fails. I watch as she looks at the time on the screen of her computer and lets out a sound of irritation. It's 10:30, and I'm pretty sure, unlike myself, Warren was not at an early morning meeting.

"You hate him, too?" I ask because she's never actually said it out loud, one of the few opinions she's kept to herself. But even if I hadn't just seen the face she made, I've had a hunch for months that my assistant hates the director of A&R as much as I do.

"How do you know I don't like him?" She looks at me in shock, and I shake my head.

"You wear your emotions very clearly on your face, Katrina." Her expression shifts to one of utter irritation, and it makes me laugh.

"That is absolutely not true. I'm a great liar." Her desk phone rings, and she turns her body toward her desk but doesn't stop glaring at me.

"Keep telling yourself that, Katrina."

"Kat!" she says like she does just about every day. "Everyone calls me Kat."

"And I call you Katrina," I say, walking into my office while she answers her phone, ready to start the day.

TWO

THEO

"And for our last topic of the week," Jeff Banks, the current president of Catalyst and my father's best friend since college, says, putting his hands onto the polished dark wood of the table in the boardroom. The last item on the agenda has held my attention since I skimmed it as I sat down.

Right at the bottom, there is a bullet point with no text beyond it. Sure, it could just be a mistake, but mistakes like that are rare, if not impossible, for Jeff.

"I've been thinking for months about how to have this conversation with all of you, and even longer trying to figure out *when*. But I'm getting old, and I'm tired of fighting with you assholes," my mentor jokes. Everyone chuckles, but I don't.

I'm not sure if I even breathe at the moment. To everyone else, that might just be another funny joke from Jeff Banks.

It's not to me.

Jeff Banks has been the sole president of Catalyst Records since he was handed the torch when my father died when I was 16. They were best friends, built the company from the ground up together, and when my parents passed unexpectedly in a car accident, Jeff took over not only the business, but raising my sister and me.

There has never been a doubt in my mind I would one day run the business my father helped to build.

Seven years after his death, I graduated college with a smile, a firm hug, and a *can't wait to run the world with you, son* from Jeff. Since then, I've always known one day, he would retire, and when he did, he would suggest I take his place as president. While the board would have the opportunity to vote for someone else, it would be a mere formality, seeing as I've been fully employed here since college, starting at the bottom and diligently climbing to the top until I was named vice president last year.

My entire life is Catalyst. I've spent every waking moment of 13 years learning the industry, gaining contacts, and building the business in my father's name.

"I'm sure it won't be a surprise to most of you, but I'll be retiring at the end of Q3." Men and women around the table nod in agreement with mumbled congratulations and *we'll miss yous*, but my stomach sinks.

It's at this moment, I realize something is horribly wrong.

Everyone is taking Jeff's announcement as if this is *expected,* and not because *he's getting old*. As I look around the conference table, the realization hits me square in my gut: the board knew this was coming, and not in an *inevitable* kind of way.

In a *Jeff told me personally weeks ago that he'll be announcing his retirement soon*, kind of way.

And I, the closest thing he has to a son, the son of his best friend and co-founder of this company, *did not know*. In fact, this is the first time I've heard of more than a whisper of retirement.

"We'll be sad to see you go, Jeff," I hear a voice say through my rolling panic, and even though I shouldn't—I really fucking shouldn't if I want to maintain my sanity and not make my blood pressure rise to an alarming rate—I look.

Warren is sitting in his chair, leaning back and congratulating

Jeff, but it isn't Jeff he's looking at. His eyes are solely focused on me, taking in every solitary reaction and shift of my body with a smug look on his face.

Unlike me, it seems Warren knew Jeff would be announcing his retirement soon.

There was once a time when I considered Warren to be my best friend. We attended the same college, both studying business so we had most of our classes the first year together. I went to school in New Jersey, a state Warren was not from, so on weekends, when I'd go to Jeff's for dinner to see my sister, I'd bring him along. Quickly, he morphed into the little makeshift family Jeff and his wife, Judy, had helped us make. But it didn't take long for things to go sour, for every moment with him to feel like a competition.

Small things started to happen, like when he started dating my college girlfriend a week after we broke up, or when I didn't get any of the preferred classes we picked out together and he got *every single one*. And even when I *did* question things, Warren would wave it off with explanations that always made so much sense, a master manipulator even then.

Finally, my senior year, we had a class together. He told me he was struggling with our final project, which I had already finished, so I sent him mine to show him how I had organized the information we'd been acquiring all year. He thanked me profusely, but when he had to present before me, I saw what he had done. Instead of using my project, which had taken weeks to do, as inspiration, he simply took my name off and used it as his own.

After class, he told me it was all a mistake and he didn't have a choice, saying his project was accidentally deleted and he froze, but that was the moment the blinders were taken off.

I saw our friendship for what it really was.

Because the reality was, Warren, the spoiled rich kid who was given everything his entire life, hated me with a vehemence that made no sense but burned through him all the same.

I had to stay up for three days straight, slapping together a new project. I lost my perfect GPA, and the rushed project barely allowed me to pass the class.

Warren graduated with a 4.0 though.

I made the mistake of telling Jeff about what happened, only to learn Warren had already told him the entire story, embellished with lies and apologies I know in my gut he didn't feel—apologies he never even bothered to give me. Jeff asked me to forgive him, to remember it was just a silly little mistake, that none of it impacted me *that* much since I already had a job lined up at Catalyst.

A fissure started that night in my relationship with Jeff, Warren becoming a constant wedge between us, especially when Warren began working at Catalyst three years ago. Suddenly, we were coworkers and competitors at every turn, and I no longer had the illusion of us being friends.

To this day, any issue with Warren I bring up to Jeff is gently and subtly accredited to the "mix-up" in college, so much so I no longer even bother to say anything. It's to the point that I've begun to wonder if he's not right, if I'm not just bitter and angry about what happened all those years ago, about our failed friendship.

And while he might not be my favorite person on the planet, I've always respected him at work, and now that he's dating my younger sister, Savannah, I am personable when I'm forced to see him *outside* of work. I was under the impression with them dating, we were under some kind of unspoken truce for her benefit. Except, now the man is smiling at me, an evil glint in his eyes, like he knows something I don't.

"Appreciated, Warren. Now, as many of you know, this company was started by my best friend, Teddy Carter, and me. When he tragically passed, I was voted in to take it over completely." This should make me feel better, the reminder that this is *my father's business*, but the look Warren is giving me like he already won . . . "And I won't be changing that history. At the end of the quarter, the board will come together for the annual meeting and will vote on who will take my place."

"We all know who you'll be voting for," Jim Clayton, one of the older board members, says. The man watched me sit in my father's office on *Take Your Child to Work Day*, not participating in any of the activities set up for the kids, but instead sitting at the small desk my father kept in there for me, tapping on a calculator and pretending to take notes, eager to emulate my idol.

I've always wanted to be my dad—there was never a time in my life when I didn't know in my heart of hearts, I was meant to run this company.

This job was always meant to be mine.

Except, the person who has the most sway with the board currently is refusing to meet my eyes before he responds, the final nail in my coffin.

"I won't be putting my support behind either candidate," he says. "To avoid any issues with nepotism or favoritism, I'll be sitting the vote out."

Murmurs rip through the room, people whispering about my father, about Jeff, probably about a hundred other things, but that's not what my brain latches on to.

Either candidate.

Either candidate.

Either. Candidate.

Either.

Candidate.

"On June sixth, we'll be voting to nominate Theodore Carter or Warren Michaels to the president of Catalyst Records."

I don't vomit until I get back to my office.

THREE

THEO

It takes a full three days before I work up the courage to walk into Jeff's office, though nausea rips through me at every single moment during that time.

From anxiety.

From disappointment.

From paranoia.

Anger.

Fear.

"I thought you'd be here Monday," Jeff says when I take a seat across from him. He's leaning back in his chair, his fingers laced together and lying on his stomach as he looks at me expectantly. "I didn't think you'd put much time between the meeting and this. Even told Diane when you came to let you right in. I'd reschedule meetings." I nod, trying to think of how to respond.

"I, uh," I say then pause. "I needed some time to collect my thoughts."

"That's fair," he says then waits for me to expand.

I had an entire well-thought-out conversation planned in my

head. What I would say and what Jeff might respond with, a million variations, and how they would each play out.

Much to some people's surprise, I'm not vice president because of my relationship with Jeff or who my father was. It's because I'm fucking *good at this job*. It's in my blood, in my bones, a position I was born to be in. I take in the reactions of others, plan out what they'll say and what will happen next, and craft my responses accordingly. The ability to find talent, that's easy. The ability to find talent and convince them to sign with your company, to convince the board to take a chance on an artist, to convince the radio stations to play their songs . . . that requires anticipating everyone's next three moves and being able to pivot when needed.

I'm *never* caught unaware. Never put in a position I wasn't prepared for.

That is, not until now.

"I'm not gonna lie, Jeff, I was a little surprised at Monday's meeting," I finally say. He sighs and closes his eyes, and I look at him. *Really look* at him. When I do that, I can see things I've been ignoring.

He's in his late sixties, once dark black hair long turned gray, the lines on his face deeper than I remember. The circles under his eyes are darker, like no matter how much sleep he gets, they won't disappear.

Jeff looks tired.

Old.

Something happens when you grow up with someone, where your mind pictures them forever locked in some moment, some vital age. Because of that, they are never changing in your mental image even if you see them regularly, even if the changes are happening right before your eyes. Somehow, despite my ability to reach people, I've missed Jeff getting older.

Or maybe I just didn't want to see it, didn't want the evidence of it happening.

Jeff laughs self-deprecatingly. "I know, son." His words cut a bit, and I'm hit with reminders of the way he's always called me son. Even when my father was alive, he called me son, like I was some kind of joint child of theirs, like not only did they share a business, but a family.

He's always felt like a father, too, especially after mine passed and he was all I really had left of him.

"I tried so many times to tell you," he says.

"Did you, though?" I ask, the anger and hurt leaking into my words when I vowed to keep them bottled up and out of this conversation. To keep it professional and business-like.

My logical side knows Jeff is allowed to run his business how he sees fit, despite whatever familial relationship we may have.

"Because to me, it looked like every person in that fucking room knew you would be announcing your retirement. They seemed to expect it. And there I was, a fucking idiot, blindsided."

"You knew I'd be—" he starts, but I've already broken the seal of my anger, it now flowing freely into my words, into my bloodstream.

"Do not act like you don't know what I'm talking about," I say, leaning forward. "Do not do me the disservice of pretending I'm speaking out of my ass." He sighs, looks out the window, and finally answers me.

"You know, I tried. So many times. Tried to tell you my time was coming, but I just . . . Each time, I couldn't do it." Once again, we fall into silence, but this time it's Jeff who breaks it with a forlorn shake of his head. "You look so much like your dad, you know. Each day, you're more and more like him. Sometimes, I walk into this building and see you and for a split second, I think it's him." His eyes shine with sorrow, but I fight the compassion I want to show him. "Gives me a heart attack every time. Looking at you, telling you I'd be retiring and that I wasn't going to back any of the candidates? I couldn't do it. It's selfish, but I couldn't do it, not one-on-one, not with Teddy staring me down."

Teddy.

I'm technically Theodore James Carter Jr, named after my father.

He was always called Teddy, and even though people would try, the only ones who were allowed to call me Teddy were my mother, father, and sister. Everyone else calls me Theodore.

Now that my parents are dead, it's just Savannah.

Teddy was my dad, and my dad is gone.

"Yeah, let's talk about that, Jeff," I say, skipping right past anything that might make me feel a pinch of sympathy for the man. "Let's run *right* past you not giving me the basic courtesy you gave random coworkers and move to the fact you're not going to put your backing behind me." He looks at me, and in his eyes, I can read his desperate need for me to understand.

"I want things to be fair, Theodore. That's how your dad would want it. How you would want it in any other circumstance."

"Fair? *Fair?* Jeff, I want this place to still be *fucking functioning* in five years. We both know I've been working my *whole fucking life* for this. And if this place goes to fucking *Warren Michaels*, it's done. Your legacy is trash. My father's legacy? Gone. How's *that* for fair?" My chest is rising and falling heavy with each breath, any shred of control obliterated. Gone is my usual calm, emotionless facade.

"Warren is extremely qualified to run his business, even if you refuse to admit that. He would not destroy your father's legacy."

I fucking disagree, but I know arguing is hitting a brick wall. But still, I can't resist questioning him as I run my hand through my hair, slumping in the chair across from him.

"Warren, Jeff? Really? That's who I'm up against?"

"I'll never understand why you have such tension with him," he says with a sigh.

"You have no idea? No idea. Really, Jeff?"

"I know there was that mix-up when—"

"Jesus, fuck, open your eyes! This has nothing to do with my personal opinion of the man. *Everyone here hates him,* Jeff. He's bad for the company. All he cares about is the fucking bottom line and making himself as much money as possible, and we both know that's not how Catalyst works. That's not how it was *built* to work." My stomach churns again at the idea of Warren coming in and destroying my father's legacy, the company he worked for until the day he died to build into something that would benefit *everyone*, not just the board.

"The board—" Jeff starts, but I cut him off, leaning forward in the chair across from his desk. Rage and irritation are filling my veins, and I think even Jeff is surprised to see it. I usually have such a painfully tight grip on any kind of emotion while in this building, working to recreate the neutral, level-headed persona, just like my father always had.

"Fuck the board!" I say, my voice going louder. "Fuck them. I'm talking about the people who keep this place fucking *running*. The *employees*. And the artists! They all hate him. He doesn't have his head all the way up their asses like he does for the board, so they see him for what he is. All those coincidences you keep ignoring, things going missing. Blacknote getting leads on artists we've been working on for months, stealing them out from under our noses. You don't think it's strange how everything he works on, everything *I* work on, suddenly they know about?"

"I don't think—" I'm on a roll now, unable to stop the flow of words coming from my mouth, all of the things I've bit my tongue on because I know Jeff believes the best in just about everyone.

"And what about all those board meetings where his first instinct is always to cut back on employee programs in order to have a bigger payout for the board? Of fucking *course,* they like him—he's going to make them a fuck ton of money if he gets the ultimate right of veto. And it's going to be at the expense of the community we've built, that my *father* built." Jeff shakes his head with a sigh like I'm a child throwing a tantrum instead of the vice president of this company bringing up incredibly valid concerns.

"He wouldn't—"

"He would, Jeff, and you know it. He's done it before. Mistake or not, I didn't graduate on time because of him and—" Now it's Jeff's turn to cut me off, his arms crossing on his chest.

"At the end of the day, Theodore, this is why," Jeff says, his voice going firmer. "This is why I'm not comfortable with putting my full backing behind you. You take these long-dead grudges and let them rule you. So you two had feuds as kids. Who doesn't? Do you think I haven't had my moments with Rick O'Connor? Or Ray Harmon? That we haven't gotten into *screaming matches* over the years and then had to smile and shake hands at the next meeting?"

My brow furrows in confusion because I *didn't* think that. I was always under the impression Jeffrey Banks got along with everyone, that everyone at Catalyst just . . . agreed with him.

"And not for nothing, but you were the first thing Warren asked about when I told him you two would be the front runners for the president position."

"So you spoke with him about it, spoke with him about *me*, but let me be blindsided?" I ask, that same fury and hurt mingling and mixing, a toxic brew of emotions in my chest, but he ignores me.

"I told him I'd be retiring and letting the board vote on who would be best suited for the president position, and the *first thing he asked* was, what about you? How would you take it when you found out? I told him you always put the company first." He raises a brow as if to say *and look at how you're acting*. "And that no matter what, you'd work with whoever to make this company and the community we serve flourish."

Bullshit. *All bullshit.*

"In fact, when I asked him if he would be interested in being considered for the president position, he told me he thought you'd be a great fit for the company." I open my mouth to argue that I *should* be the best fit, but he continues, "But he would love the opportunity to run Catalyst Records if the board found him the best fit."

This is Jeff's problem. It has been for years and is the reason we keep losing potential clients, why we can't quite seem to get the jump on the biggest talents before they blow up.

He plays business rules from 40 or 50 years ago, assuming hard work and determination are good enough, that all men will be *good* men. That everyone here has good intentions, but that's not how it *works*.

It's not our reality.

Instead of telling him that, I ask him a question that, on a bad night, keeps me tossing and turning, trying to understand and dissect his true intentions. "Don't you think it's strange that he spent ten years working with our number one fucking rivals—"

"Blacknote is not our rival, Theodore—" That's a lie, and he knows it.

"They either steal clients right out from under us or pick up every single one of our artists' *direct* competition, Jeff."

"There is no competition in music. You know people are always looking for a new song, a new album, a new artist to obsess over. There is no limit."

"Listen to yourself! My god. Of *course,* there is competition. Yes, the public has an unending ability to accept new artists, but there is only one GRAMMY given each year for record of the year. There is only a finite number of spots on the top 40 charts. They snatch up the direct competitors of our artists then use the exact same marketing plan to sell them. Don't you see how that's a *problem?*" I shouldn't even bother really. This conversation has happened so many times by now, repeated over and over until I'm blue in the face and my blood pressure is sky-high.

Jeff Banks is stuck in his ways, in his beliefs that people mean well.

"That's business, Theodore. Not everything is personal."

"So you're saying it's not strange Warren left a more prestigious position with more pay and came to Catalyst three years ago when the director of Artists and Repertoire position opened?" *Because I vacated it,* I don't add.

"He'd been talking to me for some time about moving to Catalyst but didn't want to kick anyone out of their job."

I ignore the lie Jeff clearly bought from Warren.

"Not to mention, when he started here, he sold off all stake in

Blacknote."

"He goes golfing with Travis Lane once a month!"

"He's free to have friends. He's free to have a *life*." His eyes widen, and his head tips in a challenge, and I realize it then.

There it is.

The cut I've been waiting for, the other shoe to drop.

It's not just him wanting to step away from the responsibility of putting too much sway behind me, of influencing the board's decision that has him hesitant to put his backing behind me.

It's more.

It's the same thing he talks to me about once a quarter, a gentle reminder that he's not fond of how I live my life.

Except he's taking the kid gloves off now and threatening the future of this business to . . . what? Teach me a lesson? Prove his point?

"Your problem is you're so wrapped up in your imaginary competition with Warren and in this business, you have no life." He shakes his head, and I know he's about to launch into the same conversation I've heard many times before.

"When you were born, your father made me promise to take care of you and, later, your sister if anything happened to him. I thought it was a joke, an agreement you make with a friend who is more like a brother. Never thought it would become reality. And your father . . . god, he loved this business. Fucking loved it. It was his life's dream, running this place. That man put his blood, sweat, and tears into it, worked nights and days and weekends until he was so tired, he had to take a cab home because he couldn't trust himself to drive. And that was on the nights he didn't just sleep at the office. But as soon as he met your mother, things changed. He shifted his priorities, found that balance, and when he thought I wouldn't, he pushed me, gave me shit until I found it." A soft smile comes across his face. "I don't think I'd have Judy if it weren't for your father. You know, he threatened to convince the board to let me go if I didn't take time to find someone, find time for a life. And I'm grateful he did."

I know all of this.

None of it is news to me. I know that my father met my mother and realized he'd been missing something in his life. They wanted the same for his best friend, who was just as much of a workaholic as he was.

"Your father wouldn't want this for you. He wouldn't want that life for you, working nonstop, having no social life. I know if I put my backing behind you, the business would be yours, and if that happened, nothing would ever change. Your father would never forgive me for that. If he were here, he would be so fucking worried, seeing you living like this, Theodore." He pauses, and I try not to speak impulsively and say something I might regret. He leans forward, reaching across his desk and touching my hand resting on the dark mahogany. "*I'm* worried about you. All you do is work."

"Someone has to, Jeff. Someone has to keep the place running," I say. He shakes his head, his eyes looking mournful.

"You know that's not true. An entire workforce makes this place run." I open my mouth, unsure of what I'm going to say in rebuttal, but he cuts me off. "I'm afraid to hand off Catalyst to you. I'm afraid of what it would mean for your future. You live for nothing more than work." He shakes his head. "Your father would hate this for you, and he would hate me for not stopping it before it got to this point." My teeth grind, and I grit out my next words.

"I'm not some kind of fucking hobbit who never leaves the house, Jeff." He laughs.

"Oh, I know you leave your house, trust me. To come *here*. Or to go to meetings. That's it." I groan, my head tipping to the ceiling with frustration.

"That's not true." *And even if it was, what would it fucking matter?*

"You get to work before me and leave long after me," he accuses.

"And? Isn't that a fucking *good* quality?" I ask because I thought that was what I was *supposed* to be doing: working my ass off, growing this company. This business is the one real thing I have left of my father other than increasingly fuzzy memories and a handful of photos.

Even then—all of those memories take place here, in this building, watching my father build his dream from the ground up.

"You need to live," Jeff says.

"I do live!"

"When was the last time you hung out with friends?" My face screws up in confusion, but Jeff's stays serious.

"I don't see how that—"

"You haven't dated in years," he says, speaking over me. I open and close my mouth. "Your father would want you to have someone in your life. He lived for your mother—the sun rose and fell with her in his eyes. He would want that for you."

Saying I haven't dated in years is a lie, of course. I've *dated*. I've never gone to a work event without a woman on my arm, and Jeff knows that.

Granted, has it gone beyond a night or two together or a few cordial dates?

No.

But what the fuck does that have to do with my ability to lead a company?

"And while that's not something that indicates you'll do a great job leading this business," he says, like he can read my mind. "I can't in good conscience hand over the business to Teddy's son knowing he's going to sacrifice a relationship, a potential family of his own, in favor of this place." He shakes his head.

There are so many things I could say in this moment.

So many things I *should* say.

Maybe something about how my father would just want me to be happy.

Or how my father did, in fact, put his blood, sweat, and tears into this business, and he didn't do it so Warren fucking Michaels could take over and destroy it.

Maybe something about how when the time is right, I'll find the right person, how that's not something that should be rushed. How my father wouldn't want to force me into a relationship, a marriage, a family. How, if he were alive and I told him that wasn't something I wanted, he would accept it—and I honestly believe that to be true.

Despite what Jeff might think, I've also often thought of how my father would view my work-life balance. He'd wish I would settle down, find love and family like he did with my mother, but I also know to my bones, he would just want me *happy*.

And I'm my happiest here, working, growing my father's legacy.

But I don't say any of those things.

Instead, I say the absolute stupidest thing I could possibly say.

"I'm not single, Jeff," I blurt without thinking, the words flying from my mouth without passing through my mind, as if I've been possessed.

As I say it, I instantly begin to panic. I feel it taking over completely, starting in my chest and creeping out until I'm one big mass of hysteria.

What the actual fuck am I doing?

The panic grows as Jeff's face morphs into something new, a kindness and intrigue and maybe even a bit of relief.

"You're not?"

"No, I have a girlfriend. I have for some time now," I say, digging the hole.

"Well, why haven't I heard of her?" he asks and sounds almost hurt. Fuck. *Fuck.*

"It wasn't very serious until recently, and we wanted to keep things under wraps, but we've . . ."

Don't say it, my brain begs of me. *Don't say it.*

I do, though.

I put on my best smile, the one I use to close deals, and I *fucking say it.*

"I actually just proposed."

FOUR

THEO

"Engaged!" Jeff says, his eyes wide and shock engulfing his face. "When? How?"

Fuck, fuck, fuck, fuck.

What in the fuck was I thinking?

Why the fuck did I say that?

I don't have someone to call up for fucking dinner plans, much less someone I've proposed to.

"I, uh. Recently. Last week. It wasn't . . . It wasn't anything big. Small. Simple. That's how we are."

How we are as if there's any kind of fucking we in existence.

"Why didn't—" Jeff starts then stops himself, shaking his head with a smile on his lips. "You always were a quiet one about private matters." A tiny bit of the panic recedes like a tide going out. An avoided flood.

He's buying it.

He believes me.

Now, if I could just get out of this fucking office and back into mine where I can panic and gameplay how to get myself out of this—

The relief came too soon, and the fucking tsunami hits.

"Sunday," he says, the word finite and joyful at the same time.

There it is. That dark dread is curling in the pit of my stomach, a snake preparing to strike, to sink its venom into my bloodstream.

The worst is yet to come.

There will be no easy retreat into my office, no strategizing my way out of this.

I am perfectly and thoroughly fucked.

"Sunday?" I ask, but I don't have to.

I know what he's going to say before he even opens his mouth. If I had taken a millisecond to think before I blurted out my apparent engaged status, I would have seen this as the next logical step, but alas.

"Sunday. Judy's making dinner. You bring your girl around. I want to meet the woman you've been hiding from me." His smile goes wide and genuine, and guilt rips through me.

He's happy for me. Elated, even. My single status was genuinely worrying him. Which is fucked because this is the twenty-first century, and no one needs to be in a relationship to be happy, but he means well. It's not malicious, and neither is his concern.

"Jeff, I—" I start, no idea where I'm going to take that.

I panicked and lied?

I can't even be trusted, to be honest with you, but please let me run this company because it's my only tie to my father?

I am a lonely man with no real social life, just like you fear?

I don't have to finish because Jeff's phone rings.

"Gotta take this," he says with a smile.

I don't know the last time I saw him this happy, this excited.

And it's because I've just told him I'm not a fucking loser with no life, that I have some kind of life outside work after all. It's almost like a weight was lifted off his shoulders.

"Sunday, yeah? I'll have Judy call Katrina, put it on your calendar." And then he lifts the phone to his ear. "Evan, old friend. How are you?"

And I turn to leave, walking to my office to panic.

Unfortunately, even when you're having a crisis of faith and lies, the world keeps turning. Clients continue to get into sticky situations, music keeps being made, and radio stations keep ranking artists, so I spend the rest of my day putting out fires and trying to figure out a way out of this mess between bites of lunch and conference calls that could have been emails.

I pace.

I curse the world.

I curse myself.

I have a bit of a panic attack, and then finally, I sit down with a pen and a blank sheet of paper and plan.

My breathing calms.

My heart rate slows.

And I write my options.

Option 1: Tell Jeff everything and lose any shot at running Catalyst.

Option 2: Avoid Jeff and Judy until the vote and probably piss off Jeff along the way. Potentially lose the vote anyway.

Option 3: Find a fiancée.

The answer is obvious, and I just so happen to have the right connections to maybe make it work. So long after everyone, including Katrina, has left the office, I pick up my phone and scroll to an old friend.

See, Jeff? I think to myself. I have friends. I don't admit to myself that the last time I spoke to my friend from college was maybe four years ago. But I did have my assistant send over flowers when he got married, so at least there's that.

"I fucked up," I say, groaning into the phone when Luke Dawson answers.

FIVE

THEO

The next day, I'm confident in my new plan. When I pass Jeff in the office and he reminds me about dinner on Sunday, I don't cringe or feel the all-consuming panic when I nod in agreement because I have a plan.

When I leave the office at five on the dot and Katrina questions me in the elevator with a, *hot date, boss man?* I don't even think I scowl at her. As I drive to the restaurant my friend Luke directed me to for my introductory meeting with his wife, the owner of The Ex Files, there's a sense of delusional confidence that this is all going to work out.

I met Luke in college, a friend of a friend, and while I don't see him too often, I do remember the last time I spoke with him, he told me about the business his now wife runs. She vets men for red flags, and if they pass her rigorous testing, she begins the matchmaking process, setting them up with dates. Apparently, she has incredibly high success rates, and it's even how he met his wife Cassie.

While I'm not looking for a wife, I told Luke about my predicament and he set up an appointment for me.

"Can't make any promises, man, Cassie's pretty particular. But I'll see what I can do," he said.

Everything seems to be falling into place, and I think I might just make it through this ordeal unscathed.

That is, until I walk into the restaurant, and before I even open my mouth to tell the hostess who I am or why I'm here, I stop short.

I'm on an embarrassing last-ditch effort to find a fake girlfriend, and my assistant is right in my sight. Sitting alone at a table not far into the restaurant is Katrina Delgado, and instantly, I regret coming.

This is a terrible idea.

A terrible fucking idea.

She's going to see me on my fake fucking date and have questions at work. If she finds out what's really happening, she'll laugh until she's blue in the face, never letting me live it down.

I won't have to worry about not getting the job—I'll have to quit from embarrassment.

At that moment, I almost turn around and send a quick email to my contact at the agency, apologizing. But then the hostess asks my name, and I'm running on autopilot, telling her who I am. I start to follow her to my table, ready to give a small wave as we pass Katrina if I catch her eye and pray she doesn't ask me tomorrow at work.

Except . . .

I'm brought to her table.

"Here you go, Mr. Carter," the hostess says, placing a menu in front of where she clearly intends for me to sit. "Your server will be here to take your drink order in a moment."

"I'm sorry. I—" I start, ready to tell her this is wrong, that I'm not supposed to sit here. We must have somehow been here on a work meeting once and I forgot. It must just be that the hostess remembered us and made an assumption. But before I can say anything more, Katrina cuts me off, smiling at the hostess.

"Thanks, Katie, appreciate it. Theo, sit." Her words are sharp and leave no room for arguing. I do as I'm told, like a child ready to learn his punishment for drawing on the walls.

"Funny to see you here, boss man," she says, and I don't miss the humor in her words or the smile playing on her lips.

I also don't miss how she exchanged her work outfit of a skirted suit for a black dress with a low, scooping neckline and a delicate pendant around her neck.

"I'm sorry, Katrina. There's been a misunderstanding. I'm supposed to be meet—" Once again, she cuts me off, not unlike the way she does at the office in her bantering way.

"Me. You're supposed to be meeting me here." She raises an eyebrow, and I shake my head.

"No, I'm sorry. This isn't—" She crosses her arms on her chest and smiles before cutting me off again.

"This is. You're here to speak with someone from The Ex Files, yes? Cassie Dawson owns it?" My blood cools, and my stomach churns.

Fuck.

No, no, no.

"I . . . Yes."

"Lucky you, this is my part-time job," she says with a smile and a flip of her hair. "I go on dates and vet potential clients for The Ex Files."

"You . . ." My brain doesn't focus on anything she just said or how it links to the current hole I've dug myself into; instead, I jump to something else. "Do we not pay you enough?" She laughs, loud and hoarse.

"Dear lord. No, you pay me just fine. I just get bored at night because all of my friends are happily paired up, so I use my secret talent for good."

"Your secret talent?" I ask. I must still be in shock from simply seeing her here because I'm asking questions that really don't matter in the grand scheme when I should be getting up and running from this restaurant before I make a mistake I cannot undo. A mistake like telling Katrina I accidentally told Jeff I'm engaged, and I'm contacting a dating service to try and find a temporary fiancée.

"I'm very good at reading people. You know, like when I read my calendar and saw your name on it." My mouth drops open.

"You knew this was happening?" She nods. "Why didn't you say anything?" She gives me a disbelieving look, putting her hand to her chest to show faux shock.

God, she's a pain in the ass.

"And miss this glorious view of you stuttering, thrown off your game? No, sir." I glare at her again. "And because if I did, you would have inevitably clammed up and I would never have figured out why you were reaching out to Cassie in the first place, since I can almost guarantee you're not looking for the love of your life." I open and close my mouth a few times.

"Why would you think I'm not looking for the love of my life?" Now, the look turns into one that's more pitying.

"Theo, you haven't been on a simple date in at least three months, and that one did not lead to a second."

"How do you know that?"

"Because you're neurotic with your calendar, and I manage your calendar."

That's fair, I suppose.

"How do you know I'm not ready to turn a new leaf? I could be ready to settle down." She sighs like this whole conversation is a waste of her time.

"Because if that were the case, you wouldn't contact a dating service on your own. You'd have me doing it. And you'd probably just open up your Rolodex of women who have been throwing themselves at you for the past eighty years, I'm sure, and pick one you can tolerate and just commit to her." I stare at her. "You don't have the patience for casual dating. It would take up too much time and take away from work."

"Why does everyone think all I do is work?" I ask, exhausted by this entire ordeal. She lifts an eyebrow at me. "I don't only work!" I say, my voice rising. Katrina smiles that stupid, pitying smile and reaches across the table, patting my hand in consolation.

"Okay, Theo, you keep telling yourself that."

I should fire her.

I should, but I won't because I would crumble without her, but if I didn't rely on her so heavily, I would absolutely fire her. "Now, why don't you tell me why you're really here? No matter what you want to convince yourself or whoever else, you don't date. Why are you trying to get vetted by The Ex Files?" Katrina leans back, crossing her arms on her chest, a small smile playing on her lips, and suddenly, my irritation is gone and nerves settle back in.

Which is fucking insanity because I'm her boss, not the other way around.

I take a deep breath before confessing.

"I fucked up and told Jeff I'm dating someone," I say under my breath, not even bothering to argue any further.

"What?" she asks, a laugh in her voice.

I run a hand through my hair and sigh. "I don't know. I panicked, okay? I panicked, and Jeff told me he couldn't, in good faith, hand me Catalyst because I have no life, allegedly, and I . . . just blurted it out." She nods like this makes sense.

"So you told your boss you have a girlfriend that no one has ever met because . . . ?"

"Fiancée," I mumble, remembering once again, not only did I tell Jeff I have someone in my life, but I told him I'm getting married.

Fucking married.

Maybe Jeff is right. Maybe I shouldn't get the position. I'm too impulsive. I make shitty decisions under pressure. I—

"Fiancée?!" I close my eyes at her well-deserved shock.

"I told him I was getting married." I clear my throat and avoid her eyes. "That I had recently proposed."

"Oh, Theo," she murmurs, shaking her head. "Why did you do that?"

"Because he's retiring." It doesn't answer her question, but her face perks up with a bit of understanding all the same.

"Jeff's retiring?" I nod but don't elaborate. She pauses, trying to put the pieces together. "And he wants you to be in a relationship before you take over?" I sigh.

"He's worried I have no life outside of work." Katrina scoffs out another laugh.

"Am I supposed to pretend he's wrong?"

"I absolutely have a life outside of work!" I'm defensive even though there's no real reason to be. I don't have anything to prove to Katrina.

"Theo, I see your calendar. Other than your weekly dinner with your sister and the occasional doctor's appointment, you only have work events on there."

"How do you know I don't have things you don't see? I don't have to tell you everything I do."

"You don't have to, but not having something on your calendar makes your hands sweaty."

She's not wrong.

"Okay, so he won't give you the position—" I cut her off, frustration boiling in my veins.

"He won't put his backing behind me if he thinks I'm never going to settle down." There's a pause.

"Put his backing behind you? What does that even mean?"

"He's putting it up for a vote with the board to see who takes the president position. He doesn't want a hand in it." Her mouth is open as she stares at me, my words processing before she speaks.

"He doesn't want a hand in it? What does that even mean? Who would be a better option than you?" She laughs incredulously. "Warren?" she asks sarcastically. I lift an eyebrow. "Warren? You're telling me it's you or Warren? He doesn't even do anything. Everyone hates him."

She sits back, crossing her arms on her chest. "I'll quit if he's CEO, Theo. And I won't be the only one, I can tell you that much."

This, among many, many other things, is what I'm worried about. Warren has the wool pulled so far over Jeff's eyes, so far down the board's eyes, they can't see how terrible he is for the company. This label was started with heart—with the push to make money, yes, but also to create a family. To support artists. To give back. To do good, if only in our own little community.

Warren doesn't see that; he won't. If he gets Catalyst, the entire business will change, and not for the best. I know some of the board members would be fine with that and happy to take a larger cut at the expense of the employees and artists, the backbone of this entire corporation.

But it doesn't mean I won't do everything in my power to keep it from happening.

"I know that. I do, which is why I have to do everything in my power to try and win Jeff's approval. We both know that if Jeff puts his weight behind me, most of the board will follow." She nods, but anger is still splashed across her face, red on her cheeks and her jaw tight.

"This is fucked, you know that, right? You deserve that position. Fuck, the fact that you have no life is proof enough—"

"I don't have no life, my god."

"You know what I mean." There's a pause before she leaps forward, her face moving to the one she uses when we're brainstorming solutions before shifting questions.

"Why not tell Jeff Warren is a piece of shit?" I pause, unsure of how to respond, and she gives me a *come on* face. "I mean, I know you know he's a piece of shit."

"Yes. But I want . . ." I sigh. "There's no tangible proof that he's bad for Catalyst other than the employees not liking him much, which isn't criminal." I pause, looking at her. "Wait, how do you know he's a piece of shit?" I ask, my gut churning at the idea of Warren having done something to her. She rolls her eyes.

"Keep it in your pants, Carter. I have a sixth sense."

"A sixth sense?"

"My friends call it my ick factor. It's why I have this job." Her hands move to indicate me, this dinner, before she continues, "I meet people and most of the time, I just know if they're good or bad."

"You just know if people are good?" I don't buy it, nor do I understand.

"Yeah. I get the ick if they aren't. Sometimes, it takes a few times, but Warren? It took a millisecond. That man's not right in the head."

Interesting. It explains a lot, like how Katrina never hides her opinions on things and I implicitly trust her instincts.

"Is that why you're single?" I ask without thinking, the words tumbling out without my permission, and she smiles like she caught me in some gotcha moment.

"As a matter of fact, yes. My ick factor is much too strong for the average man." She doesn't expand, but it's clear she doesn't want to, so I ask another question.

"And me? Do I have the . . . ick factor?"

"No, you're cool. You're a good person. Knew that from my first interview." She opens her mouth to say . . . something, then shakes her head. "Enough about me. What's your plan?"

"My plan?"

"You booked a vetting with The Ex Files for a reason. I don't think it's because you want to find your future Mrs. Carter. So, what's your plan?"

"No, I definitely am not looking for a Mrs. Carter." I pause and then sigh, playing with my napkin before leaning forward. "I have a proposition for your boss." Her eyes go wide as she shakes her head.

"Oh, no, we don't do that. We respect sex workers, but—"

"Jesus Christ, not that kind of proposition," I start, ready to start rambling out what I'm really asking to make sure she doesn't misinterpret me, but then I notice it.

She's smiling.

She's *smiling*.

I understand. "You're fucking with me, aren't you?"

"Maybe a little," she says, propping her chin up on her fist, and that smile widens.

"Katrina."

"I'm sorry, I'm sorry." She straightens her shoulders and makes her face look comically stern. "I'm all business now. Tell me your proposition for my boss. The one who isn't you." I glare, but she gives me a *go on* look and wave of her hand.

"I need a girlfriend."

"No shit," she mumbles, and once again, I glare at her. "Sorry! Sorry. It was too good to pass up. Go on."

"This is a terrible idea," I say, ready to stand, but she reaches over and grabs my hand, her face going serious, but not in a joking way.

"No, Theo, really. I want to help. I'll stop being a brat." The statement, that word . . . it does something I fervently ignore.

Something I always fervently ignore.

Because Katrina is a gorgeous woman.

Katrina *knows* she's a gorgeous woman.

I'd be an idiot not to see it.

I have noticed over the months she's worked for me. Everyone in the office has. And the idea of Katrina being a brat to me scratches something in my brain that should never be scratched.

Ever.

"I should fire you."

"That would look great to the board, firing your incredibly competent, if I do say so myself, assistant after you propositioned her."

"Jesus, fuck." I groan as she laughs wholeheartedly.

"I'm joking, Theo, god." She rolls her eyes and then wipes a tear from them, clearly enjoying my misery. "Okay, really. How did this all happen?" She leans forward like this is a work strategy meeting instead of some fucked-up, failed attempt at getting a fake girlfriend.

Maybe if I treat it that way, I can hop over this consuming embarrassment.

"Like I said, Jeff told me he's not comfortable choosing me as his successor because I have no life, and as you know, he's all about family. So I told him I had a girlfriend I proposed to recently. I panicked. I—"

"You panicked and told your incredibly nosy boss you have some kind of imaginary fiancée no one knows about."

"Jesus, can you let me finish? I'd like to relive this story as little as possible." She smiles wide. "After my meeting with Jeff, I started to do the math. I need at least four votes, five if I don't think I can rely on Jeff's as a tiebreaker. Ray's all pissed the date he set up with his daughter and me didn't go well, so he's definitely not voting for me, and Jay is always pissed we pay the employees too much, cutting into his profit. So that leaves six people, max. The reality is, I'm fucked if I don't have Jeff's backing." She nods like it makes sense, which is kind of her since it doesn't.

"So you lied and told him you have a girlfriend. A fiancée."

"And now he wants me to bring her to dinner Sunday. I was hoping your boss could match me with someone temporarily. We could date until the vote, and then we'll break up a bit later."

"What would it entail?" Katrina asks with that face she has when we're trying to figure out how to fit three meetings into the same hour.

"A few dinners. The gala in May. Maybe a few other dates just to prove it's not fake. I'm not exactly sure." She sits, contemplating, and I think for a moment there's hope she'll go back to Cassie Dawson and tell her about my situation, plead my case.

But then she says the unexpected.

"I'll do it."

SIX

KAT

"What?" Theo asks, shock in his words after I speak. He looks like he might implode, but the gears in my mind are moving, the clouds clearing and making everything obvious. It's the only thing that makes sense.

"I'll do it. I'll be your fake fiancée," I say.

There's a pause, and I try not to laugh at the eight different emotions and thoughts crossing his face simultaneously, each of which I'm uniquely qualified to read.

Coworkers have told me Theodore Carter is an enigma. A robot. He's all business and nothing else. I've had people groan and ask how I can bear to work with him, with his lone emotional setting being grumpy and his expectations being sky-high.

Personally, I don't see it. In fact, Theo is one of the most expressive people I know, a million emotions crossing over his face at any given moment, his mind silently dissecting which one is the most efficient to use in any situation and then responding. It's part of the reason this whole situation is interesting to me.

It's so not him. He does not just make in-the-moment, leap-of-faith decisions without thinking about the consequences first.

Thoroughly.

Which means he thinks there's a high probability of Warren getting the job over him.

"Absolutely not," he says with a finality I know he won't hold on to for long, not once he sees this corner he's backed himself into for what it is. I give him a small smile, the kind you give a child who doesn't want to take the medicine you know will make them feel better.

"It's the only thing that makes sense." He shakes his head, the front of his hair falling onto his forehead, his fingers brushing it back. That's how I know he's frazzled—his normally perfect façade is melting before my eyes.

Theo is never not perfectly polished. His dark brown, nearly black hair is longer on the top and neat on the sides, always brushed back and kept in place by some mysterious hair product that can withstand his hands running through it when he's stressed. His eyes are a dark, dark blue, like the night sky in summer when the sun is down, but it's not pitch dark. And right now, they're filled with dismay and futility.

It does something to me, that look. The utter loss of control and the panic that he feels because of it. It makes me want to fix all of his problems like I always do.

"None of this makes any sense, but that? That makes the least." His arms, clothed in his dark blue suit jacket, the same one he wore to work today, cross over his chest.

"Oh, really? How are you going to explain to Jeff why you've hidden your girlfriend from him for however long you've been dating? Warren's dating your sister, right? Is she going to buy it? That you're marrying some random woman she's never met, who you've never spoken of? You need to pretend you've been together for a while or else it looks like the lie it is." He opens his mouth and then closes it, and I take that as my cue to continue.

"If you were, say, dating your assistant, it would make sense as to why you haven't told anyone. You didn't want anyone to think poorly of me, or we wanted to make sure it was going to work before telling people. We didn't want to muddy the waters at work. We can figure out the exact reasons later, but this makes sense. At least, more sense than you hiding some random ass woman."

His face starts to change from absolute indignation and hesitance to neutrality, and I realize I'm getting through to him.

"Plus, with anyone else, you'd also have to teach her about Catalyst, about the board members, and about Warren. She'd need to know what kind of issues to avoid, who to sweet talk, who to run far away from. I know everyone. I know what to say and who to say it to and how to convince them we're real. How to convince them this isn't just for you to get a job."

He sits there, slowly letting my words sink in. I watch the gears turn and the pieces fall into place as he realizes this is the only solution that'll work.

If we want him to get Jeff's backing, for him to get the job, to, in essence, save Catalyst, this is the only option. The alternatives are to confess he lied or inevitably get exposed when he brings some random person who knows nothing to Jeff's on Sunday.

We sit in silence for long minutes as he tries to fit in different pieces, different answers to this complex problem he's created. I watch as each one he tries, fails, and he gets closer and closer to my solution.

Finally, he breaks it. "Why?" he asks, surprising me.

"What?"

"Why do you want to do this? What do you want from it?" He's staring at me the same way he does potential new clients and acquisitions. I've seen it a million times, his strange ability to read someone, to see their intentions, and always wondered if that's what I look like when I'm deciding if someone is good or bad.

From the day I met Theodore Carter, I had a gut feeling he was a kindred spirit in our ability to know what makes people tick.

"Money? A new job? Bragging rights?"

I roll my eyes.

"I don't want your money, Theo. You pay me plenty."

"You have student loans. Those? I can pay those off," he says, and it's not an accusation, but an offer.

He's slowly coming on board.

"I don't need you to pay off my loans, boss man. They aren't even that much anymore." He raises an eyebrow, silently saying, "Well? Then what is it?" And I sigh before telling him the truth.

"I'm thirty and I've never had a job I liked for longer than three, four months. I get bored, lose the will to be there as soon as the excitement wears off, as soon as I realize I'm stuck. I have never felt that at Catalyst or with you. I like my position. I'm never bored. I get paid well. I have a million different tasks to do, and I like the people I work with, for the most part. If Warren takes over, I won't like this job, won't like this company, and I'll need to start from scratch." I shrug, trying to play it off, trying not to let him know how much this means to me.

I might be an assistant, nothing glamorous, but it's the first time in my life I've felt like it's a good fit. I haven't felt that boredom creep in, the dread when I wake up.

Haven't gotten the ick.

Because unfortunately, the ick factor doesn't just apply to men in my life. It applies to everything. Friendships. Food. Relationships. Jobs. Interests. Hobbies.

I get excited about something, hyperfixate, and mold my life to fit my new obsession. I think I'm good, this one is different, that I'll be able to maintain the interest, and then one day, I wake up and it's . . . gone.

ADHD will do that to you: a constant cycle of excited hyperfixation and the sudden drop as soon as that hit of dopamine is gone.

It's a real bitch.

"You like your job."

"I do. I like Catalyst Records. I don't want to risk anything fucking that up."

I don't tell him that before I started here, I was starting to feel the panic of entering my thirties with no real ambition, no real career. All of my friends have jobs they love, careers they wake up each morning excited for. I've felt like a failure, like there is something wholly wrong with me.

And then I started working for Theo.

Silence encompasses our small table, the sound of plates scraping and people talking, laughter, and life going on just next to us as Theo continues to stare at me, to take me in.

To decode me.

I hate it, being on the other end of this, so I cut in.

"It can't be someone random, Theo. Unless you want to confess to Jeff you lied, it has to be me," I say, staring at him, and he stares back, contemplating my words.

He has to know I'm right.

It's the only thing that makes sense.

And I'll be damned if I let Warren fucking Michaels ruin what is rightfully Theo's just because Jeff has some fucked sense of who he should be.

SEVEN

THEO

I barely sleep the night after Katrina and I made plans for our ruse, tossing and turning and panicking about what tomorrow will bring.

Will she quit?

Will she even show up at work?

When she inevitably and rightfully files a report, will I be called into HR before or after lunch?

Will Jeff let me keep my job, or will I be fired on the spot?

Contacting The Ex Files seemed like a solid idea when I made the call, my Hail Mary at redeeming myself with my major fucking screw-up, but somehow, I made it worse.

I left the restaurant feeling pretty good—Katrina was in on my plan, and everything was falling into place. Maybe I wouldn't have to confess to Jeff what I did, wouldn't have to tell everyone I made up a fucking fiancée to try and get a job. But as I drove back to my place, the uncertainty settled, morphing into all-consuming panic.

Of course, she was on board while we were in the restaurant.

Of course, she was offering a solution. She was backed into a corner, her boss staring her down while she worked her part-time job. What was she going to do other than humor me until she could get to work the next day and contact human resources about my abysmal and inappropriate behavior?

All these years of helping to curate and ensure a good, safe community at Catalyst Records and I'm the one making the most dire of indiscretions.

After hours of tossing and turning, I decide to just get up for the day and attempt to get some extra work in before everything comes tumbling down. I arrive barely after six in the morning and well before anyone gets to the office, ready to dissociate with work while I can.

This is why, when Katrina pokes her head in a bit later, a smile on her lips, I jump, not even hearing her coming.

"Hey, hubby," she says, stepping into my office, grabbing her chair, and dragging it across the way until it's in front of my desk. "Her" chair is slightly larger and more cushioned than my normal guest seats. It usually sits next to my door with my briefcase on it, only moved in front of me when Katrina is in my office. She stole it from the lobby months ago after deciding that the normal guest chairs weren't comfortable enough, and since she was spending a fucking decade in here, "listening to you ramble about shit" (her words, not mine), she wanted something comfier.

It's never been returned to its rightful place, just becoming Katrina's chair in my office.

"Jesus Christ," I mumble to myself, my hand going to my chest as my heart races. She laughs that laugh that is so very Katrina, deep and rolling for such a small woman, and for what feels like the millionth time, I wonder what the fuck I'm doing. "Could you not shout that out loud for the world to hear?" I ask, the panic at her calling me her hubby before we even figured things out sinking in.

Maybe Jeff is right not to give me the job. Clearly, I can't be trusted with adult decisions if at any moment, I thought this was a good idea.

"Oh, shut up, I'm just joking!" she says. "It's just too easy to poke fun at you, you know?"

"I actually can't say I do," I grumble.

"God, you're boring. No wonder you're single. No wonder you need a fake fiancée." My eyes widen and I look toward my open office door.

"Could you please be a bit less . . . loud about it?" She shakes her head and sighs like I'm an idiot.

"Theo, there is barely anyone in the building this early in the morning." I check my watch, time not making any sense since Jeff's retirement announcement, and I'm shocked when it says it's barely 7.

"What are you doing here so early?" She usually comes in at 8:30, despite her official start time being 9.

Then she tugs at the yellow plastic protective wrapping on the candy in her hand, revealing a chili-coated mango lollipop and putting it in her mouth, despite the early hour. She once begged me to try one, telling me they were a nostalgic snack her grandmother used to but down the street in her town in Mexico and bring her as a child, then laughed her ass off when I couldn't tolerate the, admittedly, mild spice.

"We need to have a talk now that you've slept on everything."

This is it, I think. *She's backing out and going to report me to HR. Not only am I not going to get the job, but I'm going to get fucking fired.*

"Look, I know what you're going to say, and before you do, I just need to apologize. Dragging you into my mess wasn't professional. I wish we could just put it all behind us and forget last night even happened, but if you need to report my poor behavior, I'll understand. I—" She cuts me off with an incredulous look.

"Jesus, Theo, take a chill pill. I meant we have to talk to make sure you're still game and about how this will work."

I blink at her.

"You . . . You still want to do this?" She gives me a strange look.

"Well, yeah. I have to." I groan.

"Katrina, please. I went about this entire situation incredibly wrong. You don't have to do anything, I promise. You don't have to worry about me treating you differently or retribution. I value your work here more than I value a position. It was inappropriate for me to even take that dinner with you. I—"

"I don't have to do it because I think if I don't, you'll fire me, Theo," she says, giving me a strange look. I don't reply, confused, and she continues talking. "I have to because I want you to be president of this company over Warren, very much so."

Oh.

Oh.

"Yesterday, I told you Warren would ruin this company, at least for the people who work here. He'll probably make it better for the investors, for the board members, but it will be at the cost of the employees. In contrast, you will continue to make it great. You'll take care of the little people." I sigh and shake my head.

"But that's not your responsibility."

I don't know why I'm arguing—she's offering me this opportunity to save face and salvage my lie and get the job that's rightfully mine. But I won't feel right about this if she feels dragged into this uncomfortable arrangement.

"If not me, then who?" she asks. "Because I can tell you right now, Cassie isn't going to be gung-ho about setting up someone with you for a fake, temporary fling. That goes against everything she believes in. And if, by the grace of God, you find someone else, you'll need to info-dump months', if not years' worth of information and relationship building in." She looks at her watch. "Less than 48 hours. If you feel equipped to do that, God bless. But I know you pretty well, Theo. That's not your thing: relationships, talking, people." She smiles. "No offense."

I can't be offended because she's not wrong. I wouldn't be in this position if she was.

"I just . . ." I pause, trying to find the words. "I value our working relationship. I don't want to jeopardize things in that sense." She rolls her eyes.

"It's fine, Theo. We're doing this. It's gonna be fun!" She smiles and strangely enough, I actually think she believes that.

I think she might need her head checked, if I'm being honest.

"A little . . . challenge in the day-to-day." Suddenly, she looks excited and claps her hands together like this is actually going to be a fun thing for her. "Okay, so what's our plan?" Katrina asks, leaning forward.

She looks the same way she does when I tell her we have a busy day with a lot of tasks, and she grabs her iPad, ready to make a list instead of dreading the extra work like my past executive assistants.

"What do you mean?"

"How are we going to get at Warren? Make sure you get the job and he doesn't?"

"Oh, that's not the plan," I say with a shake of my head. "We're just making sure my social status isn't a factor in whether I get the job or not." Her head moves back in shock.

"What? What do you mean? We need to sabotage him." She says it so firmly, like there is no other option, but I shake my head again.

"I'm sorry; I thought I made that clear last night. I just need you to be my fiancée for a bit. To go to dinner at Jeff's and a few events, make it seem like we're together so Jeff won't worry that if he gives me the job, I'll have no life." She pauses for a long minute before squirming in her seat and pouting, almost looking defeated. The woman pouts.

"Well, that's no fun." Now, it's my turn to be confused.

"What?"

"That's no fun. We should . . . do something. Make him fuck up at work, make you look even better. Something. We need to make sure he does not get this job, period. He's an ass, Theo. He's an ass to you and to everyone who works here."

"I know it seems that way sometimes, but—"

"I know your moral compass is perfectly tuned and Jeff likes him, but I know you're not stupid. You have good instincts." She smiles a bit then adds, "Maybe not as good as mine, but you've got them. You know he's not a good person."

I don't respond because I don't want to encourage her. She's not wrong. But he's still a high-level employee with a lot of sway in this business. It wouldn't be professional to talk poorly about him. Plus, he's dating my sister now.

"We should do something!" she says, getting excited when I don't argue her point. "Put fish in his office so it stinks and people think he has poor hygiene. Hack into his email and send nudes to people. Order him some kind of food he's allergic to so his face blows up right before a big meeting. Or maybe—" I cut her off, my face a mask of horror and confusion.

"Are you okay?" She looks at me like I'm the insane one in this room.

"Are *you* okay? Warren's an ass, and he's going to ruin your father's business. He wants your job. I'm pretty sure he wants it to fuck with you, but also because he has some kind of nefarious plan."

"Yes, but—" I say, not necessarily agreeing with the nefarious plan part but not disagreeing. I'm not as delusional as Jeff to think Warren is all sunshine and rainbows, but he's not a horrible person. I don't think he would tank the entirety of Catalyst on purpose just because he hates me. Before I can expand, she continues, her face passionate and her hands moving as she speaks.

"So, we should fuck with him!" I shake my head.

"We can't do that, Katrina." Her shoulders slump again, and if I wasn't her boss and if it wasn't alarming, it might be cute.

Maybe.

"Why not? Don't you want this job? You deserve it, Theo." Suddenly, it all clicks into place. She's loyal to me. She wants me to win this, and in her strange sense of justice, the best way to do that is to take Warren out of the running. I clarify, telling the truth for the most part.

"Yes, but I want it on my own merit. Not because we fucked him over. I want the board to know I'm the best option for this position or else getting anything done will be nearly impossible, especially if Warren is still in their ears, telling them to do things his way. As fun as . . . fucking with him might sound, it's not the best option long-term. I simply want to remove the aspect of me not being in a relationship in the final decision. I think we can both agree that's a fucked way to choose a president of a company."

Kat looks completely dismayed by me putting my foot down.

"Can we make him look a little bad?" I groan. Maybe having her help me was actually the worst idea.

"Are you okay? Should I send you to some kind of evaluation?"

"I should send you to an evaluation for not wanting to do everything in your power to get him out of here! We need to go all out, Theo."

"Katrina . . ."

"Nothing crazy!" I don't tell her that sending nudes to the office, that poisoning him with allergens is, in fact, insane.

"Katrina . . . ," I repeat. She pouts. I wonder how often that works and if she's used to men seeing her pout and letting her get her way. I wouldn't doubt it. "He's a friend, Katrina," I lie.

"He is not," she says with a disbelieving laugh.

"Yes, he is. I've known him since we were in college." She gives me a *be fucking serious* face she actually gives me pretty regularly. "I've known him for a long time, and he's a family friend. I want what's best for him; I just want him to do that outside of the head of the company my father built." Suddenly, her face goes soft. Sad. Pitying, almost.

"He's not your friend, Theo. At best, he's your frenemy."

"Frenemy?"

"God, you're so old. Your friend-enemy. He's your frenemy at best, but he's also trying to take this business that is rightfully yours from you."

"I don't think he's—"

"He is." Her look has all joking removed and my brow furrows.

"How do you know?"

"My gut. I told you, it's incredibly in tune." I stare at her, and she stares back, a battle of wills colliding until finally, she sighs in defeat. "Fine. We won't do anything to make him look bad." Then, under her breath, she says, "Yet."

"Katrina."

"For now," she says, speeding right past that little yet. "We'll just make you look so freaking good, it won't matter who you're dating or not dating or marrying or divorcing." She smiles.

"So you're in?" I ask. "For real? This whole fake fiancée thing?" She smiles.

"At the very least, it's going to be hilarious. I get to fuck with you in front of everyone, and you can't even do anything about it. This is a dream, Theo."

I like that about Katrina, the way she doesn't give a fuck. She has never beat around the bush when it comes to me, never treated me differently because I'm high up on the ladder or because I make good money. Others do—men and women—but never her.

I think it's part of why I trust her to be able to do this fake fiancée thing. If I were actually engaged, ready to settle down and marry a woman, I'd want someone like Katrina. Someone who doesn't kiss my ass.

I roll my eyes like I'm annoyed, but still, I smile at her and stick out a hand.

"Then, we have a deal?"

"We have a deal, Mr. Carter."

EIGHT

THEO

I'm starting to wonder if I agreed to this chaotic scheme because I haven't slept in almost a week.

It would make sense—don't they use lack of sleep as a form of torture?

Unfortunately, this isn't necessarily something new for me, insomnia getting the best of me most of the time, but after that meeting, I spent my nights trying to figure out how to convince Jeff to back me, and once Katrina and I spoke, I sat at my computer for hours upon hours, digging to try and understand how to make things look natural with Katrina, how to prove to Jeff I'm the best candidate for Catalyst.

But right now, I'm regretting not taking something to force myself to get even a modicum of normal sleep last night as I pull into the parking garage for Katrina's apartment, thinking about how on point I have to be tonight.

It's Sunday, and I'm about to pick her up to go to Jeff's for dinner.

To introduce my fiancée to my boss.

To the man who has kept me under his wing for nearly 20 years, helping to raise me and to climb the ladder of his business.

And I'm here at an alarmingly shitty apartment building to pick up my assistant who has, for some reason, agreed to help me attempt to pull off the lie of a century.

> Which apartment is yours?

> Are you downstairs?

> I'm parking now, then I'll come up.

> You shouldn't text and drive.

> Voice-to-text is a game changer, Katrina. Which apartment is yours?

I can almost see her eye roll from here when she replies quickly.

> No need to come up, boss man. I'll come down now.

> That's incredibly rude. A man should never make a woman come down to him.

> Save the energy. We're not worried about chivalry right now.

I've worked with Katrina for nearly a year, and in that time, I've seen her stubborn streak come out to play more than once. I've also learned that when it does, it's best if I just let her be rather than argue. She's right—I need to save my energy for Jeff's and I can't bring her to this dinner already annoyed with me. So with that, I park and wait for her, the entire interaction rubbing me wrong.

It really shouldn't annoy me as much as it is, not coming up to get her from her place like a gentleman, but it does all the same.

It's my upbringing, I tell myself. My mother would murder me if she knew I was waiting in a parking lot for a woman I was taking out on a date, legitimately or not. That's all.

It doesn't take long for my overthinking and upbringing to win, though, and I step out of my car, walk to the entrance of Katrina's apartment building, and stand outside like a fucking idiot, but fuck it.

She told me not to come up, but she didn't tell me not to stand outside, waiting for her.

A few minutes later, and with a few strange looks from her doorman, a woman walks out wearing a fitted lilac dress that ends at the middle of her shins, a slit up the side ending just above her knee, and tons of gold jewelry. On any other woman, it might look modest, but on this one, all curves and temptation, it looks anything but.

Her full hair is down, dark brown with some lighter strands woven throughout, loose curls down the middle of her back, the kind of hair a man instantly thinks about putting his hands into. Draped over one arm is a tan coat and a white bag with a gold chain, but it's unseasonably warm today, so it's not necessary for her to wear.

She's fucking beautiful, and my eyes can't move off her.

Then, suddenly, I realize I'm staring at Katrina as she smiles and makes her way toward me.

Katrina, my assistant, who is giving someone else a smile as they walk into the shitty apartment building with the crumbling brick and trash pushed into a corner.

"What are you doing here?" she asks as she walks through the door. Her polite smile is gone when she sees me, the look turning into confusion.

"I'm waiting for you," I say.

"I told you not to worry about it and I'd just meet you at your car." I begin making my way toward said car, and she follows. My manners fight with the urge to place my hand on her lower back, to guide her the right way, to tell her to watch her step at the curb.

Something tells me she would argue that as well.

Instead, I make excuses.

"My mother would have murdered me if she found out I was picking a woman up and making her walk to my car." She looks at me like she's not entirely buying it, but she doesn't argue. "These are for you," I say, lifting the small bouquet of pink tulips, suddenly feeling like a fucking moron. Momentarily, her face lights up genuinely before it turns silly, her hand moving to her chest as she lets out a faux gasp.

"You bought me flowers?!" I roll my eyes at her as she grabs them. "I'll cherish them forever." I ignore her, moving to the passenger side, opening the door, and waiting for her to pull her legs inside before slamming it and walking slowly to the other side.

As I do, I take a deep breath, trying to calm myself.

It's the fact that I'm about to go to my boss's house and lie to him about my relationship that has me anxious, I tell myself.

I definitely don't touch on how seeing Katrina in that dress is fucking with me, and I absolutely don't listen to the tiny voice telling me that despite the nerves, this feels normal. Comfortable. Easy.

When I sit down, I look at her, her phone in her hand, texting in what appears to be a group chat.

"Just letting my friends know I'm with you and the type of car you drive. You know, in case you turn out to be a psycho." She smiles at me, and I furrow my brow.

"We've been working together for almost a year. You aren't sure if I'm a psycho yet? I thought you said you have some magical power of ick?" She rolls her eyes.

"Yes, but I've also never been *alone* alone with you. We've always been at work."

"And?"

"And maybe you're a psycho killer who wants to wear my skin." My face screws up with the horror I feel, and she laughs, that wild, unhinged laugh I hear all day long from my office. It's the kind that tells you she doesn't give a shit about anything, about what people think about her. It's not practiced or polite or feminine.

But it's all Katrina.

If there's anything besides her work ethic I've ever allowed myself to admit I like about her, it's her laugh.

And I hear it a lot because Katrina likes to laugh.

Clients call my office and get her first? She tells some kind of small-talk joke and laughs.

Jessica, the receptionist, walks past her desk? She laughs at some kind of face she makes at her.

I fuck up something and inevitably need her help?

She laughs.

All day long, the woman laughs at anything and everything. I've often wondered before what it's like to find such joy in the mundane of life.

"I don't want to wear your skin, Katrina," I ensure when her laughter dies down.

"Good. It would look terrible on you," she says, deadpan, and when I stare at her in confusion, she laughs again.

See?

It's incessant.

"So, what's the story?" she asks when I continue to stare at her. "I'm your fiancée, right? You told Jeff? Was our engagement recent? What's the engagement story? Does he know it's me?"

I continue to look at her as she pelts me with question after question, and I feel that uncontrollable tide of my panic rising again.

"This is a terrible idea," I mumble as I wade through it, my mind moving through scenarios of how to get out of this. "Maybe we should—"

As she tends to do, Katrina sees the terror and waves her hand at me.

"Jesus, no. Stop. I've got it." She rolls her eyes when I look at her. "God, you're such a man."

"I'm a man because I haven't successfully created an entire relationship out of thin air?"

"You're a man because you have absolutely negative creativity." I shake my head in disagreement.

"That's not true."

"You wear the same outfit every day." I look down at my outfit: a white button-down, a dark gray tie, and a dark blue suit. She's not wrong. I wear the same outfit, more or less, every day, each piece in my wardrobe chosen to be able to grab and go without wasting too much time.

"It fights decision fatigue. Steve Jobs did it."

"God, listen to you. If I didn't work for you and see your calendar, I'd ask what the fuck you do for fun, but I know the answer is absolutely nothing."

"That's not true. I—" I pause, trying to think. What do I do for fun? "I . . ." She shakes her head at me when I come up empty.

"Exactly. But don't worry. As always, your fabulous, beautiful, creative assistant has it all covered." She smiles, digs in her bag, and pulls out a folded piece of paper. "It's our history. Read it and memorize it later. Do not bring it into the house because if you drop it and someone finds it, we're so fucked. For now, you can play dumb man, and I can play excited woman."

"Dumb man?"

"Yeah, you know. The one who remembers absolutely nothing about his relationship, and his partner has to fill in the gaps constantly? The kind that absolutely gives off mommy's boy and can't find the clit energy?" I'm offended.

"I can find the clit," I blurt without thinking, and for the first time in our year of working together, I shocked the words right out of her.

It doesn't last long, though.

"Can you now?" she says, eyebrows raised and her smile wide, clearly entertained by me.

My face burns something awful and my mouth opens and closes and opens, not a single sound leaving my lips as my mind runs through the hundreds of ways this entire "engagement" is a terrible idea.

It's a minefield of inappropriate actions, begging for a lawsuit on Katrina's end.

Watching my fish out of water show, she begins laughing, the sound filling the car and ricocheting off the close quarters, sending me deeper into my spiral.

"God, you are way too much fun to fuck with, you know that?" She reaches over and brushes her hand over my shoulder, grabbing a piece of lint I must have missed. "Moving on, here's the deal. I'll handle relationship questions, but you can't leave my side. And don't go off script. Next week, we'll have a meeting, compare notes, and make sure our stories line up for the future."

The future.

Because this won't just be one dinner and done. We're stuck.

Because the world now thinks she's my fiancée, and it has to stay this way until, at the very least, the board vote in June.

Fiancée. The word reminds me of one other thing.

"Shit, before we go, I have to give you something."

"A gift? Oooh!" She claps her hands in excitement. I roll my eyes, and she punches me in the shoulder. "You're so dull, Theo." I ignore her dig, instead grabbing her left hand, sliding the ring from my pocket onto her ring finger. "A ring," she says, her voice suddenly whisper quiet.

"A ring. We have to make it look legit, after all." My eyes can't leave where the ring slid onto her finger, a perfect fit.

"I suppose we do, don't we?" Finally, I force my eyes to leave her hand and move to her face, to gauge her response, but she doesn't look at me, instead staring at her finger with the diamond in a gold band that somehow fits her perfectly without resizing. "Wow."

"It's nothing crazy. I—" I start to explain, suddenly embarrassed. Maybe I should have asked what her style was or gotten something big or—

"No. It's not that. It's exactly what I'd want if—" She pauses and looks at me with a smile. "If this were real."

"You want that? A ring, marriage?" I ask it without even thinking. She smiles and nods, but the smile is sad, even to my untrained eyes.

"Yes. Very much so. My friends call me a hopeless romantic."

"Why haven't you done it then?" She's gorgeous, kind, too fucking smart. A man who wanted that, who wasn't hyperfocused on work and business, he'd go insane to make her his.

"I . . ." She pauses like she wants to say one thing, but then says another. "I just haven't found the right one. But this?" She lifts her hand with a smile, wiggling her "engagement ring" at me. "This looks super cool, ya know?"

I, too, almost say one thing, and then say another.

"Yeah. Looks good, Katrina."

Then, I drive to my boss's house with my fake fiancée to convince him I'm a family man who can be trusted to run the company my father built.

NINE

THEO

"Oh, Katrina!" Jeff's wife, Judy, shouts as we walk into the mansion of a house and into their kitchen. She turns to Jeff and smacks him in the chest with the back of her hand. "Jeffrey! You didn't tell me his fiancée was Katrina!"

This is far from the first Sunday dinner I've been to in this house and probably won't be the last—unless tonight goes so terribly and I'm cut off from the Bates family forever. Before my parents passed, we'd come here at least once a month for dinner, and after, when Jeff and Judy took in Savannah and me, the only day we could guarantee Jeff would pull himself from his desk long enough for a family meal was on Sundays.

The tradition continues to this day, with nearly every Sunday spent here with Jeff and Judy. Sometimes, it's just me, sometimes, it's just Savannah, and sometimes, it's both of us.

Judy loves family but was unable to have children, so she's always treated my sister and me as her own.

Because Catalyst often has events throughout the year, Judy also has had many opportunities to meet Katrina, and, of course, Jeff knows her from the office.

"If I had known, I would have," Jeff says with a smug smile, crossing his arms on his chest and leaning back. "So this is why you kept everything under lock and key, huh?" There isn't the disapproval or disappointment on his face I would expect, but, instead, humor and joviality.

He's enjoying this and loving watching me squirm with discomfort.

He doesn't understand, of course, part of my discomfort is because Katrina is pinching me in my side, her way of saying, "I told you so," without any words because he's basically quoting exactly what she told me at the restaurant.

"Makes much more sense," he says, pushing off the counter and dropping his arms. He pulls me in for a hug, patting me twice on the back before turning to Katrina, who has a hand outstretched for a handshake.

"Oh no," he says with a deep laugh, his arms out. "We're family now. We hug."

"Jeff, I—" I start, because I'm the one who dragged her into this mess and I don't want to make this experience even more miserable for her.

"Oh, good, I'm a hugger," Katrina says with a smile, and then she's hugging my boss like they're old friends.

Her boss, in a way.

"I'm so happy for you guys!" Judy says, coming in to hug Katrina again and holding her close to her side. "I can't believe he didn't tell us!" She looks at me and shakes her head. "Actually, I can, and your mother is probably rolling in her grave, Theodore Carter, at just the thought of you hiding away this precious, beautiful woman like she's some kind of dirty secret."

She would, if this were real. Instead, my mother is probably rolling because she always hated lies and I've found myself in the middle of a huge one.

Please forgive me, Mom. It's for the business.

"Oh, hush, Jude," Jeff says. "We can't really talk, now can we?"

There's a wave of Judy's hand as she lets out a *pssht* sound before she walks past me and to where the wine is.

"Who wants wine?"

"Me!" Katrina nearly shouts, and even though I try, I can't fight the smile and small chuckle. She turns to me, punching me in the shoulder before smiling and walking toward Judy. "Red for you, Theo?" I nod and watch her walk to the kitchen, her voice low as she compliments something, making Judy blush.

"Now I see it," Jeff says, and when I look back at him, his arms are crossed on his chest, a small smile on his lips. "Now I see it. I'm actually annoyed with myself that I didn't before."

"See what?" I ask, my eyes moving with a mind of their own to the kitchen again, Katrina's laugh dancing through the entryway to us.

"You two. It's so obvious. Always together, always working late." I just barely remember to hide my shock when I shift my eyes to him. "Always laughing. She's the only one you ever let give you shit."

"Well, I—" I start, ready to defend Katrina because while she might like to pick at me, I wouldn't call it giving me shit. She's never stepped out of line professionally, or insulted me, or—

"No, no, in a good way. That's what you want in a good woman, Theodore. Men like us, we get used to everyone telling us yes. We get used to people kissing our asses to get whatever it is they want. Get used to people at our beck and call, telling us how wonderful even the shittiest ideas we have are. Men like us? We need good women to keep us down to earth."

I open my mouth once more to speak, though I have no idea what to say, but I close it when the women come back, Katrina handing me a glass of red wine. A glass I accept eagerly, taking a large sip. She hides a smile in her own wine glass.

"What are you boys talking about?" Judy asks with a narrowed gaze at her husband. I can kind of see it now, what Jeff was talking about. He might run a label worth hundreds of millions of dollars, but Judy treats him no differently, never kissing his ass or babying him. If anything, she mocks and teases him in a way that, for anyone else, he would never tolerate.

But with Judy, he just smiles, hooks his arm around her waist, and presses a kiss to her hair.

"Oh, nothing. Just about how men with big egos need good women to bring them back to earth every once in a while." Judy nods like this is sage advice, turning to Katrina with a severe face.

"More than once in a while. Daily. Sometimes multiple times a day."

"Oh, don't worry. If there's one thing I know how to do, it's pick on Theo." Judy's eyes widen, something registering, but before she can speak, the front door creaks open, all heads in the room swiveling.

And in walks my sister, her boyfriend behind her.

"Are we late?" Warren asks, and my entire body goes stiff.

"No!" Judy shouts, removing herself from Jeff's side and walking with outstretched arms toward my sister. Savannah drops Warren's hand and starts dashing toward her surrogate mother with a smile. Everyone watches, and a small chuckle escapes Jeff's lips as she does, acting like she hasn't seen Judy in years rather than what is probably just days.

But my eyes are stuck behind them, where Warren is slowly walking into the house with a shit-eating grin because he fucking knows.

I don't know what, but he knows something.

Something that makes him think he has the upper hand on me. Even worse, on Katrina. Something that makes him think he has this job in the bag. My eyes leave him, skip over my sister, and move directly to Katrina, who is staring at Warren as well, but instead of the panic and shock I'm sure I'm barely masking, there's determination in her eyes.

Vengeance, even.

I step back, aligning my body next to hers, and slowly, anxiously, I move my hand to the small of her back. We never talked about this part of our deal, if we'd touch each other, where her boundaries lie, and at this moment, I realize this was a huge misstep.

We should have planned better.

We should have talked more.

We should have . . . anything, and now I'm wondering if I'm going to get kicked in the balls for touching my assistant's lower back, even though I'm only doing it in case I need to grab her and hold her back from attacking my sister's boyfriend.

But instead of tensing when I put my hand on her, her head moves to look at me, breaking her hyperfocus on Warren, and she smiles.

She smiles like this is normal, like this is us, like we're both not freaking the fuck out about this douche being here.

Her head moves closer to me, her breath grazing my ear as she whispers to me. Based on the tone of her voice, even though the words are far from loving, I know instinctively her face looks serene and kind and a small, simple smile is playing on her lips when she says, "What the fuck are they doing here?"

Without thinking or weighing the consequences of my actions, the hand on her back slides until I wrap my fingers around her waist and pull her in closer. Again, I'm surprised when she doesn't fight it, when she doesn't tense up and, instead, puts a hand to my chest, turning her face closer to mine so she can hear my low response.

"I have no fucking idea, but I don't like it."

I don't like it because I texted my sister on Friday and asked if she was coming this week. I didn't want her blindsided, and while I wasn't sure if I would tell her the truth or the lie, if she were to see me with Katrina, I wanted her to be prepared.

Relief flooded me when she said no, she had plans with Warren, but I should have fucking known it wouldn't be that easy. And the look on his smug face tells me every moment of this is intentional.

It's nearly identical to the day Savannah brought Warren to family dinner months ago, her eyes downcast when they walked through the door and announced they were dating.

The look Warren gave me that time was filled with something I didn't like, something that made me worry for my sweet, trusting sister. That day, I almost tossed out the unspoken truce I had with the man to play nice.

"Brother," Savannah says, stepping up to where I stand with Katrina. She steps back, but not too far, one hand moving down to grab mine, squeezing once in support or solidarity.

"Savannah," I say, accepting the hug she gives me but never dropping Katrina's hand. It feels like a lifeline in this moment.

Because there is no shot in hell we're not about to crash and burn tonight. No chance in hell this first test of our fake status isn't going to be the last.

"This is my fiancée, Katrina," I say and watch my sister's eyes go wide, knowing everything's about to come tumbling down.

TEN

KAT

We should have talked more is all that's going through my mind as Theo holds my hand so tightly, it is starting to go numb. It's as if he's channeling all of his nerves and panic into that one touch, the rest of his body completely lax and at ease.

We should have talked more about what was okay, if I could touch him, if I could comfort him. Code words and boundaries and what was an absolute no.

Instead, I'm flying by the seat of the pants I'm not even wearing.

"Fiancée!" Savannah yells.

"Yeah, I was going to tell you before tonight, but . . ." Theo pauses, his face going skeptical. "Wait, I thought you said you weren't coming?"

I wonder if she can hear the careful control he has on his patience or if I'm uniquely qualified since I've listened to him speak to agents and coworkers and artists a million and seven times this same way before hanging up and saying, "That guy is a fucking twat," with absolute venom in his voice then asking me to schedule a golf outing.

Somehow, I feel like my normal joking response of patting his hand, giving him a faux-concerned face, and saying, "Let it out, sweetie," won't go over well in this situation.

It would be funny though.

"We weren't, but—" Savannah starts, but Warren cuts in, his hand on her hip instantly quieting her in a way I very much do not like and speaking over her.

"I heard you were bringing your new fiancée and I needed to come meet her," he says.

Not we, I note.

He doesn't say we needed to meet her.

It's then I know for sure: Warren suspects this isn't real and is out to prove it.

Too bad for him, I'm really fucking competitive and I just made winning for Theo my new life's goal.

"So, I must know, how did it happen?" Jeff's wife, Judy, asks over dessert, leaning in with her chin in her hands, her eyes glazed over with adoration and romance.

It's been an . . . interesting meal, to say the least.

After a rushed round of introductions, the men were shooed into the living room to talk business by Judy, and then I sat around her kitchen island with Savannah, picking at a phenomenal charcuterie board, drinking wine, and getting to know them.

That part was amazing. I'd met Judy a few times when she was in the office, and I'd been introduced to Savannah once or twice in passing, but I learned tonight that I like both of them very much. Theo's sister is sweet and funny and way too good for Warren, and Judy is hilarious, takes no shit, and absolutely loves to make fun of Jeff in a loving way.

When dinner was ready, we all sat down in a gorgeous dining room to eat a delicious home-cooked meal, and that was when things got . . . uncomfortable.

Jeff joked and laughed, creating conversation everyone could join in on. Every single time, Warren would turn it to something work-related and when he could, mention something either he did well or something he decided was a fumble on Theo's part.

For example, he mentioned a new artist he had just signed (based on a recommendation I had given Theo, I didn't say) and then immediately gave his condolences to Theo because one of the artists he brought to the table at a meeting recently signed with Blacknote.

"How did what happen?" Theo asks.

"We obviously know how you two met," Judy says with a laugh. "But how did it go from work to . . . more?" She looks at her husband and blushes. "I don't know how much you know about Jeff and me, but I was his assistant once upon a time."

My mouth drops open in surprise and when I turn to look at Theo, his face has the same glimmer of shock and confusion.

Judy's straight, shoulder-length brown hair with generous streaks of gray sways as she shakes her head.

"Jeff here used to be a workaholic, never leaving the office before seven, coming in early every day. Hell, I think if I wasn't working for him, he never would have settled down."

The irony doesn't go over my head.

If he had known, would Theo have been easier to convince of this sham of a relationship? It would have been an even more obvious bonding moment, another pebble in the scale of Theo vs. Warren.

I open my mouth to answer, to throw in some bullshit story about how we started up a workplace relationship, but before I can, Theo starts talking.

The stone in my stomach sinks as he veers completely off the plan we agreed to on the way here.

"One day, we were working late. The entire office was gone, Katrina was sitting on her chair in my office, and she had a pencil in her hair."

My body stills slightly because that's not a rare occurrence. I do sit in a chair in his office after hours, in a chair I call my chair. A chair he puts his stuff on during the day so no one ever uses it, so I always have a place to sit if I'm called in to take notes for a meeting.

"She was rambling on about an idea she had for the gala last year, how to add a fundraising aspect, and I looked up at her, and she was smiling. I realized she was joking, picking on me, and . . . I don't know. Something snapped. I looked up at her and it was like something had shifted and I needed her to be mine. The world stopped spinning for a moment; everything felt hot and cold at the same time."

I remember a moment a few months ago when we were working together late. We were brainstorming what charity the gala could benefit, and somehow, I found a list of chaotic foundations. One was a group of clowns who did a yearly naked clown calendar to fund MS research. I'd had tears in my eyes, laughing so hard because his face when I jokingly suggested we buy a bunch for the gift bags was one of the most hilarious things I'd seen in a long time.

As I came down from my high, I realized he wasn't laughing with me. He was just . . . staring. I asked what he was doing and if he was okay because the look was . . . so different than his normal gaze. He shook his head, his hair shifting a bit before he told me he just thought of a solution for a different issue we'd been working on earlier in the day. It was mapped out and we left the office maybe thirty minutes later, max.

But I never forgot that look, or how it made my belly flip in a weird way.

But that's not what he's talking about, of course. He's not remembering a moment that's kept me up at night more than once with any kind of true fondness. It's just . . . a useful moment he also remembers for some strange reason.

"I think it's her laugh," Theo continues, his eyes moving around the room, confirming everyone is watching, enamored by his story.

And then they stop on me, warmth and kindness and gratitude there.

See? I tell the hopeless version of myself who has read too many books and watched too many movies and listened to too many songs. It's a convenient story. He's grateful I'm here, grateful I'm helping him. In fact, he probably knows I'm annoyed he's going off script.

"Her laugh?" Judy asks, but his eyes stay on mine. I smile and shake my head, playing into it, masking how his intense gaze burrows through me.

"It fills a room. It's magical. I could have the absolute worst day of my life, hear her laughing at her desk, and instantly feel better. If laughter is medicine, Katrina's is my cure."

See? He's so full of shit. My laugh is hands down the most obnoxious part of me, and he's poked fun at it more than once in our time working together.

It's all part of the façade.

"When did you become a goddamn poet?" Savannah asks with a laugh, and finally, it breaks Theo's gaze from me until he's glaring at his younger sister.

"Theo's a romantic," I say because it feels like what I'm supposed to, and I can't think of anything else with the way my face is burning.

"Theo?" Savannah asks, shock and a hint of humor in her words, and I look at her.

"Uh, yeah? His name is . . ." I pause, suddenly unsure.

"He hates being called Theo," Savannah says, and my stomach churns. "He hates nicknames generally." I think I did something wrong, but then she smiles wide. "I call him Teddy because I have since I was little and he'd have to fight me to make me stop. Do you know how hard it is to pronounce Theodore when you're eight and have lost both of your front teeth?" The entire table laughs, and I take a deep breath, happy the strange, electric air that was holding me hostage seems to have passed.

"Yeah, I don't know," I start. "On my very first day, I asked him if he wanted me to call him Mr. Carter or Theo. He picked Theo."

There's a small smile when his eyes meet mine again, and for not the first time since this all started, I question everything.

"I never had a shot, even from that first day," he says to me then looks to Jeff. "So, what are you looking forward to doing on your first day of retirement?" With his words, his tone shifts completely, like he's changing the subject or moving from a private conversation to one for the entire room, but I still feel his words ricocheting through me.

As I look around the room, catching Judy's eye as she winks at me, I know we've somehow managed to pass this first trial by fire.

ELEVEN

KAT

"So, that went . . . ," I start a minute into the drive back to my place.

I don't quite know how to sum tonight up to be honest. It's rare I'm at a loss for words, but that's how I feel right now.

Dinner was uncomfortable, but shockingly, it was not because I was in a room full of near strangers and my boss, pretending we've had some kind of solid, quiet, secret romance for months.

It was because of the way Warren's douchey gaze was dissecting every single thing I said or did, trying to find the crack in our "relationship" I knew he was searching for to blow our plan up.

"Terrible. It went terrible," Theo fills in. I knew he'd say that, of course. It's all in his jaw that has been tight since he turned his back to Judy as she waved to us from the front door, the way his thumbnail has been scraping the side of his pointer finger nearly raw, something he only does when he's incredibly frustrated or anxious about something.

You work closely with someone for at least eight hours a day, five days a week, and you learn their tells.

"I think it went well!" I say with a smile. He sighs, running a hand through his hair, making it go askew, and leaving it there. He might actually be a bit more anxious than I calculated, if he doesn't even care that his hair looks a mess.

"You don't know Warren," he says through a grumble. I roll my eyes. I hate the man and don't trust him as far as I can throw him, but if anything, tonight was even more of a success because he was there.

Warren tried every avenue to trip us up all night, and somehow, we miraculously passed each test.

"Well, we're not selling Warren our romance, are we? We're selling it to Jeff. Though, I really don't trust his intentions with your sister," I say, even though it might be an overstep. "I told you, he gives ick. And your sister very much does not. She deserves a million times better than that asshole."

Theo sighs and nods, turning to me at a red light. "I know, but Savannah's the type of person that, if I tell her he's bad news, the next thing I know, she'll be in Vegas, marrying him."

"My kind of woman."

"Why does this not surprise me?" I just smile sweetly and move to the next topic.

"Anything I should know ahead of time before I schedule a lunch with her?" I ask. Between dinner and dessert, Savannah and I chatted quite a bit, ending in, to my surprise, Theo insisting we meet up soon for lunch. She instantly agreed, saying she was dying to chat one-on-one, "Without my annoying brother breathing down your neck."

Lunch with Savannah Carter should have made me nervous, but with that statement alone, I was sold on her, trying to figure out how to stay friends with her after this all blows over and if she would be willing to go to lunch with Abbie, Cami, Liv, and me one day, too.

Theo groans like this is just another painful moment from his night. "Yeah, sorry about that. I didn't mean to drag you into her chaos."

"I think she's sweet!"

"She's a pain in my ass, but she's my sister. She needs more good friends, less of the spoiled brat daughters of Judy's friends."

"You're a good brother," I say, my voice low.

"How do you know anything about how I am with my sister?"

"Theo, I think you forget that I've been working very closely with you for nearly a year. I field almost all of your calls and see your calendar. You have every little thing related to her in there, from her birthday to random anniversaries. I buy her flowers from you and send her random coffee gift cards just because weekly." He sighs and lets the quiet span for a bit before he speaks.

"We're all we have, and I got more time with our parents. I was sixteen when they died, but Savannah was barely eight. I'm . . . I'm filling that gap."

My stomach dips at the sweetness. I thought they were just a close sibling pair, but this makes so much more heartbreaking sense. This is the kind of thing that makes me wonder what the fuck is wrong with Jeff Bates to think Theo needs a relationship in order to have a life, to prove his worthiness of running Catalyst.

"But she has a hard time making friends, and I'm obviously no help there. That's why I kind of threw you under the bus. I can tell her you're busy, or—" I roll my eyes and cut him off, digging in my purse for a baggie of pretzels. The bag squeaks open as I reply:

"Can you please shut up? I just told you I'm happy to meet with her. She seems cool. Much cooler than you," I say with a smile, and he glares, his eyes moving to my hands on my bag of pretzels as I toss one in my mouth.

"Are you really eating?" he asks.

"Yup," I say.

"We just ate."

"I was too nervous to eat much. And this ass is fed on a constant supply of snacks," I say with a smile. For a split second, I think his eyes almost move to said ass, then the red light turns green and his eyes are back to the road.

"You're going to make crumbs."

"And? You make enough to hire someone to get this thing detailed once a week. A few crumbs won't hurt you." He grumbles some kind of response I don't bother to ask him about, and we drive back to my place in relative silence.

"You can leave me at the door," I say as we pull up to my apartment, but he keeps driving and glares at me.

"I won't be doing that," he says, and even though I want to, I don't respond. He's got that look in his eyes, his jaw tight, like if I argue with him, he might actually snap.

Is it fucked that a small part of me wants to see what uptight, always put-together Theo looks like when he's snapping?

I shake my head, trying to get that unhelpful image out of my mind.

Theo parks and then gives me a look as he reaches for his door handle, and somehow, I know that look means *stay the fuck where you are*, so I don't move. He walks around the car, opening my door for me.

"Wow, what a gentleman," I say with a laugh as he puts a hand out to help me from the low car.

"I told you, my mother raised me well. And you've met Judy. I have no choice."

"You know, your commitment to not dating is really only hurting the women of New Jersey. The dating pool could most certainly use a gentleman like you," I say. He squeezes my hand but doesn't say anything as we walk to the entrance of my building.

He also doesn't let go.

"You can leave me here," I say, and he glares at me once more.

"I'm walking you up, Katrina." I glare back.

"This isn't a real date."

"This place is sketchy as fuck, Katrina. I'm walking you up."

"You know I come in and out of this place regularly, right? Like, every day?" He just stares at me until I resign myself to the fate of him walking me up to my place, and I push the door open.

He doesn't follow me; instead, he stares at the box that requires a passcode, clearly confused as to how I got in without pressing a single button.

"Oh. That doesn't work. It's totally for show," I say, and he begrudgingly follows me.

"That's unsafe."

"That's living in an apartment in Hudson City. I chose a slightly nicer part of the city, but the trade-off was things aren't . . . perfect." He harrumphs in response, eyes moving to where the elevator says out of service.

I should really shut up, but . . . "I don't think that elevator has ever worked if I'm being honest." He gives me and the elevator a death look before moving his annoyed gaze to the empty front desk. "Someone does, in fact, man the front desk," I say, but I leave out that it's only from 9-5, so I'm not actually sure who or if they actually do sit there because I leave before they get there and get home after they're long gone.

When we get to the stairwell, Theo's hand tightens nearly painfully in mine.

"Jesus fuck, Katrina. Do I not pay you enough?" he asks, eyes stuck on the lightbulb in the hallway that's been out for at least four months. I've submitted a report to management, but alas . . .

"Oh, you do. I just like shoes better than I like apartments. It's a balance, you know?" He walks up the stairs with me, but each step sounds angrier than the last.

"You're telling me you chose to live in an unsafe apartment building so you can buy shoes?"

I don't tell him that it's not about the shoes: it's the dopamine hit I get when impulse buying a pair of pretty shoes that caught my eye. Having ADHD means I have horrible impulse control, so living in a more affordable apartment is actually a point of fiscal responsibility, something both of my parents always hammered into my mind my entire life. By saving a bit on a cheaper (though still safe, despite Theo's dramatics) apartment, I'm leaving a cushion for myself to both buy what I want and set some money aside for savings.

Instead, with a wise smile, I say, "And dresses. I like pretty dresses, too."

"Jesus Christ, Katrina. We need to . . ." We reach my floor as his voice phases out, his mind going somewhere, calculating. I walk him down the hall and stop in front of my door.

"This is me," I say, digging in my purse for my keys.

"You know, we never talked," he starts, finally dropping my hand to scratch behind his neck, suddenly uncomfortable. "We never talked about what you'll get from this. I can pay you for your time, or —" I was waiting for this, knowing there is no way Theo, who thinks all things should be just and equal and balanced, would just let it go.

Wishful thinking and all, I suppose.

"No," I say firmly, cutting him off. "Nope."

"No?" He looks at me, confused.

I'm starting to realize he does that quite a lot, looks at me like I'm some kind of alien, a species he doesn't understand in the least.

"No. You're not paying me." I say it firmly because I believe it firmly. I'm doing this because I like Theo as a person and I think he's the best fit for Catalyst. I'm doing it because this is the first place I've actually liked working and I know Warren with fuck that up.

"I already pay you," he says like that's his leg to stand on.

"Not for this, you don't."

"Well, I'd like to. I—" I cut him off, putting a hand on his shoulder and looking into his eyes.

"I'm doing this as friends. I'm doing this for Catalyst. I'm doing this because I'm a little fucked in the head and I love schemes." I shake my head, my hair swaying against my back as I do. "But I will not be doing this for money."

"Katrina, be reasonable—

"I am. And I'm not taking your money."

"This is ridiculous," he says, his face going a bit red with irritation. It's strange because I've seen him talk calmly to people who are vowing to ruin him, his company, and not bat an eye. But refusing to let him pay me for this is making him angry. "You deserve to be compensated for the time and energy you're using to help me."

"We're friends, Theo," I explain, my voice low. I don't know if I've ever told him this, but now seems the right time to confess it.

Because that's how I feel about Theodore Carter, despite the fact that he's a grumpy asshole who likes to boss me around. "Friends help each other. That's it, Theo."

He stares for long moments where I question if I made a mistake, if I just made this super fucking awkward, before his brow furrows and he speaks.

"We're friends?" He sounds . . . baffled. Shocked, even. Not in the way I was nervous for, in the pitying, *oh, you poor, silly thing, you think we're friends* way. More in a *wow, I can't believe anyone could think I'm their friend* way. It's a bit heartbreaking if I'm being honest.

It's then I start to wonder, if only for a split second, if Jeff wasn't right.

Theo's life revolves around Catalyst. He has no outside relationships I'm aware of, and I know when he goes to the doctor and the dentist and when he has dinner with his sister.

But there are never dates on that calendar.

Never social outings with friends.

Does Theo . . . Does Theo have friends?

"Well . . . yeah, Theo. We're friends. What else would you call this?" I ask, my hand waving between us, indicating the two of us.

"Employee, employer? Coworkers? Colleagues?"

"I mean, yeah, but I always thought . . ." Now, I feel stupid. Really freaking stupid. The hand holding my keys moves, and I try to find the lock, to end this uncomfortable conversation before it somehow gets worse. "I should get into my apartment. It's late, and like you said, this is kind of a sketchy building. I—" I don't know what I was going to say next, but I can't say anything because suddenly, my wrist is in a strong grasp, my body is being turned, and my back is pressed to the door of my apartment.

And Theo is pinning me in place, his body pressing against me, his face mere inches from mine.

"I would be absolutely honored to be your friend, Katrina," he whispers, his warm breath coasting across my lips in a way I shouldn't find intriguing. Not when he's my boss and this is fake and he's in an emotional state.

So I smile up at him and speak, ignoring how my heart is beating out of my chest.

"And I'm honored to be yours, Theo."

TWELVE

THEO

On Monday, Katrina's laugh fills up the small reception area between my office and the rest of the floor, the sound loud and joyful.

"Yeah, that works! I'll get your number from Theo," she says, piquing my interest. It's not uncommon for Katrina to be friendly with anyone who calls to speak with me; that's just her personality.

But getting their number . . .

A curl of irritation and something else too close to jealousy for my liking spins in my stomach at the mere idea of her getting close to one of my clients.

Who could it be?

That crooning singer, Patrick? He's single, I believe.

Maybe Hudson from The Saturn Experiment? The last time he was here, he stared at her ass for a moment too long for a professional setting.

Or it could be—

My phone ringing interrupts my mental breakdown of every man who has ever come into the building and breathed the same air as Katrina because I'm obviously going out of my goddamned mind.

"Who is it?" I ask.

"Oof, you good, boss man?" Katrina says with a laugh in her voice.

"I'm fine. Who is it? Is it Hudson Jones?" That seems the most likely suspect.

"It's your sister?" she replies slowly with a question in her voice. "Are you okay? I can tell her you're busy if—"

My pulse, which I didn't realize was racing, slows, and I take a deep breath.

What the fuck is wrong with me?

"Yeah, I'm fine. Sorry. I just . . . I, uh, I got an email that is frustrating me."

"Anything I can help with?" she asks, nothing but kindness in her voice.

Kindness I don't deserve since I just assumed she was making after-hours date plans while "engaged" to me.

"No, no. I've got it. Just dumb shit. Send Savannah over," I say. She hesitates before answering.

"Okay. Well, let me know if you need anything after, okay? I can run and get you one of those matchas you like from the shop on the corner."

I don't deserve her.

"I'm good, Katrina. Thank you, though."

"Alright," she says, then I watch more than hear her press a button, transferring my sister to my line.

"What can I do for you, Savannah?" I ask, my pulse still regulating itself, still coming down from a high I didn't realize was suffocating me.

"I like her," she says, completely ignoring my question. "I like her a lot, and I'm really pissed I just met her yesterday. I can't believe you hid her from me for so long!" There's a whine in her voice that has me rolling my eyes. Despite the trauma of our parents dying when she was young, no one on this earth is even close to as spoiled as Savannah Carter is.

"It wasn't intentional," I say with a sigh, leaning back in my desk chair.

"Wasn't intentional," she repeats in a mocking, deep voice. "What do you mean? It was fully intentional." Her disbelieving glare is almost audible through the line. I know right now, her eyebrow is probably arched, a disapproving sneer on her lips.

"I didn't want to mess with her employment," I say, sticking to the plan Katrina and I made that seemed to work well at Jeff's. How I didn't know that Judy was once his own assistant, I don't know, but it absolutely helps in the grand scheme of this lie.

"You're her boss," she says, deadpan. "What were you gonna do, fire her if you broke up? You'd never do that."

"It wasn't about me. I didn't want other people to think differently of her. She's a hard worker and has a lot of pride." Not a lie. Maybe that's the key to getting through this without a full-blown ulcer: to tell the fewest actual lies as humanly possible. To weave the lies in with the truths until it's a seamless tapestry of bullshit.

"So, she's not pregnant or something. You really like her, don't you? This isn't just you checking off a box on the checklist of what you think you *should* be doing." my sister asks after a pause, her tone shifting so there's awe and softness in her words with just a hint of shock.

"I do," I say, ignoring the first part. It isn't a lie, either. I do enjoy Katrina's presence—it's why we work so well together. She just doesn't have to know that I mean it in a platonic, coworker way. There's a long pause while she seems to process this information.

"I'm forcing her to go to lunch with me," she says in a way that sounds more like a challenge than an announcement.

"Savannah . . ."

"She's going to be my sister-in-law," she starts, and that guilt ratchets up in my chest. There's excitement there, in the voice of my sister who has always longed for any sense of family nearly her entire life. More of it. Lots of. "I want to get to know her. She's nice. Plus, you hid her for long enough. It's my turn to roast you in private to her."

"Roast me?"

"Oh, for sure. It's fully my job to tell her about all of the dumb, embarrassing things you did when we were kids. She needs to know what she's getting herself into."

"Savannah, Katrina has a life, you know," I start. But then I look to the doorway of my office, Katrina standing there, leaning on the side of the wall, a manila folder in her arms and a smile on her lips.

"It's fine," she mouths with a smile and a shake of her head. I widen my eyes at her, and she does the same back, a challenge.

There's a silent conversation of, *this is a bad idea* (me) and something along the lines of, *wouldn't it be strange if your new fiancée didn't want to get lunch with your sister?* (Katrina), and I don't really know when Katrina became the voice of reason in this chaos, but here we are.

"Fine. It's fine." My sister squeals in excitement, and guilt floods me once more. It's hard for her to make friends, and here is Katrina, not only helping me, but helping her in a way. "You're right, you should get to know her." I pause, my eyes on my assistant, a strange surge of gratitude rushing through me. "She's great. The kindest person I know." There's a pause I barely register as I watch a blush creep over Katrina's cheeks before she waves the folder at me and flips me off with a roll of her eyes.

But I think it's then something in me snaps, like a glow stick. The cold, unfeeling part of me suddenly blooms with neon warmth and light, the urge to continue on breaking everything I once knew until everything is aglow overwhelming. Suddenly, I want to see just how much I could make her blush, what other compliments I could give her to get that reaction, and even more, what other reactions she might show me.

"You know, I wasn't sure at first," my sister says, bringing my attention from where it had drifted off. "But that? That seals it."

"Seals what?"

"That she's really, really good for you, Teddy."

"What do you mean?"

"You don't . . ." She pauses, like she isn't sure how to say it, then continues, "You don't like people."

"I like people just fine," I say, my eyes still on Katrina, and she snorts out a nearly silent laugh. I give her a glare and she lifts her hands, turning back to her desk while I try to think of who I can use to convince my sister I do, in fact, like people. "I like you."

"I'm your sister. You have to like me."

"Millions of siblings who never talk beg to differ." I just know she's rolling her eyes when she huffs.

"Besides me. Who do you like?"

"I like . . . I like Jeff," I say.

"You idolize Jeff."

"I do not idolize Jeff." She makes a sound that somehow says *sure, you don't* without saying a thing. "I like lots of people, Savannah," I say with exasperation.

"Who?" she asks bluntly.

"I like . . ." I swallow before I say it, the words tasting sour. "I like Warren." My sister snorts out a laugh.

"You tolerate Warren, which is fine. He takes some getting used to. He's sweet, though," she says like she's trying to convince me. "You'll see. You just need to be around when it's just us more. He's different with me. And outside work."

"Yesterday was outside work," I say, and I wish I hadn't.

"But Jeff was there," she says, justifying.

"Jeff is always going to be there, Savannah. You know that." Silence fills the line as she tries to figure out what to say and how to respond, and I wish I had let it just die before speaking. But at the very least, it got her off the subject of me having no friends, I suppose.

With that reminder, I decide it's time to change the subject before it goes poorly. "So, when are you meeting up with Katrina?" I ask, thinking we should probably have a meeting before then to fill her in on anything my sister might ask about that she might not know.

"She's sending me her schedule later, and we'll cross reference. My weekends get kind of crazy, and she has a big-girl job," my sister says. She did not go into the family business; instead, she went to school for a degree in photography, specializing in family photography and weddings.

"Can you do lunch?" I ask.

"We need to go shopping, too," she adds.

"What? Why?"

"Because you have events coming up that your new fiancée will have to dress for. The gala, for one. I'm sure Judy will throw you two a big engagement party." Dread fills my lungs. "And, of course, there's the fundraiser luncheon in April."

Katrina is going to murder me.

But on account of her refusing to let me pay for anything, my mind starts to put together how I can have Savannah make sure she buys everything and anything she needs with my card.

"That makes sense. Can you do it on a weekday if I get Katrina out early?"

"Yes, are you saying she can go to lunch and shopping with your sister on the clock?"

I don't tell her in a way, all of this is on the clock. "Yes, hold on," I say, pulling up the joint calendar Katrina makes for me, mostly green chunks of time blocked off for my calendar. However, there's the occasional purple line for times Katrina is unavailable. Unlike me, she keeps only work appointments on this calendar, but I know on Tuesdays, she meets up with a friend for lunch, and on Fridays, she leaves the office early to avoid traffic.

"Tuesday, she goes to lunch with a friend, and Wednesday, we have a meeting with Jeff, but she could leave early on Thursday, to go to lunch and shopping with you."

My sister is silent.

"You know her schedule?"

I roll my eyes.

"I mean, I can read her calendar that I also have access to." There's another pause before she speaks.

"Does she put personal events on her calendar? That's kind of overstepping, Teddy." Quickly, I correct her. See, this is why I need Katrina. She helps to buffer me from putting my fucking foot in my mouth.

"What? No. I'm not intruding on her personal calendar or anything."

"But you know she goes to lunch with a friend." Her words are filled with hesitant skepticism.

"She does it every week." I pause, starting to worry. "Why, is it weird that I know that?" It's been so long since I've dated, much less been in a serious relationship, and suddenly, I'm worried I'm doing a pretend one wrong.

"No, it's normal, I guess. I just didn't think . . ." As her voice trails off, I begin to panic. She doesn't believe we're real. She doesn't think this relationship is actually happening. She doesn't— "I didn't think you'd be the type, you know?"

"The type?"

"The type to take note of a woman's schedule, to try and make plans for her. That kind of thing." I pause before sighing.

"Jesus, Savannah, you really think I'm that big of an asshole?"

"No, no, I just . . . I don't know. Maybe? You're so wrapped up in work. You dating was a shock, much less being engaged. I just . . ." If she were in front of me, I'd see her shrug. "It's a surprise. A good one, but a surprise nonetheless." There's another pause before she adds on, "I'm happy for you. I was worried you'd never settle down, never find someone."

Why does everyone think that?

I know I work a lot, but when did that become a crime?

"But then you found Kat," she says, wistful happiness in her voice.

I glance over to where Katrina is sitting at her desk, chatting to the receptionist whose name I can never remember, leaning over to grab a snack from her drawer. The receptionist says something, and her head tips back, that melodic laugh finding its way into my office.

"Yeah. Then I found Kat," I whisper, wondering not for the first time what I would do without her.

THIRTEEN

THEO

"Can you come into my office, Katrina?" I call through my open door to where Katrina sits. She doesn't respond, but she doesn't have to. A few moments later, her body, dressed in pink pants and a black blouse today, is in my doorway. "Close the door and sit, please?" She scrunches her nose at me but steps inside anyway, putting her iPad on my desk before moving my briefcase to the floor and beginning to scrape her chair across the carpet.

"You know, if I didn't know your deepest, darkest secret, I'd be nervous you were about to fire me."

"I can't fire you if you know my deepest secret?" I ask, joking, but clearly, it doesn't come across well when she freezes, the chair halfway between its place by the door and in front of my desk, her eyes wide.

"What?"

"Jesus, I'm joking. It was a joke, Katrina." She rolls her eyes and sighs before sitting down finally.

"You really need to work on your delivery," she says with a groan.

"Why would you get fired?" I ask, confused because never once have I even contemplated letting her go.

She's much too valuable to me.

To the company, I correct myself.

"Theo, every time you tell me to come into your office and close the door with that grumpy, no-nonsense tone, I assume I fucked something up big time and you're ready to fire me." I stare at her, and she looks at me like that's the obvious conclusion.

"You never fuck up," I say.

"That's kind, but untrue." She leans forward, grabs her tablet, and leans back in her chair, crossing one long leg over the other.

"How often do you think I'm going to fire you?" I ask curiously as she opens the cover of her iPad and flips it back, grabbing the stylus she keeps tucked into the case.

"Oh, at least once a week. The most in one week was four times. That was a rough one." She smiles blindingly at me. "It was the week Blacknote got to Piper Shaun before you. Thankfully, I usually just have to remind myself you will absolutely crumble without me and I get less panicky."

That was a shit week, and even though I've never said it aloud, my gut tells me Warren was part of the issue there, too. I don't know why, but I blurt out, "I think Warren gave them that information, you know." It feels like a dark secret I'm admitting out loud, even though the evidence that he's done that exact thing recently is fresh in my mind.

"Oh, he did. One hundred percent."

"You think so, too?" She nods. "You never told me?" Her smile dips, and she leans forward.

"I like working here. It's the first job I've had where I haven't gotten violently bored." She's mentioned this a few times before, explaining that it was incredibly important to her parents she go to college, but she knew she needed a degree that was flexible and versatile, choosing a degree in Communication for that reason.

"What else have you done? Work wise?" She smiles.

"Oh, everything. I worked in the makeup section of a department store. That was fun because I worked with my best friend, but having to touch people's faces gave me the ick. I've tried pet grooming, which was fun until I got bit by a Papillon. I started to get my cosmetology license, to do hair, but people are super gross, so that was a no. Hmm, let's see, what else." She taps the stylus to her chin, thinking. "I worked at a sandwich shop for a few weeks, retail in a clothing store." A pause before smiling. "One summer, I worked at a zoo. That was a blast."

"What did you do at a zoo?"

"I fed the lions." I sit in shock at her response, and she waits a beat before dissolving into laughter. "Jesus, Theo. You're so gullible. I did not feed the lions. I sold lemonade. But I got to wander a lot and met so many cool animals. Gertrude is a giraffe there. I still like to go visit her." She says this like it's a common phrase.

"You're friends with a . . . giraffe?" I ask. My mind goes to my conversations with Savannah, where I couldn't name a single real friend, and here Katrina is, making friends with fucking giraffes.

Honestly, it fits if I really think about it. She would make friends with a giraffe.

"Yeah. She's cool, and she loves leaves." I stare at her and shake my head.

"You're a conundrum, you know that?" She shrugs. "Okay, so why am I being called in here?"

"My sister." Her face clears and she nods with a smile.

"So precious. I love her already."

"You're going to lunch with her on Thursday."

"I am?" I nod, and she smiles. "How do you know I don't have some extravagant plans, Mr. Carter." There is no fucking reason for me to shift in my seat when she says that. It's fucked really.

But the reality is, it's always been that way.

On Katrina's first day, she asked me if she should call me Theo or Mr. Carter, and I fucking froze. Something about my last name on her lips tipped some kind of scale in my mind, contorting it in a way that was absolutely the furthest from professional it could possibly be.

I chose Theo, even though not a soul in my life has ever called me that at the risk of meeting my wrath.

"I can see your calendar, Katrina. And despite you, along with everyone else in my life, getting on my ass for not having a social life, you don't have much of one yourself outside your small group of friends. You have the same schedule every week. All I had to do was check that you didn't have anything else I wasn't privy to." She stares at me for a full minute, I think, before she bursts out in laughter.

"I didn't even know you knew how to open my calendar," she says, wiping a tear from her face.

"Well, I do."

"Interesting. Does that mean you're not completely incapable of looking at your calendar and don't need incessant reminders of when your own appointments are?" I fight the urge to chew on my bottom lip, a habit I picked up as a kid and thought I had dropped in high school until Katrina, with her constant needling, brought it back to life.

I don't admit I like her reminding me of what I need to do on any given day or how I like her having an excuse to pop her head in and nudge me about something, instead giving a basic, canned response.

"I'm unbearably busy, Katrina, you know that. The less time I have to spend digging around on my calendar, the better." She hums a noise that sounds very much like she does not believe me.

Fair.

That's fair.

"Anyway, is there anything you need to prepare for lunch with my sister?"

"Prepare?" I sigh, forgetting she doesn't actually know Savannah.

"My sister is incredibly nosy and needling. She'll ask you a hundred questions." Katrina stares at me and then gives me a soft smile.

"No, I don't need anything from you, Theo. I'm a big girl. I'll be fine."

"I'm serious. She's going to ask you everything from how we met to when we first got together to how many kids we want to have one day."

"Do you want to have kids?" she asks, tipping her head to the side, reading me in a way no one else does. But then again, I don't allow anyone else to.

"What?"

"If she asks, how should I answer? Do you want kids?"

"I mean . . ." I pause, confused, but answer anyway. "Yes. I do. One day."

"Hmm," is all she says in reply. I feel like this is the spot where a normal human would ask her the question in return, so I do.

Uncomfortable and awkward because I think that's all I know in this woman's presence, I start:

"Do you, uh . . ." I pause, my hand reaching behind my neck to scratch there, watching as her smile spreads across her face. "Do you want kids?"

"Yes," she says, that smile in her voice as well as on her lips. "One day." I know without her saying it, she's enjoying my discomfort.

"Hmm," I say, clearing my throat. "Well, that's good, I guess." She doesn't speak, and the silence is killing me, so my dumbass keeps going, filling in the void. "That's good. You'd, uh. You'd be good at that. Being a mom and whatnot."

I'm a moron. I don't know how to speak to anyone. Jeff is right. I can't run this company. I can't even have a basic, getting-to-know-you conversation with my assistant of a year. I should—

"Alright, alright, bud, don't give yourself a coronary," she says, letting me off the hook. "No need to ask all the deep questions. I'm sure I'll be fine with your sister."

"Katrina, I know you're capable, but my sister is . . . She's a pain. She won't stop; she's going to ask questions incessantly—" She cuts me off.

"And I'll be just fine, Theo."

"Katrina . . . ," I start.

I don't know why I'm panicking because we don't have any other option. I pushed Savannah on her, and now she's making plans. That's what happens. I wanted my sister to have more friends, and now she has one. I got us into this mess.

"Theo." Katrina sighs, her eyes going soft. "Tell me who in this world, for better or worse, knows you better than I do? It might mostly be on a professional work level, but I know you, Theo. I'll be fine."

I stare at her and can't argue. It's the truth.

For better or for worse, Katrina Delgado knows me best of all.

FOURTEEN

THEO

When Katrina pops her head into my office on Thursday before leaving to go have lunch with my sister, I barely even look up. Instead, I sit staring at the thick piece of cardstock Jeff handed me a few minutes prior, my stomach churning with nausea.

Our next trial by fire has arrived.

"Earth to Theo. Everything good?" she asks, leaning in the door-frame, her brow furrowed in confusion. I don't respond, and she steps farther in, her heels sinking into the plush carpet soundlessly. "Theo?" When I look up, she's barely a foot from me, standing behind my desk with me.

"What are you doing on March first?"

"Why do I feel like I suddenly have plans?" I hand her the invite Jeff brought to me, and she flops into her chair, which is already in front of my desk from an earlier meeting.

"I have a stack more, in case you want to, uh, invite anyone," I say with a sigh.

"An engagement party." She looks at me with raised eyebrows.

"Yeah. Judy, she, uh, she loves parties." Her smile comes out, though even now, it's a bit uneasy. Nervous.

"Who doesn't?"

"Me," I say, and she rolls her eyes.

"That's because you're boring as hell and don't like people."

"I like people." I sigh through a groan.

"Yeah, okay. You like your sister, I think. And you like Jeff in a weird, contrived way."

"I like you," I say without even thinking then instantly wish I could take it back.

"You like me?" she says, a wide smile on her face and her hand holding the invite going to her chest.

"I mean, I don't . . . You know I like you, but I don't . . . We don't . . . ," I stutter out. She lets me flounder for a full minute before she starts laughing hard, needing to wipe her tears and catch her breath before she can speak.

"God, Theo, you should see your face!" I lean back in my chair and sigh with what I hope she doesn't realize is relief before glaring at her.

"Why are you like this?"

"Funny? I don't know. I was just born this way. A gift, you might say." I harumph in response, and that pulls another laugh from her. She stands, stepping around my desk before resting her ass, and I sit back in my chair, a small smile on my lips despite her driving me insane.

For a moment, I can't help but think how, to anyone walking past my office, this would look exactly like we want it to. A fiancée sitting on her groom-to-be's desk, giggling with him before she leaves for the day.

But it's just us.

"So this party," she starts, flipping the thick cardstock over and reading the details. "What's the dress code?"

"Dress code?"

"Yeah, like, is it fancy? Jeans and a tee shirt? A dress? Heels, flats?" I stare at her and feel my eyes getting wider. She rolls hers in response and tosses the invite onto my desk.

"God, you're useless. Is Savannah going?"

"What?"

"Savannah. Your sister. Is she going too?"

"I mean . . ." She stares at me, waiting for me to speak, and suddenly, I feel like an idiot. Like someone who is supposed to know answers but doesn't.

The only person on earth I've ever felt that way around is Katrina.

"It's fine. I'll ask her today."

"What?"

"Your sister. I'll ask her today what the dress code is. We're going shopping anyway. She can help me figure it out." There's a pause as she reads the card before she mumbles, "It's dressy. Shit."

"What?"

"The dress code is dressy. Black tie." I'm understanding slowly.

"Okay, why is that shit?" She sighs.

"I have to wear white."

"What? No you don't."

"Yes, I do. I'm the bride-to-be, Theo. Brides wear white."

"Oh. Is that a problem?" I look at her and try and picture her in white. I don't think it's a color she's ever worn. Maybe she hates wearing it? Maybe—

"No, it's not, but it means I'm going to need to find a fancy white dress." She sighs. "You're a real pain in my ass, you know that, Carter? Gotta go buy a whole new wardrobe now." She says it with a smile, but my gut churns all the same.

"You don't have to—"

"I do. It's fine. If I can't find anything with Savannah, my friend Abbie will have a blast figuring out what I should wear. She's going to be in heaven. Not so much when I tell her the budget, but—"

"Budget?" Her mocking glare returns.

"Yes, Theodore, some of us have them. Some of us don't basically run a giant conglomerate on our own."

"I know what a fucking budget is, Katrina. I'm just not sure why you think you need one." She gives me a strange look.

"Well, you see, I don't run a multimillion-dollar company, as much as I like to joke that I basically do."

"But I do." Her confusion doesn't clear, so I explain, "You're doing this for me. I'm footing your wardrobe bill. Obviously." She shakes her head, her long, dark hair swaying, the ends brushing past her breasts in a way I am not allowed to take note of.

I do all the same.

Fuck me.

"Oh, god, no, I didn't mean it like that. I don't need you to—" She starts to argue, but I cut her off.

"I know you weren't looking for money, Katrina, but I'm paying. You're doing this for me. It's basically a write-off." She looks at me dubiously, as she should because buying your fake fiancée clothes is most definitely not a write-off, but we don't have to touch on that just yet.

Or ever, really.

"That's not necessary, Theo," she says, her voice firm. I ignore her, pulling my own phone out and looking for the cash-sending app I've used in the past to pay her back for food or coffee.

How much do clothes cost? I think, but I know if I ask, she'll lowball me, if she even bothers to give me a number.

I type a few digits out, delete and add a bit more, hit send, and then put my phone down, crossing my arms on my chest.

"There. Will that do?"

"Wha—" she starts, then her phone beeps with a notification. Her eyes drop to her hand where her phone is and she glares at me. "Theo."

"Is that enough?"

"You really don't have to—"

"Not my question," I say, my voice going firm. "I asked if it's enough." She looks at me with shock on her face, and I don't know if it's the money or the fact that I'm speaking to her like that, but either way, she nods slowly.

"I, uh . . . yeah. That will do." A beat passes before she shakes her head, and I reach for my phone to send more. "Actually, fuck, I can't do this. This is too much."

I should have known that was much too easy. Not nearly enough arguing.

"It's not—"

"A dress costs one, two hundred dollars max, Theo. Shoes another hundred. This is five thousand dollars," she says, showing me the screen of her phone as if I didn't just make the deposit myself.

"Buy a nice dress. Buy nice shoes."

"I can't do that, Theo. Seriously, I can't."

"You can. We have events to go to, Katrina. The gala, family dinners, this engagement party. There's a charity luncheon Judy runs and a bunch of other shit I'm definitely forgetting. I want you to feel comfortable. It's the least I can do. Please. Go spend my money on pretty clothes."

She stares at me, her face and resolve softening, and I know I'm almost there. I've almost won.

"You told me yourself you'd rather spend money on clothes than a safer apartment."

She continues to stare, then her looks turn catlike and for the first time, I see it. The nickname everyone else calls her, how it fits her perfectly.

She is a cat.

"What if I need more?" she asks, and I fight back a smile of my own, instead leaning forward to grab my wallet from my back pocket. I open it up and grab my personal credit card, putting it in her hand and curling her small fingers around the black plastic.

"I got you stuck in this situation; you get whatever you need. Make it hurt, kitten."

I don't know what makes me do it, calling her fucking kitten like she's actually mine and we're to the point where we have fucking pet names, but it fits.

It fits her.

For a moment, I wonder if she purrs when she's content before I scrub that out of my fucking mind.

Then I do another ridiculous thing, lifting her hand wrapped around the credit card and wrapped in my hand and pressing my lips to her soft skin. Her own lips part and her eyes widen as she watches every single movement, but she doesn't say anything.

It's a bad idea.

A terrible one, even.

But I can't find it in me to stop.

FIFTEEN

KAT

I'm still confused as fuck by the time I get into my car and drive to downtown Hudson City, where I meet Savannah, because what the fuck just happened?

Theo called me kitten.

And he kissed my hand like I was some duchess and we were at a ball. I don't even remember what happened after because I basically ran from his office with not much more than a see you later.

Lunch is at a precious little café Savannah takes me to, and I instantly put it into my mental list of places to take Abbie. She would love it here, with gold and pink accents everywhere and cutesy little names for all of the dishes.

I was worried the meal would be uncomfortable, that it would take us a bit to get into an easy conversation, but Savannah proved me wrong, instantly asking me a bunch questions about myself, my friends, my family, and, of course, Theo.

I'm surprised when for most of my answers, I don't have to lie. She asks me things like the most annoying thing Theo does (when he has a call he is anxious about, he's grumpy all morning, the nerves getting to him and resulting in short, irritated answers and working with his door closed. Not an ick, but something I like to make fun of him for) and when we're thinking of for the wedding. (We're taking it slow and trying to survive Jeff's retirement before we decide, which Savannah agrees is smart.)

Originally, I had planned to use this meeting as a fact-finding mission, to learn more about my rival (Warren) and of course, get some dirt on Theo so I could make fun of him later. When Savannah mentions how happy she was when Warren decided they needed to go to dinner at Jeff's on Sunday, I use it as my opportunity.

"So, how long have you been dating Warren?" I ask, trying to be as casual as humanly possible. I have a theory, one I haven't told Theo yet, and I don't know if I ever will, knowing how he feels about his sister. He calls me protective, but I know somewhere beneath his cool, calm demeanor, he is the ultimate protective big brother.

Savannah blushes and smiles, looking down at her plate and running her fork through hollandaise from her eggs Benedict. "Almost eight months." Her smile is coy and my stomach hurts because it's clear from her face, she really likes him. She likes Warren.

Fuck. She likes the creep. She does not have an ick factor unfortunately.

Sadly, this also means that if I somehow convince Theo that we should fuck with Warren and craft a revenge plan, we might have to play it more carefully than I expected. Than I hoped.

It also complicates things.

It complicates things because I could have sworn just six months ago, Warren came to a company event with a woman on his arm who was absolutely not Savannah.

"It was under wraps for a bit," she says with a conspiratorial whisper and smile, leaning in like she's sharing a secret. "Warren had a feeling Jeff was going to retire and didn't want our relationship to impact anything. He didn't want Jeff to treat him any differently because he was dating his pseudo-daughter, ya know? He's so chivalrous." I give her a forced smile because even for this scheme we're pulling off, I can't lie and call Warren a good guy.

"So what changed?" I ask because they haven't been dating out in the open for long. I remember the day she announced it because Theo was in a shitty mood for almost a week. I have a gut instinct on what happened, but . . .

She shrugs with a smile. "I don't know. A little over a month ago, he came to my place and told me he didn't want to hide anymore. He said he loved me and wanted everyone to know."

A little over a month ago was probably around when Jeff began quietly telling people he was thinking of retiring.

A little over a month ago, I noticed Jeff and Warren had a closed-door meeting, Jeff's office being directly across from where I sit at my desk. When it was over, there was a hug with a lot of back-patting and Warren looked so damn smug, I remember taking note of it, adding another red flag in my mental file.

But maybe he was told Jeff was retiring. Maybe that night, he went to Savannah's and told her he wanted their relationship out in the open, his way of looking like a better candidate to Jeff. My mind starts making what-ifs and potential situations, explanations for what could have happened and how it could have gone down.

Did Jeff tell Warren he was worried about Theo, about how he was single and his father wouldn't want that for him? Was then when Warren told him he was dating Savannah, a check in the Warren for president column?

Savannah, oblivious to my mental calculations, continues speaking.

"I had the biggest crush on him for forever, since he and Theo became friends in college. I thought he didn't notice me at all, you know, being the little sister. We're eight years apart, after all. He'd come over and wouldn't even look my way. Last year, he came to a family dinner at Jeff's. Theo couldn't come, and we just . . . hit it off."

Her smile is wistful now as she shrugs, her mind clearly elsewhere. She looks at me after a beat and shakes her head. "I know he's a bit of a grouch. Rough around the edges and kind of competitive. He's probably so much different at work than he is with me, especially now that Jeff is retiring and . . . well . . . you know."

I do know.

I know that Warren is a fucking tool who is doing everything in his power to sabotage Theo from taking the lead at the company his father helped to start.

"But once you get to know him outside of all of that, he's good. We should set something up soon! A double date!" She says it with such sweetness and excitement, I can't help but smile and nod.

"Yeah. We should." I have no intention at all to willingly see Warren outside of work hours. "What's your take on the whole company thing?" I ask, my eyes moving to my soup and pretending it's just a simple, basic question.

Theo would never ask his sister this, but I'm not Theo.

I think it also shocks Savannah because her face transforms a bit and she drops her fork, sitting back in her chair and crossing her arms on her chest, a smile on her lips. She looks . . . impressed.

"You know, no one ever asks my opinion on that kind of thing. Not Jeff, not Theo, definitely not Warren." That definitely has my ick flaring even more, but she continues, "But I've met you twice now, and here you are, jumping in and asking."

"I'm sorry. I didn't . . . I didn't mean to say something I shouldn't. I'm just curious. I—" God, Theo is going to kill me for offending his sister.

"No, no, no," she says, leaning forward and reaching for my hand across the table. "I'm happy. It's good. It's just, no one ever thinks I have an opinion because I chose not to go into the family business."

"But you do? Have opinions?" She shrugs.

"I mean, I don't know the business as well as any of them, of course," she says, sitting back once more and keeping her eyes on her hands, where she's playing with a thick linen napkin.

"That doesn't mean you don't have thoughts." Finally, she sighs.

"I think Theo is the best choice for the business. I love Warren."

My stomach churns at the confirmation of how deeply she feels about the douche. "But Theo is Catalyst Records. He loves that place. He knows the business. He has personal connections with all of the artists. He works really freaking hard to make sure everyone who works in the building is happy to be there, is paid well, and is taken care of. That's what my dad would have wanted. Not a business, but a family."

"And Warren?" I ask, trying to toe the line between asking too many questions but understanding her take.

Again, she shrugs. "He's smart. He's good at what he does. But his focus is the bottom line. Sometimes, he . . ." White teeth pop out to bite a red-painted lip. "Sometimes, he talks to me about the business. He doesn't like how Jeff does things and thinks Theo is too soft."

"But you . . . ?"

"I think it's how my dad would have wanted it, and that's how it should be." Again, she bites her lip before taking a deep breath, like she's preparing to say something that's going to hurt her to confess. "I think Jeff is making a mistake by not backing Theo."

"Have you told him?" Her eyes go wide and she shakes her head.

"God, no."

"Why not?"

"Because I'm just . . . Savannah." Something in my gut twists, and I reach out, grabbing her hand this time.

"You know, your brother loves you very much. He talks incredibly highly of you all the time. He doesn't talk about pretty much anything in the world outside of work stuff, but he talks about you, Savannah." And it's not a lie or an exaggeration, not a part of my plan to win her support but the truth. The only person I've ever seen Theo speak about as if he enjoys their company on a personal level outside of work is Savannah. Even with Jeff, he there's a bit of idolization in his words, like he thinks he's larger than life.

Savannah gives me a half-hearted smile and shrugs, looking down at where my hand is holding hers, her eyes going wide with whatever it is she sees.

"Is that . . . ?" she starts, pulling it closer. "I can't believe I didn't ask to see the ring at Jeff's place."

"It was kind of crazy, you know, just meeting me and everything," I explain as she turns my hand a bit, touching the diamond ring gently before looking at me with a small, surprised smile.

"It is," she says to herself in awe before she lets go of my hand gently, eyes dancing as she leans back with a widening smile, arms crossed on her chest. When she doesn't say anything, I give her an uneasy smile and break the silence.

"I'm sorry. I'm a bit . . . confused." Now, she shakes her head like she finds the whole situation crazy. Same, girl. Same.

"He didn't tell you, did he?"

My mind starts running through all of the things Theo could have told me but didn't, things his sister would know. Maybe she's in on our ruse? Considering her dating Warren, I doubt it. But then—

"That's our mother's ring."

The world freezes.

"Well, her first ring. She has another one that's to be mine. Judy's holding on it for me, even though I'm not sure I'll use it when the time comes. On our parents' tenth anniversary, Dad got Mom a new engagement ring. Big thing, gaudy as all hell, but very much Mom. She gave that one"—her chin tips to my hand—"to Theo. Told him give it to his future wife."

I'm wearing Theo's mother's engagement ring.

And he didn't tell me.

"No way?" I ask, looking at the ring on my finger in a new light, a small smile playing on my lips.

"It is your style?" she asks, suddenly moving from happy to annoyed. "Theo so would just give a woman a ring without figuring out her style. He's very utilitarian and practical that way."

"No, no, no," I say quickly, shaking my head vehemently.

"Strangely enough, it's exactly what I'd have picked for myself." It's the truth, and as she tries to read me, I know she sees I mean it.

"Well, then it's meant to be, I guess." Her smile is genuine, and something on her face looks almost like relief, like she's glad her brother has someone who likes her mother's ring.

"Yeah, I guess it is, isn't it?"

On our way to the clothing boutique Savannah told me we had to check out, we pass a small corner store with a huge display of spring flowers, both bouquets and in pots, nearly spilling out of the store and onto the sidewalk with color and vibrancy.

"Oh! It's almost tulip season," I say, looking at the wide display of plants with green stems, not yet bloomed.

"You like tulips?" Savannah asks, a strange curiosity in her words. I nod.

"I love them, they remind me of my *abuela*. She loved them, had paintings all over her house of them. She'd always say they were a lesson, how they have to be literally frozen for like, five whole months and somehow still make a pretty flower. I see them and it reminds me of her and how sometimes we have to go through something hard and excruciating to make something beautiful and magical." I shrug and smile, suddenly feeling silly. "Ignore me. Sometimes, I get strangely introspective."

"No, it's true. I never thought of it like that." She stops in front of the display, touching the stem on one that's marked as pink. "Do you have any? At your place?"

I shake my head. "Unfortunately, no. I live in a shit apartment. Maybe one day. I have a friend, though. She's an amazing gardener. She always grows tulips in the spring so I get to see them when I go to her place," I say, thinking of Olivia. "I also have this friend, she lives on a Christmas tree farm," I continue when we start walking again. "She has two daughters and the oldest is obsessed with flowers. Last year, her mom's boyfriend helped her make a little cut flower garden, and she sold the flowers on the weekends at a little stand."

"Oh, my goodness, that's so precious."

"It was. We all drove by and had shifts to make sure she was never disappointed by not having any customers, but it wasn't necessary. She was always sold out by the end of the day regardless."

"You all drove by?"

"Yeah, my friends and I. We're all close. Kind of a little . . . family of our own, I guess. It's nice."

"It sounds it," she says, something wistful in her words, and I remember Theo telling me she has a hard time making friends. "Have you ever been to one of those tulip farms?" she asks abruptly. I shake my head.

"No, but it's on my bucket list."

"You should go one day. There's one down in South Jersey. It's gorgeous." She smiles and hip-checks me like we're old friends, and I like it. I like her. "Maybe we should have Theo take you, you know?"

I smile, my lips tight because I like her and could see us being friends if it wasn't for the fact that I'm lying to her.

"Yeah. Maybe," I say as we stop in front of the store.

"Alright, ready to spend all my brother's money?" I smile wide.

"Absolutely."

SIXTEEN

THEO

I get absolutely nothing done from the moment Katrina leaves the office, dread curling in my gut. This situation keeps getting more and more fucked. I fucking called Katrina *kitten,* some insane mental breakdown *once again* proving I clearly should not have the privilege of ever running Catalyst.

Maybe we should enact a psychiatric examination before anyone gets any kind of high position. I'm sure that would violate some form of HIPAA laws, but at least it would probably also rule out Warren.

And when I'm not stressing about calling my assistant *kitten* and kissing her fingers like some kind of chivalrous duke, I'm panicking over her lunch and shopping date with my sister.

Somehow, I just *know* something terrible is going to happen while they're together.

Maybe Savannah will ask something about how we started dating and Katrina will crack.

Or maybe she'll say something to my sister that will tip her off, and instead of talking to *me* about it, she'll go straight to Warren, who will use it as ammunition.

Or, worst of all, the two of them will create some kind of insane pact together, some grand scheme to get me the president job. I can see it happening, Katrina talking Savannah into one of her crazy revenge plans she keeps trying to convince me to enact.

That's why, when my phone beeps nearly three hours later with a text and a photo from Katrina, my stomach sinks to my feet.

A million worst-case scenarios run through my mind, but none wind up right where we are—with a mirror selfie of Katrina in a skin-tight black dress that flares out near her knees, a slit almost to her hip. Her hair is tossed up into some kind of haphazard bun, her tan leg stepping out of the slit. It's the kind of dress her short frame would absolutely need to wear heels in, so it pools a bit on the floor. The neckline dips down to her breastplate, leaving the swells of her breasts exposed.

She's absolutely breathtaking.

I can't even stop staring long enough to reply, my eyes zipping to different parts of her body in the photo, before another hits my messages.

This one is red, stopping at her knees and somehow even tighter, a single strap wrapping around her neck, keeping the top up.

A third photo comes in, this one a creamy white dress, tight up top with puffy, short sleeves that would be almost sweet if her generous breasts weren't boosted up in the tight top and the skirt that flares out at her hips wasn't so short, I have to wonder if her ass shows at all.

I'm lost in my head, flipping from photo to photo in a way neither a fake fiancée nor a boss should be doing, when a fourth comes through.

This one is less worrisome, Katrina in a dressing room surrounded by clothes, a hanger with a different white dress around her neck, her face panicked and goofy.

Finally, a text with words comes through.

What do you think?

I think I want to peel all three off you, is the first thing that pops into my mind, making panic fill my veins.

That is *not* something I can say to my employee. I know she likes to fuck around and flirt sometimes, but it's just because she likes to watch me squirm.

Another text comes through.

> I'm thinking the white for the engagement party?
>
> Do you think it's too short?

Yes, because every man at that party is going to have his eyes glued to your gorgeous long legs and your perfect ass, waiting for the wind to move the skirt and give them a view of what's mine, that voice says.

Not mine, I remind that voice. *Katrina is the furthest thing from mine, and these intrusive fucking thoughts are so dangerous.*

Dangerous for me.

Dangerous for my . . . friendship with Katrina.

And honestly, it's dangerous for my *career.*

> Savannah says it looks shorter in the pictures and that it's not so bad in person.
>
> I really like it, though.

Without thinking, my fingers start moving on my phone screen.

> Do you feel good in it?

I hit send before I can even really read what I typed out, and when I see it's not some fucked variation of, *I'd like to flip that skirt up and fuck you,* I'm relieved.

God, what is *wrong* with me?

It must be because I haven't had sex in what feels like an eternity, but probably is closer to six months. I've been working hard to secure the resigning of Hometown Heroes, the extra work diminishing what little time I used to devote to my social life.

Maybe Jeff was right, that douchey voice in my mind says. I kick him down the mental stairs in my mind.

> I do. I feel like a princess.

> Then that's the one. I'll cover your ass all night if I have to. Wear what makes you feel beautiful, Katrina.

> Okay.

That's all she replies.

The talkative woman who never has less than three sentences to say when you ask her what she wants on her *pizza,* says just a single word.

Fuck.

> For the record, I think you look gorgeous in all three.

Then, because I can't stop apparently, I add on more.

> Buy all three. And whatever else makes you feel good.

> What about lingerie?

Jesus fucking Christ, this woman.

> Lingerie makes me feel pretty.

I take deep, calming breaths, counting down from ten to calm both my pounding heart and the jolt of my cock from thinking of all of Katrina's lush curves in fucking *lingerie.*

What the actual fuck?

> Whatever makes you feel pretty, Katrina.

> I'm racking up quite the total, Mr. Carter.

Again, my cock twitches.

I'm a fucking idiot.

What made me think I could have a platonic, fake engagement with my gorgeous assistant who loves to fuck with me and try and get under my skin?

> Good. Make it hurt. Call it payback for getting you into this mess.

I scroll back to look at the dress photos again, spending much more time on them than I should, saving each and applying one to my phone's background, telling myself that's something a fiancée would do.

Finally, she replies with a devil emoji, and when I lock my screen, seeing her in that white dress, I know she's right.

Hell is *exactly* where I'm headed.

SEVENTEEN

KAT

We make it nearly three weeks of being "together" before it happens.

Three weeks of sly smiles from my coworkers, of congratulations, both genuine and skeptical, of eating lunch together with the door closed instead of open. None of it is different, how we act, but it's giving off a different vibe, and everyone picks up on it.

And we make it three weeks before Warren becomes tired of our game and decides to show what a fucking ass he is.

I nod at Rick O'Connor and Cheryl Rowland as I walk into the break room to make a coffee for Theo and myself, and they smile back, though their eyes linger a bit longer on me than they would pre-engagement. It's as I'm adding sweetener to my own coffee, waiting for Theo's to finish brewing, that Warren comes up beside me. I can smell him before I see him, that thick haze of too-strong cologne he wears like a warning signal.

"Where's your fiancé?" he asks, and even though he's now close enough that I can feel his physical presence next to me, I don't look up from stirring my coffee.

"Theo is probably in the boardroom, preparing for the meeting in"—I look down at my watch—"five minutes." He doesn't respond and I don't bother to give him anything more than he deserves.

As I reach for the shots of espresso I brewed for Theo, his voice comes again, his time louder, as if he wants someone else to hear.

Which, he does, of course. This is nothing if not a planned attack, something he's been trying to find the right time for since we announced our engagement. He needed an audience, a way to introduce doubt into board members without Theo being there to step in or stick up for me and definitely without Jeff to witness him questioning what is none of his goddamn business.

He leans his hip against the counter, not even pretending to make himself coffee or have any reason to be in this room other than to fuck with me, before he speaks. "It just seems strange, you know? Jeff has a conversation with Theo about him not wanting to put his full backing behind him because he's a loner, and suddenly, he's engaged to his assistant."

Well, seems like my theory that Jeff told Warren he was unsure about backing Theo is right, but how does he know about Theo's and Jeff's private conversation?

I don't let any of my surprise show on my face, though, instead pouring milk into the frother and pretending like he's just an annoying gnat, which he is. "Theo and I have been dating for some time, not that it's any of your business," I say, turning to face him, my arms crossed on my chest. My face is calm and collected, but I know the ears of the board members are on us, and probably the eyes. They're looking to see how I react, how I respond.

And the way Warren is smirking at me, like he knows something I don't or something I don't want him to, makes my need to win this tête-à-tête bubble in my veins.

"Well, he's practically family, you know. I'm just looking out for him." He says it in that good ol' boy tone that might convince someone else, if they didn't know how full of shit Warren is.

"Ah, yes, I forgot you're dating Savannah. That's a pretty recent thing, too, isn't it? A few weeks? Also seems pretty . . . strange, doesn't it? You starting to date the current president's pseudo-daughter just a month or so before the announcement that he's retiring? Interesting, since Sav confided in me that you were dating for months in secret. I thought it just seemed a little odd when she told me that, considering you brought a pretty brunette to the Twigz release party a few months ago. I remember you two getting pretty rowdy in the corner." I'd gone back through the photos the event photographer had sent Theo for promotional materials and found I wasn't imagining it either.

Warren's jaw goes tight, and he lets out a small, fake laugh before turning to the two board members. When I look at them, their attention is rapt on Warren and me, and I can't help but wonder who, in their view, is winning this battle.

"Would you two mind letting Katrina and I have some privacy? I think there's been a miscommunication." They look at Warren, then me, then at each other before nodding and mumbling something about seeing Warren in the meeting. When they leave the room, I cross my arms on my chest and pout.

"What, you don't like it when I fire back those same accusations in front of the buddies you're trying to impress?" Suddenly, the concern and decency are wiped off his face, though, and all that's left is vile anger and hatred.

I fight back the panicked shiver that runs through me and hold my ground.

"Cut the shit, Katrina. You're a smart girl. Not sure what Carter has on you, what's making you fall for his bullshit, but whatever it is, it's not worth it." I tip my head and play the part of the dumb assistant.

"I'm not sure what you're insinuating, Warren. Surely, you're not making an accusation against Theo." He steps closer, and I take a step back.

"All I'm saying is it's really interesting timing, and I wouldn't want this to impact your future here at Catalyst, especially when I'm in control." I raise an eyebrow at him.

"Funny, I didn't know they had voted for president yet," I say. He glares at me with cold, lifeless eyes, but then his hand moves, grazing my forearm in what I assume is meant to be a soft, warm caress, a come-on.

It turns my stomach, and my eyes look to the door, to check if it's open. I don't think he would do anything that stupid, but when it comes to men and pride and power, I've learned you never actually know how far they might go.

"I could really help you, Katrina," he says, his voice low, an attempt at seduction falling flat. I pull my arm back and fight the urge to step farther from him, turning toward the coffee again.

"What are you trying to say, Warren? How could you help me?" Maybe it's as easy as this. Maybe it's as easy as asking what his plan is.

Unfortunately, he doesn't seem to be as much of a dumb frat boy as he seems.

"That's fine. You can play dumb all you want," he says, and I curl my fingers into a fist, reminding myself that punching out my fake fiancé's competition would not really be doing what I've agreed to. He steps back with a douchey smile, and I reconsider once more.

I could punch him, knock one of those pretty fucking veneers out. He takes another step back toward the door and suddenly, I can breathe again, out of his reach. Over his shoulder, I can see Cheryl there, standing and looking worried, like she decided the situation made her uncomfortable and she wanted to check on me. "But really, you should tell him all this is going to do is ruin his integrity and the ability of the board to believe in him." It's then I realize he's speaking louder now, loud enough for Cheryl and, now, Joe, who, from the look of the empty white mug in his hand, is grabbing coffee before the meeting as well, to hear.

When he turns, he looks at the board members and acts like he didn't expect to see them there. I want to fucking strangle him.

"Sorry, guys, I was just talking to Katrina here. I'm worried about Theodore, you know? Things with them are moving so quickly."

I fucking hate this man.

Theo just wants to get the job, to leave little to no collateral damage, and to save the business he loves from being destroyed by Warren, and I'm going to help him do that however he needs me to. But more and more each day, I can't stop feeling like I want to destroy Warren in the process.

And when Joe Ruiz, who has never looked at me with anything other than kindness and decency, gives me a new head-to-toe like he's wondering what I look like naked, the professionalism I once held stripped from me with one subtle, misogynistic accusation, that anger bubbles.

Then they all leave for the meeting, and I continue to stand there, attempting to collect my thoughts, to remember what the actual job is.

But as he's guiding Cheryl and Joe out the door and toward the boardroom, Warren looks over his shoulder with that shit-eating grin, like he won this battle. It's then I realize he has no fucking clue who he's messing with.

I'll just have to show him.

EIGHTEEN

KAT

Fuck that guy.

He thinks he's got this figured out, has me figured out. Warren thinks he's smarter than Theo, smarter than me, and that might be his first mistake.

Underestimating me is always a mistake.

Because Theo might want to keep things copacetic, might not want to tell Jeff and the board and the whole world what a piece of scum Warren is in order to play nice, but I've never really liked playing nice.

No, I've always preferred to play dirty when it really mattered because I always play to win.

And I'm here to win this war Warren started.

My heels don't make much noise on the carpet of the office, which is annoying because, in my head, I'm walking toward the meeting room where Warren and Theo and the entire fucking board are gathered like a movie montage before a big battle scene. A woman on a mission. In my head, my chin is tipped high, a small, sneaky smile playing on my lips, my heels clacking in a furious staccato against hardwood, the soundtrack for my revenge.

I open the door that just barely shut behind Warren, the folder of papers Theo needs still in one hand and the coffee I made for myself in the other, and walk right to my boss, and I know—I know all eyes are on me. I don't have to look around to know it, and I don't have to double-check that Warren is staring at me with a mix of anger and irritation and that same stupid smugness that follows him around like the fog of his shitty-smelling cologne.

"Katrina," Theo says in greeting, the sweet, sweet man so oblivious to what is about to happen.

We never did have that boundaries talk I wanted to have when we were at Jeff's.

Here's hoping he'll just go with it.

"Here you go, honey," I say, my voice sugary sweet as I hand Theo my coffee mug with a lipstick print on the rim. I lay down the folder of documents he requested for the meeting and step closer to him.

And then I do the unthinkable.

I put a hand flat on his chest, feeling his heart beating beneath my palm before I move to my tiptoes because the man is unbearably tall even in these heels, and I press my lips to his.

For a split second, he's stiff, confused, and probably a bit panicked.

I don't know for sure, seeing as my eyes are closed.

My lips are on Theodore Carter's and they're warm and they taste like the spearmint gum he chews religiously when he's stressed and he smells like whatever subtle bodywash he uses, and I'm realizing now this is a terrible, terrible fucking idea. He's nervous and I'm crossing a line and whether I'll admit it aloud or not, if and when he denies me, when he steps back and rejects this kiss, my feelings will be hurt.

But it turns out, I don't need to worry about that at all, as the hand not holding the coffee wraps around my waist, tugging me close as his lips soften, and he kisses me back.

My body is electric with the gentle movement of the brush of his lips on mine, the warmth of his body. I feel every tiny millimeter of it, of his front pressed to mine, of that hand on my back. I feel how my body melts a bit, comfort and bliss and something akin to coming home after a long day flowing through me.

It's a good fucking kiss.

A great kiss, even.

It's definitely the best kiss I've had in a very, very long time. Maybe ever, if I'm being honest with myself.

And just my luck, it's with my stupid fake fiancé. My boss.

It feels like a century but I know it's just a few seconds before I let common sense slide in and break the kiss, stepping back just a bit. His hand doesn't move from my back, though, the very tips of his fingers digging in a bit reflexively, like he also doesn't want this to end, like he also thinks that was the best kiss of his life.

It wasn't anything substantial, wasn't a long or particularly hot kiss, nothing groundbreaking or soul-searing. It was just a simple, easy kiss partners would give each other in the presence of colleagues, but it felt . . .

Different.

Otherworldly.

"Have a good meeting, Theo," I say, patting his chest, and my voice is unintentionally throaty when I do.

What the fuck?

The same what the fuck is in Theo's eyes, even though his face is loose and easy, like this is normal for us, as I step back and turn toward the door.

I take note of the eyes watching us as I do.

Jeff looks pleased.

Cheryl, Rick, and Joe from the break room look intrigued.

And Warren looks absolutely feral.

I smile and give him a triumphant small wave of my fingers as I leave.

Mission accomplished.

NINETEEN

THEO

It was smart, kissing me in front of everyone. It added a layer of *real* to our relationship that hadn't been there yet. In fact, I've made a very strong effort to maintain our regular level of *real* for my own sanity. Part of me thinks it should have been more planned, should have been talked about.

But another part of me knows I would never have been ready for it, for that kiss.

That fucking kiss.

That fucking kiss that has me well and thoroughly distracted through the entire meeting, only able to pop in with helpful commentary or the correct projections because, as always, the file Katrina prepared based on the meeting agenda was impeccable and had everything and more I might need in it.

Even when Warren tried to catch me in a slip, mentioning an increase in PVC from the vinyl supplier I suggested we move to, I was able to ensure everyone I had secured a two-year long price hold, the signed contract and email communications already in the folder and duplicated so each member could have a set for their files.

"Good initiative," Jeff said with a smile, and I didn't miss the way the board members looked to one another, smiled, and nodded *or* the way Warren's glare burned through me.

And *that* is why it should have been planned. Because every single move I make right now is being dissected by Warren, scanned for insecurities and weak spots he can chip away at and show he's the right—the *only*—option for president.

I attempt to convince myself to pay attention and stop thinking about the way Katrina tasted of coffee and spice throughout the rest of the meeting. When it ends, we all stand, doing the required handshakes, Warren gripping mine a bit too tight and too rough to be cordial, Jeff giving me a knowing smile and a wink, before I walk to my office, using every ounce of restraint I didn't know I had anymore not to run there.

When I approach Katrina's desk, I see she has a bag of snacks opened, but her eyes are on mine.

"My office. Now," I say under my breath, not even pausing at her desk as I walk straight through the door, standing to the side as she comes in, snacks in hand.

She doesn't even argue as she moves her chair, placing it in front of my desk and sitting down while I close the door and blinds.

I'm sure the office will be abuzz with whispers and speculations, but I can't put this off to a time that is less inconspicuous.

"What was that?" I ask, beginning to pace. To my irritation, Katrina smiles, crossing her legs and tossing what I see now is a piece of technicolor candy into her mouth, crunching it between her teeth.

At least she doesn't bother to pretend she doesn't know what I'm talking about. In fact, I've always liked that about her, how she never beats around the bush, never avoids a conversation that needs to be had.

"Staking my territory." I stop my pacing and stare at her with wide eyes.

"*Staking your territory?*" I ask, fighting the urge to let my voice rise.

"Yup," she says, popping the "p" as if this is just another silly little quirk of hers. I take a deep breath, close my eyes, and scratch my thumb along the side of my pointer finger. At this rate, by the end of this quarter, I'll be down to bone.

Here I was, thinking the biggest issue with this whole fucking thing was Warren digging too much or Jeff finding out, but *no*. I somehow forgot my assistant is absolutely *insane*.

"Can you please explain to me *why* you felt the need to stake your territory on me? In front of everyone at a board meeting? Also, that was *not* my fucking coffee, considering it had about a gallon of sugar in it."

She rolls her eyes.

"It was maybe three tablespoons of creamer. Cool it, boss man. I was on a mission and forgot to grab your coffee instead of mine. Plus, I thought the lipstick on the mug was a nice touch."

Of course that's the part she chooses to explain.

"Katrina . . . ," I start, and she rolls her eyes again, reminding me of when I was a kid and my mother told me my eyes would get stuck like that if I didn't stop.

Clearly, that was a lie, or else with the frequency she rolls hers, Katrina's big brown ones would have been stuck staring at her brain years ago.

"I was in the break room, making your coffee and one for myself for your meeting. Rick and Cheryl were in there, too, and then Warren rolled on in." She pauses for dramatic effect, and I circle my hand, telling her to hurry the fuck up.

"Okay . . ."

"And he started being an ass."

Suddenly, my skin feels hot. Suddenly, the neckline of my dress shirt is too tight. Suddenly, I want to go back into that boardroom and turn that handshake into a punch in his smug face.

The simple idea of Warren bothering Katrina is doing this to me.

"An ass, *how*?" I ask through gritted teeth.

"He started making . . ." She tips her head left to right, like she's trying to decide how to phrase it, taking in my body language as she does with everyone, calculating and reading me. "Insinuations. About us. Loudly, so the board members could hear, and before you say anything, yes, he knew they were there, and yes, I think it was intentional."

"Okay . . ."

"So he left, and then I decided he shouldn't be allowed to do that. He shouldn't be allowed to make me feel like he's *winning*, to make insinuations about us in front of other people just because he wants your job."

"It's not my job. It's a job I *want*," I start, but she shakes her head.

"That's your problem. It *is* your job, Theo. By *right*. It's your job, and everyone knows it." I glare at her because, as kind as it is, it's not the truth, but she just rolls her eyes again. "So I left the break room, and I walked into the boardroom, and I kissed you because I needed to wipe any hint of doubt he had embedded into their minds." I don't speak. I don't know what I would say if I did.

"And the way they looked at me after, the way I could tell they *believed* in us, the way they suddenly doubted Warren, that fucked with his credibility. That did exactly what we needed it to do."

Finally, I'm starting to understand, to see how her brain worked to get to the only decision of, *I have to kiss my boss in front of a ton of people to prove a point.*

And it makes sense.

"Okay," I say. "I see it. Some warning though, next time, would be good." She smiles and gives me a thumbs-up and throws a few more pieces of candy into her mouth.

The way she is so unbothered by all of this is honestly kind of admirable.

Also kind of terrifying.

"Next time, I'll give you a heads-up. Maybe I'll tug my left ear?" she asks, referencing a sign we've *already* established. Even though she's joking, I nod.

"Perfect." I sit as well, sighing with relief as I decompress from that meeting. I didn't even take notes or anything, though it was just run-of-the-mill with no new information, mostly just reiterating things that have been gone over every week for months.

"It was a good kiss, though, wasn't it?" she asks, her voice slightly lower.

"What?"

"I said, it was a pretty good kiss. Like, for relative strangers, for a first kiss. It was good, you know?" Her lips are spread wide in a smile, her shoes kicked off onto the ground and tucked beneath her, as always making herself comfortable in my office.

"It was . . ." I pause, trying to figure out how to explain it.

It was amazing.

It was better than I expected.

It was better than it should have been.

It was distracting as hell.

It was addictive, and I want another and another and another, but that can't happen.

"It was very good. It definitely seemed . . . real," I land on finally. She seems to like that response, her smile widening.

"I told you, Theo. If I'm doing this, I'm gonna make it look real."

And even though we move on from talking about the kiss to work, I can't help but think about how good *real* feels.

TWENTY

THEO

"What's this?" I ask, tossing an announcement on Jeff's desk with utter fury in my bones a week after the kiss incident.

"I don't know?" His eyes scan the printed paper noting the announcement of a last-minute signing of Oliver Porter to Blacknote. The artist I found on social media six months ago, who I carefully watched for weeks before approaching, taking in how they used their small but powerful social media platform, how they interacted with fans, and how they used new and exciting marketing techniques to get their name out.

Two months ago, I had Katrina create an extensive document on the artist and a week later, I shared it with the board as a new, potential client. I might not be the director of A&R anymore, but I saw the potential there, and most everyone else did, too.

Except for Warren.

"I have a few questions," he had said. "I'm just not sure they fit our current portfolio."

I remember the anger flowing through my veins at his words because it was so unbearably clear this person was meant to be a star, and everyone knew it. I also knew we had little time to work because while their videos weren't reaching the masses, other labels would soon see their potential.

I knew every fucking management team and label in the country would be nipping at their heels within a month.

Jeff had looked to Warren with skepticism, but he believed everyone on this team brought value, had a new and interesting perspective that could cushion the business from future issues. "Why do you feel that way?" he had asked, and Warren gave a smile that I could see right through before telling Jeff it was just a gut feeling.

"Can I set up a call soon? One on one. Maybe I just need to get to know them." Jeff instantly agreed before I could argue, and I was told to give Warren their contact information.

Then suddenly, the offer Jackson in A&R and I had worked for weeks on wasn't good enough. Their team requested more money and more promises. They wanted guarantees of what we could offer and what type of stardom we could shoot them up to. I couldn't figure out why this artist was suddenly asking for it all when they'd originally been over the moon to hear an offer from us, but now it makes sense.

They were getting other offers.

Offers from Blacknote, it seems.

We'd been waiting for them to agree to the final terms for over three weeks, the contract sitting on my desk now fucking useless. "Is this that social media folk singer you were working on?" Jeff asks then looks at me. He must see the answer there because he curses under his breath.

"He isn't viral, Jeff. I found him on a whim, by chance. I told the board, Katrina, Jackson, and the contract division about this. I trust Katrina with my life, and the contract division is all fucking lawyers who know if they even whisper something, we'll sue them for everything they're worth. Jackson would get a hefty percentage for the duration of the contract, so it's not in his best interest to speak." I pause, building up the dramatics. "All that's left is the board. And Warren."

Jeff sighs, hearing the conversation I've had multiple times before.

"Warren wouldn't do that," he says, resignation in his words as he pushes the printout away from him.

"He would, Jeff! He would. I know you love this company and you trust everyone in it implicitly. That's how you and my father built this place, trust and respect. I value that too, but Warren does not. His loyalty lies with himself, bonus points if he can make a dime doing it."

The accusatory thoughts I've been sitting on for years continue to swirl around my mind. What is Warren getting from Blacknote? He doesn't have stock in them anymore, doesn't have any skin in that game . . . not above the table at least.

"I know it's frustrating, being in competition with him for president, but—" Jeff starts, and my blood begins to boil.

Just then, Warren pops his head into Jeff's office, a small frown on his face that, to some, might look genuine. To me, though, all I see is the fucking smugness hiding behind it.

"I see you guys heard about Porter," he says.

I want to strangle him.

I'm bigger than him.

I could do it.

I once read it takes up to five minutes to kill someone through strangulation, though. I wouldn't have that much time before someone pulled me off him.

Not worth it.

"All part of the game," Jeff says with a good ol' boy smile Warren returns.

I continue to glare, letting my anger swirl around me, a near-tangible flame.

"Strange that Blacknote found them, though," I say, crossing my arms on my chest. "They don't even have more than ten thousand followers on any platform. No notoriety, nothing. Not a single viral video."

"Huh. Well, maybe they were giving demos to other agencies, or maybe when you sent them that offer with no contingencies for reaching out to other labels, they approached Blacknote. Not uncommon."

Even now, he tries to make it a dig to me. He disagrees with me not adding a line into my contracts forbidding artists to reach out to other labels. Normally, it's not an issue, seeing as it's typically seen as a good thing, a sign we work above board, that we're never trying to fuck over the artists.

Warren hates it and never misses an opportunity to throw it in my face.

But I know when I approached them, Oliver Porter didn't even have a demo. At the time, they were focusing on writing, looking to do ghost songwriting.

I was the one that convinced them they had the opportunity to be the whole package and personally bankrolled the first stages of making that happen, of making a demo, not that I told Warren or Jeff that.

It was something I knew my father had done many times over the years when he saw an artist with potential but no way to afford the required demo.

"Or someone told Blacknote about them," I say, accusation clear in my words.

"Theodore . . . ," Jeff says, his voice exasperated. A small, almost undetectable smile forms on Warren's lips as he takes another step into Jeff's office.

"Now, who would do that?" he asks, challenging me to call him out. "Only a handful of us here have heard the demo."

"Didn't you post two weekends ago you were golfing with Travis Black?" I ask. Katrina sent me the post, a photo of Warren with the owner of Blacknote, and my blood had boiled.

"He's allowed to be friends with our competitors, Theodore. There's enough talent for everyone."

"If it makes you feel any better, Travis and I never talk business.

We're just old friends," Warren says to Jeff. "You can call him, have him confirm. I'd never put Catalyst at risk."

"It's fine, Warren. I'm sure Theodore didn't mean it like that. Right, son?" The word son twists like it always does when he says it like this, like a weapon he's using to remind me of who I am.

I usually like it, being called son by the only father figure I have left in this world, until it's used against me.

But it does the job all the same: I remember who I am.

And what I'm supposed to be.

And the game I'm supposed to be playing.

I'm not supposed to be Warren's nemesis, not if Jeff is going to feel comfortable with me being named president.

"Yeah. Sorry, Warren. Just a little frustrated, you know?" I say, the fake smile almost painful, and I put a hand out to the man I hate.

Suddenly, I can't help but think maybe Katrina is right.

Maybe we need to go beyond just dating. Maybe I need to let her chaos and insanity off its leash a bit and tarnish the perfect image that is Warren Michaels.

Warren grabs my hand with a wide smile, gripping it much too tight, pulling me in too way hard, and slamming my back with his hand like we're the old pals Jeff wants us to be.

"Game on, motherfucker," he whispers in my ear before stepping back, winking at me, and walking out with a wave to Jeff.

TWENTY-ONE

KAT

"Wait, so you're fucking your boss? Hell yeah, Kat, I didn't think you had it in you," Cami says when we're out at our monthly Sunday morning friends brunch, and I swear to God, I have such hatred for my friends.

I love them, of course, but my god, I fucking hate them sometimes.

"I'm not fucking him, Cami. I'm pretending to date him," I say with a casual shrug.

"Yeah, not gonna lie, that didn't work out too well for me," Liv says with an apologetic cringe, and I roll my eyes.

"That's because you're unhinged and somehow, Andre loves it, and you two were absolutely meant to be." Liv just smiles, agreeing.

"So, you're not fucking him? You're just platonically pretending you're engaged? No funny business at all?" Cami asks, a perfectly formed eyebrow lifting in disbelief.

The problem with Camile Thompson is she can see through bull-shit faster than anyone I've ever met in my life, and she's always willing to call you out on it.

We all have superpowers, in a way. Cami can see through the

bullshit, I have the ick factor, Abbie can charm literally anyone into doing anything for her, and the insane way Liv's brain works at solving any problem is actually alarming.

I sit there momentarily, biting my lip as I try to decide how to move forward without lying, before Cami nods. "Yup, there it is."

I sigh and drop my head in my hands. "I kissed him," I admit with a low groan.

I still don't know why I did it, not really, at least. And I've spent every moment since putting it into a box, sealing it away from the light of day because if I ignore my problems, they go away. That's how that works, right?

"You kissed him?" Abbie asks, excitement in her voice.

"I feel like that's part of the expectation, is it not? You pretend you're getting married to someone, you occasionally have to kiss them so people don't think it's all bullshit? Like, you plan out how to make it seem all real and whatnot and then . . . do it? That's what Andre and I did. We would plan when the paparazzi would see me and when they'd get a good shot."

Everyone looks at me, and I bite my lip, staring down at my plate as if it might magically spell out the answers.

"It wasn't exactly . . ." I clear my throat. "It wasn't exactly planned."

"What do you mean?" Cami asks, her voice going low with skepticism, and I pause, thinking, deciding how best to explain it, but I say fuck it and spew out the word vomit.

"I was in the break room, and Theo was about to have a meeting so I was making coffee, and there were some board members in there, and fucking Warren came in. He starts loudly speculating that Theo and I aren't really dating, like an ass, which, okay, sure, valid, but who fucking says that out loud when you don't even know me? He was doing it on purpose to try and make them second-guess things."

I look up finally, and Abbie's nodding along, already knowing where this is going. Liv has a look of *how dare he* on her face, and

Cami's eyes are closed as she takes a deep breath, also knowing where this is going but clearly less impressed than Abbie.

"So he leaves to go to that meeting, and the board members give me such shitty looks, like they're buying his bullshit, and I get . . . I don't know. I get mad. I get angry."

"What a surprise," Cami says with an eye roll, but I keep going.

"Theo deserves that job, you guys. He loves the company, and he knows this business, and Warren just wants . . . I don't really know. Money? Power? But it's not to continue to build the legacy and community of Catalyst."

"We get it, Kat. Your boytoy is the one who deserves the job. You've been telling us that for as long as you've been working there. What happened after the douche canoe accused you of faking your fake relationship?" Cami asks, moving her hand in a *geton-with-it* way. I glare at her.

"Ignore Cami, she hasn't seen my dad in, like, three whole days because she's been working events," Liv says with a roll of her eyes, and Cami turns her glare to her. "Then what happened?" she asks, ignoring her not-quiet stepmother.

"I went into the boardroom."

I leave it at that, stirring the small spoon in my coffee, listening to the clinking of the metal against ceramic, as if it will hypnotize me so I can black out and dissociate through this whole conversation.

It doesn't unfortunately.

"And . . . ?" Abbie says. I groan, putting my head back to look at the ceiling, embarrassed to admit what I did next.

"I walked right up to Theo and went on my tiptoes and I kissed him. Like . . . really kissed him. Not a little peck on the lips either. In front of everyone. Without any kind of warning."

"Wait, so, in front of the whole board?" Abbie asks, excitement in her words because she, too, is insane.

"Yeah. I mean, there wasn't tongue, but . . . it was still hot, you know?"

I didn't think that actually made sense, but all heads at the table nod regardless, further proof that these are my people.

"What did he do?"

I bite my lip.

"He, uh . . . He kissed me back?" I say.

"He kissed you back," Cami repeats, deadpan.

"Well, he couldn't exactly push me away, you know? We're engaged."

"And after?" Cami asks almost clinically, like she's taking notes before sending me on a fucking grippy sock vacation.

Honestly, at this point, I could probably use it.

"He said it made sense but to give him a warning next time. So he wasn't so taken off balance." I roll my lips into my mouth and decide there's no use hiding any of it. "And we agreed it was a really good kiss."

"Jesus fuck, Katrina," Cami says.

"What? It sounds like it was a good kiss! What does that hurt?" Liv asks with confusion.

"Because Kat's going to get hurt. She's going to get her heart broken or this fuckwad Warren is going to figure out what's happening and try and get back at her. This kind of thing never ends well," Cami says, and even though her words are harsh, they're said with kindness and love, and they're an echo of my own fears.

But I don't have the luxury of worrying about consequences anymore—I can only move forward.

"Does he give you the ick?" Liv asks, his head tipping to the side with interest.

"Who, Warren? For sure."

"No, your boss." Everyone stares at me, and suddenly, I feel self-conscious.

"Theo? Oh. Uh, I've never thought about it," I say, which is both a lie and a truth. I never thought of it before, other than knowing I like his company and I've never been annoyed by him.

But now . . .

"No, he hasn't given me the ick," I answer, poking at my toast and keeping my eyes away from my friends.

"What?" Abbie asks with genuine shock in her words. I don't need to look at her to know it's reflected on her face.

"No, I haven't gotten the ick." I say the words casually, like it's just a silly, little, offhanded circumstance.

"You haven't gotten the ick yet," Cami repeats, her voice low and skeptical.

"Nope."

"Not yet," Liv qualifies with a laugh.

"Exactly." I say the word, but I'm . . . conflicted.

"Uh-oh. You've got that look," Abbie warns, setting her fork down and giving me her full attention.

I really wish she wouldn't. She gives that *tell Mama all about it* vibe, and it makes me want to hide. Even more so when Cami notices I've become quiet and gives me her full attention as well.

"What look?" I ask, playing dumb.

"The one where you're trying to convince yourself of something."

"Oh, yes, that's exactly it!" Abbie says. "It's like that time you got the ick from Samuel because he talked about his mother every five minutes, but tried to convince yourself you didn't because you had chemistry with him and he was good in bed."

"He was very nice! He just had a strange relationship with his mother." In fact, when I broke up with him, he called his mother and put her on speakerphone, asking me to tell her about our ending relationship.

"What about the time your *abuela* told you that Benson James was a creep just by looking at a photo you showed her, but you kept dating him anyway because he bought tickets to that concert you wanted to go to?"

"I stand by that decision, it was a great concert. And my *abuela*'s ick factor might be stronger than mine, but even *I* knew Benson was a creep. I just wanted those tickets."

"Or the time we were supposed to go to the Poconos and you

were getting the flu and had a 102 fever but refused to admit you were sick."

"We lost the deposit on that trip! I felt horrible." Cami rolls her eyes.

"So?" Liv asks, thankfully no situations born from years and years of friendship to throw in my face. "What is it now? What are you second-guessing?"

They all stare at me, and I almost say nothing for a moment. I almost tell them they're insane and I'm totally fine—cue high-pitched David Schwimmer, *I'm fine!* But something about the way they're looking at me, judgment-free, genuinely willing and ready to talk me off any ledge, makes me spill the dark secret that's been echoing in my ear since I suggested this entire scheme.

"What happens if I don't?" I whisper the fear that's been circulating in my gut for weeks now. "What happens if I start to like him and I don't eventually get the ick?"

"Have you ever gone this long?" Liv asks. Abbie and Cami shake their heads, already knowing the answer.

"I've never gotten past seven dates." By the then, there is always something that bugs me so much about a man, it makes me instantly unattracted to him. Something I can't rationalize my way through, something I simply can't envision myself having to endure for the entirety of my life if things went any further.

"So, seven dates? That's how long we have to get the ick?" Liv says it like it's a group project.

"And we've been on two, I guess. One The Ex Files set up and one at his family dinner."

"So, five to go," Cami says.

I don't remind her how I've been on countless dinners and lunches with him for work and I see him nearly every day and haven't gotten the ick yet.

That's . . . different, I've convinced myself. *That doesn't count.*

"I just . . . What happens if it doesn't happen?" Abbie asks. "Will you have to quit? Won't things be weird?"

"Damien doesn't give me the ick. Neither do you guys. Or Andre or Zach. Life goes on."

"But that's different. You've never been in a relationship with them. You've never kissed them, much less a good kiss," Olivia says. I look to Cami.

"Why is she here again?" I ask with sarcasm in my words. Liv balls up her napkin and throws it at me.

"I'm just saying, if we're talking worst-case scenarios, what happens if you don't get the ick?"

"It doesn't matter," I say, shaking my head. "I don't have to worry about that because I'm going to get the ick. I only haven't yet because I didn't see him that way and my brain didn't even go there. I'm going to just have fun until then. In fact, it's even better because if I want to, I can take it further and be confident that at the end of it all, we can go back to being friends. Coworkers."

Abbie and Cami look at each other and even though I don't want to, I can read their silent conversation. *She's delusional.*

"Really, guys. It's the perfect situation," I say, trying to convince them and myself at the same time. Abbie nods, deciding she's going to be the one to take me on.

"So, humor me, okay?" she asks with a light and happy smile, even though she's absolutely about to fuck with my head. "We all know it's not going to happen, but what if you don't get the ick? What then?"

I fight the urge to argue, to tell her it's a stupid exercise because I'm going to get the ick.

I always get the ick.

But I don't because she's my best friend and I love her, so instead, I let my mind go down that road for the first time. Theo doesn't want a relationship, so we would have to end things even if I don't want to.

"I'd have to quit. He doesn't want a relationship, and if I fall for him, seeing him every day would be uncomfortable," I say, forcing myself to think logically. "I'd probably get my heart broken." My words are low and soft, words I've never actually had to say out loud. They feel foreign on my tongue.

"That would be a first," Abbie says, but not in a snarky way, in a serious, concerned way.

"I'd have to find a new job. Probably in a new field because I wouldn't feel comfortable using him as a referral."

"You love that job, though," Liv says. "It's the first time you haven't gotten bored."

My stomach flips.

"You could try working with Liv and me. Doing the same type of administrative work, putting out fires, that kind of thing."

"Cici already works with you guys," I remind her with a smile. Cami makes a face like she was hoping I wouldn't remember that part. Knowing her, she would somehow create an entire position they didn't need and probably couldn't afford just to give me a job.

Have I mentioned I have really good friends?

"Wait, wait, wait," Abbie says, waving her arms in the air. "Why are we assuming it would go poorly?"

Everyone at the table looks at her with a *don't be stupid* kind of look. "What? It could go totally fine." Cami rolls her eyes.

"The man doesn't date," I say. "And the whole reason he's in this mess is because he doesn't want to. He wants to focus on Catalyst. And he doesn't like me. He's pretty much constantly annoyed with me. He just keeps me around because I'm really good at my job."

I don't know why we're still even entertaining the idea that I won't get the ick, but before I can bring that up, Cami's face of contemplation changes as she swirls a fry through ketchup and speaks.

"Didn't you say when he dropped you off, he was all thrown back by your shitty apartment?" I nod.

"Yeah. He thought I was living there because he wasn't paying me enough, but I just have a shopping addiction and need to prioritize shoes over a fancy place."

"Cheers to that," Abbie says, tipping her mimosa glass my way to clink in agreement. Cami rolls her eyes.

"But then two days later, there's someone in your building, fixing the elevator that hasn't worked in the three years you've lived there?" she asks, lifting her eyebrow again. I shrug, grabbing a roll and buttering it.

Suddenly, I feel the need to keep my hands busy.

"Yeah," I say.

"And they made sure the codebox works, so not just anyone can get in?"

"Mhm," I say around a big bite of roll. I'm definitely not trying to keep my mouth full so I don't have to respond.

"And the burnt-out lights in the hallways were all fixed? And they finally put someone at that desk all day?" I swallow my bite, and it feels like sandpaper and lands in my stomach like lead.

"Someone probably complained. Or maybe the city came and they failed inspection. I don't know. I haven't thought of it as much as you guys clearly have," I say with a shrug.

"Or maybe your boss dropped you off at your apartment and didn't like how unsafe your place was, so he called someone. The boss you've been talking about almost incessantly for the past year. The boss you have weird inside jokes with even though you tell us at every turn he has absolutely no personality. The boss who, apparently, you're the only person besides his lone living relative who calls him by a nickname."

"That's all . . . unrelated," I say, waving my hand at Cami. Her eyes are almost pitying, but I fight to ignore it.

"We're just worried," Abbie says, her voice low and kind. They're clearly playing good cop, bad cop, and I hate it. Usually, I'm good cop and Cami and I are talking to Abbie. "We don't want to see you get hurt if you get attached." I smile weakly.

"Well, it's a good thing I'm broken and I can't get attached, right?" I down the rest of my half-full drink before looking around. "Where's that waiter? I need a refill." I sigh with relief when she pops out of the woodwork, grabbing my empty and taking another order from Liv, giving me the perfect opportunity to change the subject to something safer.

"Now, on to the fun stuff. Warren finally showed his hand and on Friday, Theo gave me the all clear to fuck with him. It can't be anything crazy, just dumb stuff to drive him batshit and make him look bad. Whose got ideas?"

And even though Cami, Abbie, and Liv all give each other looks I could interpret but refuse to, they let me drop it, instead throwing out possible sabotage ideas, from super basic to absolutely insane. (All from Liv, of course.)

But for the rest of the weekend, I can't seem to stop hearing those what-ifs in my mind over and over and over.

TWENTY-TWO

KAT

I get into the office at my usual time on Monday and smile, noting Jessica's, the receptionist's, car is in the lot and Warren's is not.

The man is never early and rarely on time, which is just another reason he should never get control of Catalyst Records.

Today is my first step into truly ensuring that won't happen, because after Warren told Theo, "*Game on, motherfucker,*" he came to me and told me I was free to orchestrate revenge.

"What?!" I said excitedly. He looked at me like he was already regretting the decision, but I kept smiling.

"He gave Blacknote Oliver Porter. I know it. He's taking the gloves off, and so am I. You wanted to do revenge?" I nodded. "Then do it."

"Free rein?" I asked. He stared at me and instantly, there was regret in his eyes. "So long as it's not illegal?"

A long beat passed where I thought he might change his mind before he nodded.

"Free rein."

So this morning, I went to Jessica and filled her in on the basics of what was going on, leaving out any and all mentions of Theo. Instead,

I told her I didn't like how Warren was treating our relationship and had a plan to give him a taste of his own medicine.

"That's fucked," Jessica says after I fill her in on what happened in the break room last week. "Everyone knows you two have been circling each other from your first day here." My head moves back in surprise.

"What?" She nods, her short red hair swaying as she does.

"Oh, for sure. You two were always giggling together, and you were always picking on him and he let you. Grumpy Theodore Carter let you pick on him." My hackles rise instantly.

"He's not grumpy. He's just . . ." I pause because he is absolutely grumpy, but it feels like a betrayal to say it out loud.

"It's fine, girl. I won't talk shit about your man anymore. Now, about this douchewad. You said the package would be here Friday?" I smile and explain my entire plan to her.

When I head back to my desk and open up a shopping browser, I can barely fight the urge to do a little victory dance.

I picked express shipping, which means on Thursday, a big brown package is delivered to Jessica's desk. As she signs for it, she gives me a thumbs-up and smiles my way. I nearly snort out loud as I watch her grab a pair of scissors and open the package, her eyes going wide as she chokes back a laugh.

Closing it up quickly, she puts it under her arm with some effort (okay, so I may have gone a bit overboard with my order) and starts to walk toward Jeff's office across from me.

And I swear to fucking god, I couldn't have planned it better. As Jess walks with the box, Jeff stands from his desk and makes his way toward the door as Warren heads her way. As usual, Warren gives zero fucks about anything in his path and shoulder-checks Jess, knocking her unsteady and making her drop the heavy box.

Jeff catches her as she falls, and Warren turns to yell at her.

"Watch where you're going," he shouts before he realizes who is standing next to her, and then he pivots, his tone doing a complete 180. "I'm sorry. I'm just in a rush and—"

But his words trail off as he looks to where both Jessica and Jeff are staring.

The now overturned box's contents have spilled onto the ugly gray carpet of the office, a sizable collection of various sex toys scattered on the floor.

Three employees walk past, their steps slowing as their eyes also widen, looking at the mess, and for a moment, I regret not having the forethought to set up a camera and record this. Liv would love it.

"What . . . ," Jeff starts, and Jessica jumps in, clearly fighting a laugh.

"I'm sorry. I was just bringing this to you. It's..." She shifts her gaze to Warren and then back to Jeff. "Well, you know company policy is to open any packages and physical mail that comes in unless it's marked not to, for safety purposes and because much of it is for the artists." Jeff nods. "Well, this came for Warren and—"

"What?!" Warren shouts. "The fuck it is for me, you bitch." My eyes go wide and Jess's face goes pale, but Jeff's jaw tightens.

God, this is better than anticipated.

"Well, it's marked to you, and the credit—"

"It's a mix-up, clearly."

"The invoice says it was purchased using your company card," she corrects softly, looking at Jeff.

"Clearly, you can't fucking read, you dumbass. I don't need any of that shit." Warren's hand moves to indicate the toys on the floor.

"What's going on?" Theo says behind me, but I don't even look at him or speak; instead, I wave a hand behind me to shush him.

"Warren, my office. Now," Jeff says, his words filled with anger. "Clean up this box and bring it to me."

"What the fuck? Why do I have to—"

"Warren, I don't know why you ordered your personal items to be shipped to the office, nor why you used your company card, but we can discuss this behind closed doors. Unless you want everyone here to witness this," Jeff says. Warren stutters but doesn't respond, instead going to a knee to start violently growing items into the now empty box.

Quickly, I fumble with my phone and take a picture for posterity's sake. I snort out a laugh, no longer able to fight it when I see the image. Warren's face pops up, and his eyes meet mine. He glares, his jaw going tight, and I wiggle my fingers at him, smiling.

God, it's utterly blissful.

"Katrina, my office for a second," Theo says as Jeff closes his door, Warren inside. I do as he asks, and as soon as I close the door behind me, the tense look melts from his face, a small smile playing on his lips.

"Was that you?"

I shrug and smile back. "Game on, motherfucker," I say, and with that, Theo's booming laugh fills the room.

A good day, indeed.

TWENTY-THREE

THEO

The next day, Katrina storms into my office at noon, her face red with anger and irritation.

My mind runs through all of the things that could have made her so mad and without thinking twice, I start to match each with a solution, something I could do to counter it.

We're out of the coffee she likes?

I'll send her to the shop down the road or, better yet, go myself.

A client is giving her a hard time?

We'll cancel the contract.

Maybe Warren said something to her again? Fine, I'll let her execute the more illegal options on her revenge plan.

Her landlord raised her rent? I'll buy the building.

It's none of those, though.

"What the fuck is this, Theodore?" she asks, fury raging in her eyes as she waves a piece of paper she clearly just printed out.

Hmm.

Theodore.

I'm not sure how I feel about my full name on her lips like this, especially when venom is laced in the word.

"I don't know?" I ask, standing and walking around my desk and in front of her, trying to look at the paper she keeps waving.

"You know! You know what you did!"

"I really don't, Katrina," I say, leaning back on my desk and crossing my arms on my chest, settling in for her rampage to die down. She'll show me whatever it is that's angering her when she's calmed a bit.

"You do! You're looking right here at the receipt!" I raise an eyebrow and tilt my head toward her.

"I can't see it when you're shaking it, Katrina."

"Oh," she says then pushes it to me, slapping me in the chest with it. I grab the now creased and bent paper, trying to focus on what it says, but I don't have to once I recognize the logo at the top.

"Why are my student loans paid in full?" she demands.

"Oh."

"Oh? Oh?! You paid my student loans!" The words come out in a shout, and for some reason I can't quite explain, I have to fight a smile.

So that's what she's pissed about. I figured it would be a fifty-fifty shot of her being mad when she eventually found out—it seems like it landed on the absolutely livid side of things. I can only assume she's going to be even more pissed when she finds out what I did at her apartment.

"Yeah, I know," I say, because that seems to be the only appropriate answer when she's stating the obvious.

"You . . . You . . . You know!?" she asks, shifting to put her hands on her hips.

Okay, I was wrong. It was not the right answer.

Thankfully, I don't have to weigh the outcome of another response because she speaks again. "You can't pay for my student loans."

"Well, I already did, so . . ." As my voice trails off, her face goes red with fury.

Again, wrong answer.

"I can't believe—you paid—what were you—" she stutters out before taking a deep breath with her eyes closed and obviously forcing her body to relax. "Why did you do that, Theo?"

"You wouldn't let me pay you for helping me," I tell her honestly.

"So you paid my loans?!"

"They weren't even that much, Katrina."

"They weren't . . . You were . . . It . . . ." Her mouth opens as she tries to think of how to respond. "They were seventeen thousand dollars!" she shouts, and even though this room has soundproofing, I wonder if anyone can hear that.

"Sixteen thousand, five hundred, and nine, but you're right, rounded up, they were seventeen." She stares and blinks at me for long moments before finally, she speaks.

"Why would you do that?!" she asks, her voice cracking a bit.

But the reality of it is, I don't know.

I don't know why, but the second she told me she wasn't going to let me compensate her, I sent my private investigator on a hunt for any debts she might have, finding only the small sum of student loans.

I don't know why I saw them and instantly paid them off. I told myself that it was because she jokes about it regularly, her working for me solely because of her outstanding loans.

But if that's the truth, then why, when I left her apartment, did I go to that same investigator on a mission to find who owned the building and to get their information? And why did I threaten said landlord with calling the city and getting the building closed for being unsafe if he didn't fix things?

I don't fucking know, but I know I liked doing all of them and I did each one on impulse.

I know that none of this is like me, and I don't know how to feel about it. I am not impulsive.

I don't tell Katrina that; instead, I give her my rehearsed excuse.

Because yes, I planned for this argument because even though I'm starting to wonder if I know myself at all, I know her well.

"You're the one that keeps saying we need to make this look real. Would your fiancé let you struggle with student loans?"

She stands there, her face pinching in frustration, as if she knows I'm right but doesn't want to admit it.

"I wouldn't. Not at all, and everyone who works here knows that, too." That, at least, is the honest truth.

"But no one knows about my student loans! No one knows I'm still paying them off, so it doesn't make sense for you to do it." I groan.

"Would it help if I paid for everyone in the building's loans too? Would that make you feel better?" I don't think I could pull that off, but maybe if I set a cap or paid a portion or had the company match—

Her head jerks back in surprise. "What? No. Why would you do that?"

"So you'll stop looking at me like I killed a puppy instead of helping to make you more financially stable." Her face softens, and her shoulders lose their anger.

"I'm not looking at you like you killed a puppy, Theo. I just . . . That's a lot of money. A lot of effort. I don't understand why."

"Because you wouldn't let me pay and I don't like the idea of anything hanging over your head, of anything impacting your day-to-day negatively." She listens then thinks, and for a moment, I hope she'll let it go.

And then she asks a different question, backing me further into a corner.

"Did you call my building?" She asks it simply, with little to no emotion behind it, so I'm not sure how she'll take my answer or what kind of reaction I should prepare for. Still, I answer quickly and concisely.

"Yes." She throws her hands up.

"Jesus Christ! Are you kidding me, Theo?" I'm on a roll, though, and I explain.

"Yes, I called your landlord. I told him the building was not up to code and that if it wasn't fixed in the next week, I'd call the city. In case you're wondering, I also told him if he raises anyone's rent more than the normal amount next year, I'll be coming after him." I cross my arms on my chest and stare at her because not a single part of me feels bad for making that call.

"Why would you do that!?" she shouts.

"Because I didn't like it, Katrina, and I'm a man who gets what he wants. I dropped you off at your place and it was unsafe. There were simple safety measures already in place but not being utilized. I did not enjoy the idea of dropping you off there and then lying in bed all night, wondering if some creep made his way into your apartment building, because it's not locked and there's no one at the front desk keeping an eye on shit. I didn't like that if you were having a long day or were tired or, God forbid, hurt, you'd have to trudge up a dozen flights of stairs when there was a whole ass elevator out of service. I don't like that there were lights out in stairwells, making it the perfect place for you to get fucking hurt."

"Why do you care!?" she asks, her voice going higher. "Why do you care, Theo? Who cares if my apartment is unsafe!"

And for some reason, I snap.

"Because I like you! I like you, Katrina, and that's why I don't want you getting hurt. You're a good fucking person and a great fucking friend, and I like you. Am I so goddamned impersonal you can't even see that?"

My heartbeat races, panic and frustration and confusion running through me because why the fuck did I just say that?

I open my mouth to backtrack, to explain, to fix this, but then the unexpected happens.

She touches her ear and then leans in.

TWENTY-FOUR

KAT

I don't know why I do it.

Maybe it's because, finally, I see a crack in Theo's uptight façade and it seems like I'm the culprit. I did it. I made him so uncomfortable and frustrated, he had to raise his voice.

Or maybe it's his confession of *I like you*.

I like those three little words way, way more than I should, all things considered, especially since he probably means I like you as a person, as a friend.

Or maybe I just didn't sleep well and these are the consequences of my actions.

Whatever the reason, I reduce the gap between us, move up to my tiptoes, and press my lips to his.

Like the last time, the world stops spinning.

The room around us ceases to exist, and all there is is Theodore Carter and me.

I slide my hands up his chest, looping them around his neck as our lips meld and press against each other's, one of his arms going around my waist and the other moving up my back to bury his hand into my hair.

Though I start the kiss, he takes over quickly, using his grip on my hair to guide my mouth where he wants it, to slide his tongue inside, to taste me, to tease me.

It feels so fucking easy. So natural, like this is just something we do on the regular. Like we always make out in his office at work after we have a little tiff, like this is just . . . us.

And I like it much more than I thought I would.

The kiss stops naturally, a slow, drawn-out end with him peppering kisses to my lips and me returning the favor until finally, finally, I step back. My head is swimming, and I fight the urge to move my hands to my lips, to press them there and feel if they're as kiss-swollen as they feel or to cement how this moment feels in my memory forever.

Because I just kissed Theodore Carter with no one watching, with no expectation, for no good reason, and I really freaking liked it.

He really liked it too, if the way his chest is rapidly rising and falling and the way I could just barely feel him getting hard when he was pressed to me are any indication. My lips tug into a small smile on their own as I try and wrack my brain to figure out what to do now. I open my mouth to say I don't know what, when a loud laugh from outside in the office makes its way through our little bubble.

Reality enters.

I watch it happen in real time, watch the awe leave Theo's face, a different emotion rolling in, and him step back to the side, away from me. He looks from me to the door to the windows, like he's trying to ensure whoever laughed wasn't laughing at us, but it was just someone enjoying their Friday. *Whitney Watson,* my brain tells me, pinpointing the name of the person.

My gut sinks with the look all the same.

"What was that for?" he asks, his voice low and rough, eyes wide and panicked.

Fuck.

I fucked up.

I miscalculated.

Fuck, fuck, fuck. Come on, Katrina! Think of something! Anything!

I look around the room, panicking now, trying to save this massive fuckup, to fix it, and my eyes land on the windows.

"I, uh . . . The blinds are open," I say, my heart beating fast with all-consuming worry. "I thought I saw Jeff walk past. It seemed like a good . . . idea. In case he thought we were fighting."

"Oh," he says, giving a small, understanding nod. "Got it. That makes sense. Good call."

Something that looks much too like relief passes his eyes, and that ball in my stomach turns in on itself.

He's relieved.

I should be relieved that I avoided catastrophe, but somehow . . . I'm not.

For the rest of the day, I don't think about my loans, my apartment, or even anything work-related. Instead, my mind is occupied with battling and trying to decode why I kissed him.

TWENTY-FIVE

THEO

On the day of the engagement party, I send Katrina a text.

> What's the code for your building?

> We're not doing this again.

> You're right, we're not. Now give me your apartment number and the code I need to get up.

There's a pause and I watch the text bubble appear and disappear a few times, like she's typing a response and deleting it before I finally get a reply.

> You don't remember my apartment number? You remember everything.

I do, but I thought it would be weird to tell her I memorized where she lived the one time I walked her up because I didn't trust her sketchy-as-fuck building.

Plus, reminding her of that might bring her anger back about me stepping in, and she hasn't brought it up since that day in my office.

And that fucking kiss.

I shake my head to remove that thought and text her back.

> Please, Katrina. Make my life easier and just give me what I'm asking for.

I expect her to continue to argue, as she does, so when my phone buzzes in my hand with the code and apartment number, I'm surprised but don't question it. Instead, I'm out the door of my car and headed toward the entrance, trying the door without the code once to make sure it actually works. I'm pleased to see it does and that there is now a person at the front desk, despite the fact that it's after five on a Saturday. He also makes me sign in, takes a copy of my license, and calls up to Katrina to make sure I'm a welcome presence.

When I finally knock on her door, it opens almost instantly, and I'm stopped dead in my tracks when I see her.

"How do I look?" she asks, turning left to right.

She's wearing the white dress, and I'm happy to see in person that it does, in fact, cover a bit more of her ass, but not as much as I'd like it to when we're going to a party full of men who already stare at her all day at work.

Why do you care? that obnoxious voice in my head asks.

Because she's my employee. I don't want them staring at her, making her uncomfortable, I rationalize. That's what I'm going with, at least. It's the most logical. There's definitely no other reason.

Nope.

Not at all.

"You look gorgeous," I tell her, not even bothering to choose my words, to say something more befitting of a boss speaking to his assistant, instead telling her the whole truth. Her face goes a bit slack with surprise and she gawks at me.

"What?" she asks.

"I said you look gorgeous."

Her face moves again from shock to contentment, a small laugh coming from her lips as she puts a hand to her chest.

I fight the instinct to follow where that hand goes and look at her breasts. *Don't you dare, Carter.*

"Is that a . . . compliment from Theodore Carter?" she asks. I roll my eyes and put my hand to her elbow, moving her to the side and walking into her apartment, looking for where her coat is.

"No need to act like I have a complete inability to say something nice to you," I say, grabbing the tan coat from a hook as she laughs. "Come on. Jacket on. Let's get this shitshow over with."

TWENTY-SIX

KAT

We park outside of the venue, a large reception hall on the water in Hudson City. It's still early spring, so it's too cold for anything outdoors, but it's a popular spot for events. Just last summer, Catalyst hosted a release party here: there's a large, gorgeous outdoor space that overlooks the river, popular for sunset parties in the summer.

For a split second as we pull in, I think it would be the perfect location for a wedding, spinning my engagement ring on my finger.

"Wait," I say, reaching over and grabbing Theo's wrist, stopping him from leaving the car. He turns and looks at me, concern on his face.

"What's wrong?" I roll my eyes.

"Nothing, you worrywart. We just didn't talk about how we're playing this tonight." I meant to have this conversation at my place or on the drive here, but my mind has been stuck on the way his eyes traveled over my body when he opened the door, his gaze drawing lines of fire wherever they moved, right before he called me gorgeous.

"What?" He looks adorably confused.

"How we're playing this? Are we madly in love? Do we do PDA?"

"PDA?" he asks, and I look at him, thinking he must be joking because who doesn't know what PDA is. When he stares blankly back at me, like he's completely lost, I realize the answer is Theo. Theo doesn't know what PDA is.

"Are you kidding me? You really are old, aren't you?" He glares at me, and it makes me smile, as his glares always tend to do. "Public displays of affection, PDA."

"Oh. Okay. So like . . ." The word trails off, and he waits for me to fill in the blank for him.

"Like kissing. Hand holding, hugging. That kind of thing." I roll my lips together then decide I should touch up my lipstick, flipping the visor of his car down and grabbing the tube from my clutch.

I'm definitely not doing it to avoid his gaze that is suddenly burning on me again.

Nope.

Not at all.

"What are you thinking?" he asks. "I mean, what would you prefer? This is all kind of in your hands." I shrug, rubbing my lips together to even out the color I smeared across them then using a nail to clean up an edge that does not need cleaning up. Literally anything to avoid looking at Theo.

"Oh, it doesn't matter to me." There's a pause of silence and finally, I look at him, and only then does he speak, like he wanted to see my face and gauge my true reaction to his question.

"So if I . . . if I touch you, would that be okay?" Theo asks, and I get a full-body chill I fight to make unseen.

The words *if I touch you* run through my mind, as do all of the things that could mean.

"Touch me how? I mean, honestly, after that kiss, I'm down for whatever," I joke, trying to play it off as if the two kisses I've shared with Theo, both against his will, haven't been ruling my waking and sleeping thoughts for weeks.

"I meant . . . your waist." He stares awkwardly at me, and I can feel an embarrassed blush burn my cheeks even though I fight it. "If we're standing together, talking to someone, can I touch your waist?"

"That's fine. I'm open to anything," I say with a shrug, as if his skin on mine wouldn't destroy my mental stability. "Whatever we need to do to sell this, I'm in." He shakes his head, and I feel it like a knife to my gut.

God, why is this so embarrassing? And why am I letting it bother me? I've never had this, a man turning me down, for lack of a better term, and being disappointed or hurt by it.

Fuck, a man not being wildly into me is usually just one of my very first icks.

That must be it, I tell myself. It must just be that I'm embarrassed that he isn't into me, that it feels like this whole fake relationship is a burden to him, like it's something he dreads.

"Anything more than we've already done is a bad idea. I wouldn't want there to be any feelings or attachments causing problems. I value your work for me, Katrina. I don't want this . . . mess I'm in to jeopardize that."

I laugh, a rueful, self-deprecating noise. If he only knew . . .

God, it's ironic, isn't it? Him saying that to me, not understanding the curse that is me. That no matter what, even if we did start something up, I wouldn't have any long-lasting feelings to fuck up our friendship.

"Oh, that won't happen, trust me." His face turns to me, and I see it there for a split second before it's slammed behind his professional mask, that grumpy face he always wears.

Hurt.

Maybe disappointment?

Okay, disappointment might just be a fucked sense of wishful thinking. But the hurt? That was absolutely there.

"No, I don't mean . . . It's not you. It's me," I say, struggling to explain, and when he gives me a *did you really just use the oldest line in the book?* face, I shake my head and clarify. "No, I'm serious. I'm broken."

"You're broken?"

"Oh, yeah," I say with my normal, forced chipper attitude. "Super broken."

"I don't . . . ," he starts, his words fading off. "What do you mean you're broken?" He sits back in his seat, arms crossed on his chest and body turned to me like he's about to yell at me for speaking poorly about myself. Happiness and laughter bubble in my belly at how funny it looks on him.

"Oh, don't get me wrong, I think I'm the shit. I'm just broken emotionally." His face shifts again and his mouth opens. "And before you go all *who did this to you* on me, the answer is my parents. Trauma. You know, the fun stuff." His brows furrow together, like he's even more confused, and I sigh. "It's a really long story, but the long and short of it is, I never get past seven dates with a man before I get the ick. I told you about my ick, right? Something happens by that seventh date and I fully lose all interest in him. It happens every time." I shrug and smile wide, playing off how exhausting it is and how over it I am. How desperately I want to find love like my friends have. "Easy as that."

"So you've . . . you've never dated a man for more than seven dates?" he asks with a raised eyebrow.

"Uhm, before you judge me, please remember you're fake dating your assistant since you're so tragically single, your boss won't give you a promotion because he thinks you literally have no life outside of work." A small smile forms on his lips.

"Okay, fair. That's fair." I roll my eyes and sigh.

"Anyway, all that to say, if we did anything—if we did something . . ." I pause then shift my gaze to my hands, refusing to glance at him, to read the thoughts and emotions that undoubtedly will be written there. He's so easy to read and normally, I find that to be a good thing, but right now? I don't think I want to know. "We'd be fine. Knowing you, it won't take long. We'd be safe if we wanted to do more. There's obviously chemistry, and it would help our case." Finally, I look at him, at his face, which, for the first time in a long time, is . . . blank.

I see nothing there, nothing at all telling me how he's feeling, how he's interpreting this. He's showing me nothing, leaving me panicked and unable to shift my response to cater to his expectations.

Finally, he speaks, his voice unemotive and neutral, like he's letting me down easy. "I think it's best we keep things uncomplicated," he says. "Minimal . . . boundary-pushing."

I ignore the jolt of disappointment, telling myself it's just because I haven't gotten laid in some time.

"Suit yourself," I say with a sassy shrug of my shoulder, plastering on a self-righteous smile and reaching for the door handle to open it myself.

"Katrina," he says, my name sounding gorgeous on his lips.

"Hm?" I ask, turning back to him with a flirty smile so I don't look like a fucking idiot.

"It's not that . . ." He clears his throat, and I feel my brows furrow slightly. "It's not that I don't find you attractive. You're . . ." There's a pause while he looks me over, head to toe, and with each millimeter his eyes touch, heat rolls through me. ". . . incredibly beautiful. You know that." Butterflies dance in my belly. "But we've made this complicated enough without adding another layer, and I value your work for me and your . . . friendship."

Somehow, that eases things, even though the answer is the same.

Because now that wall on his face is down again, I see it all there.

The desire, the attraction, the confusion. He's telling the truth. It's not that he doesn't want to mess around until my ick kicks in. It's that he's nervous it could mess things up between us.

And that? That I can handle. Fuck, isn't that exactly what I've been grappling with since our first kiss? The push and pull of my attraction to him and not wanting to cross a line?

I reach over, touching his cheek, fresh shaven and smooth, letting my thumb graze over his high-cut cheekbones.

"I get it, Theo. We're all good. I value you as a friend as well."

Disappointment streaks across his expression and for a moment, I wonder if maybe he was hoping I'd argue, that I'd push the subject.

I wonder what he would have done if I had?

"We should go in," I whisper, tipping my head to the venue.

"Yeah," he says, but instead of moving, his big hand covers mine and holds it to his face. "I guess we should."

TWENTY-SEVEN

KAT

Cheers erupt in the room as we walk in after leaving our coats with the coat check, Jeff and Judy walking over to hug us both. Judy gives me a kiss on each cheek before she passes me to her husband, who engulfs me in a huge hug. Once he lets me go, I'm turned by Savannah, who squeals like we've been best friends for years, hugging me too.

"You chose the white!" she says with a wide smile. "See, I told you with the right shoes, it would be perfect." She turns me, looking over every inch of the dress she helped me to pick out and the blush stilettos with bows on the backs of the ankle straps. "Did Teddy flip when he saw it?" she asks with a laugh.

"She could wear a paper bag and I'd flip," Theo says, putting an arm to my waist and tugging me in, pressing a kiss to my hair.

It's for show, I remind myself. We're "on" right now. The spotlight is on us and we have to be.

But that doesn't stop my belly from flipping over and over.

"Carter," a voice says, and my body stiffens. Theo's arm tightens on my waist at the same moment Warren walks up behind Savannah. Strange that he wasn't by her side moments ago when we arrived.

"Warren," Theo says, sticking out a hand. His entire body jolts mine as he shakes Warren's hand, both clearly fighting for dominance with a tight grip.

"Still can't believe you two are a thing," Warren says, and Jeff laughs, but I see the true intent. "Just a few weeks ago, you were single as can be, staying at the office long past everyone else. Now, you're all cuddled up with Katrina every chance you get."

"Oh, stop it, Warren," Savannah says with a laugh, slapping his chest, but there's irritation on his face in the way his eyes narrow, the way his jaw tightens like he's annoyed by her.

I don't like that. Not at all.

"Well, let's go sit. You two are at the table with all of us, right in front!" Judy says, clapping her hands then linking her arm with mine and leading me to the table. I look over my shoulder at Theo, who is closely following behind, and my gut churns with everything happening around us, this perfect storm of chaos, but then he gives me a wink, and I think we might just survive this.

Until, oh dear god, the worst of it happens.

Little speeches. In her timeline for the event, Judy has scheduled a full thirty minutes for whoever wants to step up to a mic and talk a bit about us. As much as I like Judy, I think I might hate her a little because this is bound to be the most uncomfortable moment of my life.

Also, who has speeches at a goddamn engagement party? Even at a wedding, it's only a few people on a preapproved list. But for some reason, Judy thought it would be great to have everyone who wants to come up and say a few nice things?

Kill me now.

And when I look at Theo, the pinch of discomfort is clear on his face. If I hate this, and I'm not usually averse to human interaction, this might actually be a painful experience for him.

Surprisingly, it doesn't go as poorly as I anticipated, and with nearly all of the board in attendance, it actually leans in our favor. Judy steps up first, clearly already having planned what she would say, and lays out a tearjerker of a speech, thanking Theo for letting her help to raise him. Then Savannah comes up, tells a few jokes from their childhood, and tells the room her brother is the most loyal, hardworking person she knows and thanks me for letting her get to know me.

"I'm so excited to finally have a sister!" she exclaims, and guilt churns in my gut.

When Jeff is pushed to the mic by his wife, I'm truly unsure of what he'll say. Nearly everyone here is a work acquaintance (I was able to talk my way out of having my friends come, as that would have been an utter disaster, especially if you got a few drinks into them), and this speech could be a subtle nod toward backing Theo.

"You know, I've known Theodore since the day he was born, and I'm pretty sure that was the day he made the most noise in his entire life." The room booms with laughter, and I smile, too, despite my nerves. "He's always been a quiet man, always keeping to himself. That is, until he hired Katrina as his assistant. It took maybe a month of her working for him before every once in a while, we'd hear them laughing in his office or catch them chatting quietly at her desk. I'm actually surprised no one caught onto their relationship sooner, if I'm being honest." I turn Theo and give him a *see? I was right* look. He rolls his eyes and it makes my smile turn into a grin.

"It's incredibly similar to the relationship his father had with his mother. Teasing and fun. Cathy always was able to poke fun at Teddy in a way he would never let another person do. They'd both be overjoyed to see the two of you together," Jeff says then raises his glass, eyes locked on Theo, before taking a sip of his drink and moving to sit without any more fanfare.

I hope it's done, that this ridiculous part of the night is over, until Warren stands. Theo reaches out under the table and I move my hand to his, letting him grab it with a near-painful grip.

"We never thought Theodore would actually find someone, you know?" he says, and the room laughs. Looking at Theo's face, I see it rolling in there, the anger and irritation.

And then he proceeds to tumble into a long story about getting drunk at a party in college and then having to work on a project they had due the next morning. He goes into gruesome details, explaining every single thing that happened that night, the shots he took, the girls he flirted with, and even without looking at Theo, I know it's all bullshit.

It's clearly some kind of ploy to try and make Theo look bad, but it's such a strange angle, in my opinion. Who in their right mind would hold a drunken night nearly fifteen years ago against someone trying to get a job promotion?

"I, of course," Warren starts, his smile going slimy. "Told him we should stay in, but he didn't listen. He wanted to party. We've had quite a few nights like that since, haven't we, Carter?"

Ahh, that's where he's going—lying about parties they go to currently to set himself up as the responsible option where Theo is a party animal. And then, I know. He's nervous. He's grasping at straws since this is clearly so out of character for Theo, no one in their right mind would believe it.

"In fact, Theo keeps a bottle of whiskey in his office—to schmooze clients, of course, but—" His smile is smarmy as he speaks and with that, I stand.

I don't know what comes over me, but a wide smile graces my face that some might mistake as friendly, but it's truly lethal. I walk the few feet over to where Warren is, taking the microphone from his hands before he can continue to talk shit about my man.

I mean, my boss.

My fake fiancé.

"Thank you so much, Warren, for that . . ." I pause and exaggeratingly widen my eyes, making sure everyone can see it. A few people snicker. ". . . enlightening tale. I just wanted to come up here and tell everyone how grateful I am that all of you came here to celebrate Theo and me. It's been a long year, and we know our relationship was a bit of a surprise, but when has Theo ever been conventional, you know?" A few laughs and claps come from the crowd.

"No matter what our friend Warren over here says." I look to him with a smile that I'm sure he can read is venomous. "Theo really is an amazing partner. He always takes wonderful care of me, is incredibly attentive, and is always the responsible one of the two of us. I'm honored he's chosen me to hold his hand through the next chapter of his life." My eyes meet his and I smile, hoping he knows what I'm really saying without screaming in front of this room of people.

I'm here for you.

He smiles and nods.

"Alright, now let's party, you guys!" I say into the mic, cutting off anyone else who wants to come up and give a ridiculous speech in an effort to kiss Jeff's or Theo's ass. A round of cheers takes over, and relief visibly passes over Theo.

After I hand the mic back to the DJ, who instantly starts playing music, I walk back to our little table. Theo instantly grabs me as I sit, wrapping an arm around my waist and tugging me and my chair close. He presses his lips to my hair and I smile, but it's not at the move or the joy of being here. It's at the words he whispers there.

"Thank you."

Glancing around the table, I take just a moment to take in everyone's expressions.

Jeff looks happily surprised. My brain catalogs that to later decide if it's because I stood up for him when Theo was clearly uncomfortable or if it's because he thinks Theo found someone who is outspoken.

Judy gives me a soft smile and a nod, which I'm pretty sure is approval.

Savannah's eyes aren't directed at me, but at Warren, her brows furrowed, her face pinched into a mixture of disapproval and confusion.

But it's Warren's face making my stomach churn. He looks furious. He looks like if he could without ruining his appearance as a good ol' boy, he would love to rip me a new one and yell at me for making him look stupid.

And that means even though Theo is determined to play this clean, still rejecting the majority of my offers to help get some kind of revenge, we need to reevaluate our plan. My gut is telling me Warren's getting ready to play dirty—or dirtier— and we are not prepared for that in the least.

Unfortunately, there's no time to think much about it because just moments after the music starts, we're flooded by partygoers congratulating us and coming to chat with Theo.

But my eyes never stop tracking Warren.

About an hour into the party, Theo and I finally get a break from the incessant congratulations and hugs and small talk. He takes my hand, leading me to a dark corner.

"We can hide here for a bit," he says, sagging against the wall and sighing. I laugh.

"This is tough for you, isn't it?" I ask, but I already know the answer. Theo does not like small talk. He doesn't like talking to and hugging dozens of people. He hates this.

In fact, at work events, we have created a system for rescue missions; my main purpose at those events is to get him out of conversations he doesn't want to be in and/or into a quiet room alone so he can recharge for a bit.

I keep my eyes on him through the event, not hovering but never far, and if he raises his right hand and tugs his ear, I'm to go in and save him, make up some fake emergency that needs solving.

Unfortunately, this being our event, we can't really do that, so the corner will have to do for a bit of peace and quiet. I'm hoping the open bar and recentlyannounced buffet will keep too many people from scoping us out in the shadows.

"Jeff knows I hate this shit, but he also knows how many important conversations can happen at an event like this. People let their guard down, have a drink, say things they wouldn't in more businesslike settings." I nod, knowing this because we've had this conversation a million times. "It's just a bit different when the event is focused around me, you know?"

"I do. I'm sorry," I say then reach out to grab his hand, squeezing it once. For a moment, I panic because why would I do that when no one is watching, but he looks at me and gives me a small smile, the energy slowly coming back to his eyes now that we're in a quieter area. We sit in relative silence for a few minutes before a light to my right pulls my attention. Someone turned a light on in a hallway, two figures now standing there, facing each other, clearly in conversation.

It's Warren and a woman standing nearly a foot apart, Warren's arms crossed on his chest defensively, the woman waving her hands at him and toward the party, clearly irate. Where we are, I'm pretty sure they can't see us, so I don't bother to hide my stare, trying to understand a bit more of what's going on. I bump my elbow into Theo, tipping my head toward the hall.

"What's up with them?" I ask.

"Who?"

"Warren and someone else, they look like they're arguing." Theo's head follows where I'm staring and he nods, like this is nearly expected. "Who is that?"

"That's Melody. Ray Harmon's daughter, an old friend of mine." Ray is one of the grumpier board members who gives me the ick for sure.

"An old friend?" I ask, smelling information I'd like to know more about.

He sighs.

"She's an ex of mine, kind of," he says. "We went on one date, but she very much wanted it to be more." Suddenly, I remember the calendar event from just a few weeks after I started at Catalyst and I smile. I never saw that name again despite the rush of jealousy. The woman is gorgeous, in a tight black dress with blonde hair cascading down her back. I can't see details, but from what I can tell and what I remember from seeing her at other events, she's essentially a damn

Barbie and everything I am not. Her face changes to apologetic just then, her hand moving out to grab Warren's arm.

"Not of Warren's?" I ask because a woman does not touch a man she is not fucking like that. Or, at the very least, he's a man she wants to fuck soon.

"Not that I know of," Theo says, even though he's looking at them as well because he's a man. Men are not inherently programmed to decode every nuance of someone's body language and tone of voice and facial expressions, and it must be fucking nice.

"Hmm," is all I say, and her hand moves from Warren's arm to his chest. She steps even closer, nearly touching her chest to his as she tips her head up to look at him.

"What does that mean?" he asks, turning to me.

"Nothing."

Hmm means I'm pretty sure they're fucking, but I'm not going to say that.

He opens his mouth to ask something else, but before he can, a familiar, petite older woman comes up to us, hip-checking Theo.

"I had a feeling I'd find you back here," Judy says with a small, playful smile. Theo shrugs, so I think of it as my sign to speak.

"The noise, he doesn't like it. It gets to him. I'm kind of his noise-level watchdog. I see him start to get overwhelmed, I make an excuse and squirrel him off to a corner to recover." She smiles warmly.

"I'm glad he has that. I'm glad he has you," she says with a knowing smile. "When he was little, when we'd all have to go to these events, Jeff and Teddy and Sarah would all take off, begin the process of mingling. They were both fabulous at it, and Jeff lives for this kind of thing. But me and Theodore, we'd sneak off, go hide in the kitchen together, eating a dessert or chatting." She lets out a sad laugh before looking at her pseudo-son with concerned eyes. "Those were some of my favorite parties we ever had."

Theo casually reaches out, grabs my hand, and squeezes in a very not casual, almost unbearably tight way I know is him trying not to let any kind of emotion show on his face.

For whatever reason, those memories hurt him.

"Maybe one day, you two will have a little one who will need me to hide them away," Judy says with a smile, and usually, that shit annoys me, grown people making assumptions about a couple's future family plans, but with Judy, it just feels . . . hopeful. Not like pressure, but a kind wistfulness.

"I think Katrina will make an amazing mother one day," Theo says, surprising me, putting an arm on my waist and tugging me in, once again pressing a kiss to my hair. "And you would be a fabulous grandmother to any of the Carter kids." My belly warms and flips in a way it absolutely should not, but I don't have the heart to bring it back down to reality.

I let my inner romantic bask in the warmth of it, even if it's all bullshit.

Even more so when I see Judy's eyes shine in the dim lighting.

"I'd love that," she says. Just then, a voice not too far away calls her name. "Oh, I'd better go before I reveal your hiding spot." She moves to Theo, pressing a kiss to his cheek. "Proud of you, my boy." Then she moves to me, wrapping me up in a tight hug as well.

"Thank you so much, sweet girl," she says quietly in my ear before leaving. I don't have to ask or even wonder what that means.

And for the first time, genuine guilt fills me as I understand just how high the stakes are with this ruse, especially the ones we didn't see coming.

TWENTY-EIGHT

KAT

Somewhere along the line, we get separated when I can no longer deny my need for a bathroom break. I leave him chatting with a board member, pressing a kiss to his cheek and watching with satisfaction as the board member smiles just a bit at our PDA. When I return, though, he's nowhere to be found. I wander around the party, looking for him, and when I see him, I stop dead in my tracks.

He's in a quieter area, a blonde woman's hand on his arm, her eyes gazing at him with longing, a seductress's smile on her lips.

Fucking Melody.

Unleashed fury swipes through me, jealousy I'm not allowed to feel nipping at its heels.

How dare he make me look like an idiot at this event, my impulsive mind thinks. *How dare he sneak off as soon as I'm gone to go talk to some woman he dated.*

But then I take in Theo.

He's standing there, face made of stone and impersonal, his hands at his sides, not even bothering to attempt to look comfortable or happy to be there.

He's not there willingly.

He needs saving.

"There you are, honey," I call, coming up behind Theo, my eyes locked on the woman.

Hers narrow as he shakes her hand off his arm, and he tugs me close with an arm around my waist, his body turning toward mine like he's a flower and I'm his sun, and my free hand slides up his chest. It seems almost natural, like this is how we actually act.

"Who's this?" I ask, smiling wide at him and just barely catching the quick hint of confusion on his face, considering we just talked about her not an hour ago. When I look back at her, her eyes are fiery as she glares at me,

"This is, uh . . . Melody," he says. "Melody Harmon."

"Oh, of course! Ray's daughter!" I smile wide and fake then put out my hand to shake hers.

My left hand.

Her eyes zoom in on my ring, the ring I stare at way too often each day, the ring I'm getting way too used to wearing.

"Hi, I'm Kat. Theo's fiancée," I say with a smile. Her face goes even more sour.

"Theo?" she asks, continuing to stare at my hand then to Theo like she's . . . hurt.

"Oh, goodness." I slap his chest like this is an ongoing joke we have. "Tell me you didn't give this nice woman an issue when she didn't want to call you freaking Theodore."

"You told me you hate that name." Her eyes flit to me, and I watch her jump through her options on what to say next until a catty smile spreads on her lips. She speaks, and that smile goes plain bitchy, like she thinks whatever she says will be a direct hit, a win in this battle of wills I don't really feel like being in. "When we dated."

"Oh, that's right! I forgot you went on a date with Ray's daughter!" I say, twisting the knife a bit.

Theo doesn't react to that, but his hand tightens on my waist, pulling me a bit closer. "I guess it's just took the right person saying it. It's growing on me now," he says. He shifts his arm so he can pull me in even closer now, so my chest is nearly on his, my hand pressed between us, and kisses my hair.

I watch Melody's face, watch the anger rip through her, but I don't even feel the warmth of a win. Instead, I'm so lost in this, in him holding me close, cherishing me. I'm too busy reminding myself this is a show.

"You know, I heard he was engaged and that you both had been dating for almost a year, was it?" she asks, tipping her head to the side, a fake confused look written on her face.

I fight the urge to roll my eyes, knowing exactly what she's going to say next.

"I just thought it was so strange. Because last, what was it, Teddy?" she says, and Theo's teeth grind.

"Theodore," he says, but she finishes her thought, ignoring him completely.

"Maybe back in May? We went on a date. And it went pretty well, or at least I thought." Even though he is literally holding me, this bitch's arm reaches out and touches my man.

My boss.

My fake man. But there's no need to split hairs because for all intents and purposes, she thinks this is my fiancé. And she's touching him in front of me.

I see red.

I see red, and I go off script.

"You know, it's so funny," I start with a sugary sweet smile. "I did know that! I made the appointment in his calendar after all. And I really should thank you, you know. For asking him out." I twist the knife once more, knowing Theo wasn't the one who initiated that date because she came to the office while visiting her daddy and asked him in front of four board members, putting him on the spot so he felt required to agree.

Her face pinches up because I just know this is the kind of

woman who only asks a man out if she's desperate, expecting him to make the first move.

"And you know, that night, I could not sleep. I was so twisted up about my Theo going out with someone. That's the day I realized I was in love with him." I pause and pray to fucking God I'm right with my next words. "After he got home that night, I called him. We talked all night, and we both confessed we were feeling something for each other." I shrug happily, moving to my tiptoes to kiss Theo's cheek as if I just can't help myself. "Really, I have you to thank for getting us together."

Her face is red now, rage and embarrassment running through her. Usually, I'm not the kind of girl who likes to pit women against each other. It goes against everything I believe in.

But sometimes, bitches need to be put in their places.

"Everything okay over here?" a voice says, and I fight the urge to roll my eyes as Warren Michaels walks up like the fucking boogeyman.

"Just chatting with our friend Melody," I say with a smile. Her eyes go stone-cold and she looks at me, then up at Warren.

They are so totally fucking, I think.

"I was just telling Katrina how thrown back I was to learn of Theodore's engagement since I went on a date with him just last May," she says.

I want to rip her hair out.

I want to break her perfect little nose just so she can cry and have her daddy buy her a new one.

I want to—

Warren sighs.

"I was trying to talk to Katrina about this recently at the office. I'm so worried one of them is going to get hurt."

"Why would either of us get hurt, Warren?" Theo asks, his hand tightening on my waist.

"When a relationship like this happens, someone always does," he says with faux sincerity lining his words.

"I'm not sure what you're saying," Theo says, his words stilted. Warren's eyes go cold, the fake kindness leaching out.

"We all know this bullshit relationship is just so you can continue to shove your face further up Jeff's ass. What do you think he's going to say when he finds out this"—his hand flits between Theo and me— "was all a ruse to get a job? When you never get married and break up after he stupidly falls for your bullshit, what's he going to say when I tell him everything I know?"

His eyes move to Theo, dark and near feral now, and I wonder just how much he's had to drink. "Jeff told you he thinks you're such a fucking loser and have no life outside Catalyst, so you made up some bitch. I don't know how you think this is going to work, but I promise you, I'm getting that fucking position." His face is pure venom, nothing but anger and wrath and danger, and it sends a chill down my spine.

Theo must feel it, too, because his hand moves to my hip, and he angles his body in front of mine, protecting me. This causes Melody's eyes to flare with her own brand of anger, but I can't pay her any mind.

Theo's jaw has gone tight, and I don't have to look at him to know he's fuming, to know he's counting to try and keep his temper in check. Lucky for me, I don't have to. I'm not the one trying to play nice. I lean in just a bit and lower my voice, speaking directly to Warren. "And what's he going to say when he finds out that if you get the job, you'll destroy Catalyst? That if you get the job, half the employees will quit?" I take a stab in the dark. "Or when he realizes you're the one leaking everything to Blacknote?"

"Shut the fuck up. You don't know shit," he says, all jovial kindness now gone.

It doesn't put me off the way he thinks it will, doesn't stop me from poking the bear. "I know more than you think I do, Warren. I know you're planning some kind of bullshit and you're hanging your hat on getting the job by fucking over Theo instead of, oh god, I don't know, doing your fucking job and doing it well." I let a slow, wicked smile spread over my lips. "But what you didn't anticipate is me. I'm as loyal as they come, and I'm fucking insane. Theo might want to play this clean and keep things good, but me? I'm happy to play in the mud with you. So before you try anything, before you try and fuck with my fiancé and his legacy, just know that if you go low, I'll tunnel to the core of the fucking earth." My words are venom and anger and malice, but my face is kindness and a happy smile.

In contrast, his looks like if he thought he could get away with it, he'd hit me. Pleasure strikes through me from knowing I'm getting to him.

But while this game has been fun, I'm over it.

"Anyway, it's been just lovely getting to know you, Mel, but I must mingle before Judy yells at us," I joke. Then, to Melody's shock, I untangle myself from Theo, grab her shoulders, and kiss each cheek like we're old friends. "It was great meeting you!"

"Umm, yeah," she mumbles. We start to walk away, but as tends to be my way, I can't resist one last dig.

"You deserve each other, by the way," I say, looking over my shoulder at her, Theo's arm on my waist tightening. I can almost hear the words he's trying not to actually say. *Let it go.*

He should know by now that is not my style.

"What?" she asks. I stop walking away and turn toward her, Theo groaning as I do.

"I said you deserve each other, Warren and you."

"I . . . I don't know what you're talking about."

"Yeah, I bet you don't." Through her "confusion," though, there's panic.

I'm right.

And even though I glory in the small win, I also feel a hidden sense of urgency because if I'm right about that, I'm right about a whole lot more, and that means Theo and I need to move quicker.

But I don't have time at all to overthink, panic, or try and make a plan because Theo's long legs move faster until I'm almost running to keep up. He nods to a few people but keeps walking with a determined stride until we're in a quiet, empty hallway, not a soul around.

I'm ready for him to yell at me.

He's definitely mad at me for poking the bear, for making a mess when it wasn't necessary. He walks me into a wall, my back pressed against the cool surface, and I open my mouth to speak, to explain myself and apologize. To commiserate about what a bitch that woman is, to ask how the fuck he went on even one date with her, or maybe something about how I'm so glad it didn't last long because I could never endure her walking past my desk on the regular, but I have no time.

Because Theo is caging me in.

"I'm going to kiss you, Katrina," he whispers, hot breath playing against my lips as he does.

"Okay," I whisper because really, what other option is there?

The truth is, I want him to kiss me.

And then he is, his lips pressed to mine, and it's so different than at the office. There, it was a quick goodbye, made to seem like it didn't matter, like it was casual and pedestrian even though it was anything but. It was for an audience, to prove a point. And the second time, it was more but still . . . basic. Just a kiss.

But this?

This kiss in an empty hallway, his body lined up with mine, my jaw in his big hands, my arms sliding up to loop around his neck, is just for us.

It isn't for show.

A small noise comes from my throat with the realization, my fingers twining in the hair at the base of his neck as I rise to my tiptoes, trying to get more, to get closer, to be his.

At this moment, I feel safe admitting that to myself, even if it's just a whisper swirling in my mind.

I want to be his.

The move, or maybe the noise, seems to spur him on, and he presses closer to me until I'm glued to him, my body lined up with his and his hand running down my side. His other hand follows suit until they're both at my hips, dipping under my ass. His knees bend a bit, though he never breaks the kiss, and he's hoisting me up, encouraging me to spread my legs and wrap them around his waist. He's holding me up now, pressing me against the wall as he kisses me, inhaling me, tasting me.

His lips move down, kissing my neck, and I tilt my hips and quickly realize that like this, only his pants and my underwear are between us. He groans into my neck as I shift, grinding against him in a way that is pure torture for both of us.

But I feel him.

I feel him through his pants and my thin underwear, feel his hard cock pressing where my body is begging for him.

"Theo," I whisper, a plea. I don't know what I'm begging for exactly, but I'm begging all the same. For him. For more. For anything he'll give me.

In the far depths of my mind, his lips dropping my guard and obliterating my shields, I think I'm going to have to wrestle with that soon. I can't bury it forever.

I want Theo, and I'll take him anyway he'll give himself to me.

A loud laugh in the other room has Theo's body tightening like a bow and instantly, I know the moment is broken.

His lips leave my skin, and his hands help me down before holding me at my shoulders until my footing is sure. Once he knows I won't fall, he steps back, staring at me, taking me in. My hands swipe down the skirt of my dress, buying me time to settle my mind before I look at him. His chest is heaving, the bulge in his pants telling me he feels the same all-encompassing need I do, the flush on his cheeks so endearing, I almost smile.

"What was that for?" I ask in a whisper.

"I don't fucking know," he says, running a hand through his hair. He sighs before continuing, explaining in a way, "People don't stick up for me, Katrina. It doesn't happen." I smile, realizing that's why he kissed me like that. Because in my own way, I stuck up for him to Warren, to Melody, and he appreciated it.

"Well, now you have me," I say, my voice low. He lifts a hand like he wants to touch my face before he decides against it and drops it.

"For now," he says low, and my heart drops to my feet. "Come on. Let's say our goodbyes and head out of here."

TWENTY-NINE

KAT

I almost skip lunch with Abbie on Tuesday, not particularly ready for her to see right through me when I tell her about how the weekend went, but I don't, instead heading out of the office at my normal 11:45 and meeting her at the taqueria down the street from my building we meet at more often than not.

Truth be told, the longer this fake fiancé mess goes on, the more . . . confused I'm getting, and I don't need Abbie and her hopeless romantic, wants everyone to fall in love as hard as she has self to confuse me even more.

The regret for not canceling sinks in barely five minutes into our lunch. "So, are you going tell me how the engagement party went?" Abbie asks, lifting an eyebrow at me.

On Sunday, Abbie, Cami, and Liv each called me throughout the day, asking for updates on how yesterday went, and I gave each of them the same basic story: the event was fine, Theo was a gentleman, and Warren was a jackass. I told them about the confrontation with Melody and how I called Warren out but left out the kiss and all of the mind-boggling details.

"There's not much to tell," I lie.

"Bullshit," she says, calling me out.

"I'm serious. It was an engagement party for a fake engagement. How much could really have happened?" She gives me a look.

"So, you're telling me absolutely nothing of interest went down? Not with the boss or his sister or the douche canoe?" I don't say anything. "Exactly. Fill me in. My life is much less entertaining than yours." She then puts her elbows on the table, propping her head in her hands.

I roll my eyes but know arguing is no use. Abigail Martinez is a force to be reckoned with.

"Uh," I start, unsure of where to start but knowing the topics I don't want to touch because Abbie will take that inch and run a mile. "There were speeches. Like, a dozen of them."

"Speeches? At an engagement party?" she asks, an eyebrow raised.

"It was weird. And then the douche canoe stood up and started talking about Theo getting drunk in college and then about him drinking at the office and it was clearly making Theo annoyed and uncomfortable and . . ." I pause, knowing she's going to love this but also use it as a reason to keep pushing. "I stood up and interrupted, ending the speech portion of the night."

"Did you now?" she asks with a smile. "What other incredibly boring, run-of-the-mill things happened?"

There's no use.

"His ex was there and all over him."

"No," she says, aghast. I nod.

"And she even implied our relationship was bullshit because she went on a date with him in May."

"No!" Again, I nod. "What did you do?" I smile. I do love how she knows I *absolutely* did something.

"I thanked her," I say, my smile turning smug.

"You thanked her?" I nod.

"I told her seeing their date—and I was sure to remind her it was just one—on his calendar was the catalyst for telling Theo how I felt. How if it hadn't happened, we probably wouldn't be getting married."

"Shut up. I bet she loved that." I smile at the memory.

"Oh, she was *pissed*. Then Warren came over and started getting loud, making accusations as well. I kind of called him out for not having the best intentions if he gets the company and that did not make him happy. Honestly, I think moving forward, for Warren at least, it's going to be gloves off," I say with a sigh, voicing my concern.

"What does that mean?"

"He's going to do anything in his power to fuck with Theo and get the job. He's already fucking with artists Theo recommends and he has no problem voicing his 'concerns' in front of board members, but my gut tells me that's just the tip of the iceberg."

"So what are you guys doing?"

I roll my eyes. "Nothing good enough. Theo has a . . . moral compass."

"A moral compass does you no good if someone else is playing dirty."

"Exactly! That's what I'm saying! He let me do a few little things. I sent his work number to a million telemarketers, and I ordered sex toys to the office using his company card." Abbie snorts, covering her mouth as she laughs, and I smile too. "Yeah, that one went even better than I thought. But Theo won't let me do anything to actually sabotage him. I think he wants to get the job on his own merit. He'd rather us work at making him look better than Warren worse."

"Well, that's dumb." I give her an, *I agree* look.

"Plus, his sister is in love with Warren. They're dating. But I . . ." I shake my head and sigh. "I don't think it's real. Which, I know, is ironic. But I think she doesn't know it's not real."

"Warren is dating the sister to fuck with him?"

"Yes? Maybe? Or to get on Jeff's good side or to prove a point that he's a more solid choice than Theo. My theory is Jeff confided his concerns about Theo to Warren and he ran with that, leaned into the family man shit. In my head, the timelines add up."

"But he doesn't actually like her?" I move my food around on my plate, suddenly not very hungry.

"He's cheating on her," I say, sure it's true. My gut just knows.

"He is?" Abbie asks with shock on her face. "Have you told her? Have you told Theo? What did he say? What did *she* say?!"

"Well, hold on. Let me clarify. I *think* he's cheating on the sister. I have no proof other than him being strangely chummy with the woman at that engagement party and my gut."

"But your gut is never off," she says like it's obvious. I shrug.

"Yes, but I can't just make an accusation based on a gut instinct."

"Yes, you can. Women's code and everything."

"We told you Richard was a douche and you're my best friend. You didn't believe me. At least, not in a way that made you get rid of him." Abbie's face screws up before she nods.

"Okay, fair. What does Theo say?" For some reason, I love that. I love Abbie calling him Theo, like he's part of this group of people I trust most of all, like he's already one of us.

"He agrees, but doesn't know how to approach it with Savannah. We have no proof, after all. He tried to bring it up to her when they first started dating, and it caused a rift between them." I remember that night, the drive home, trying to explain my gut feeling to him.

"That was kind of hot, you know," I said finally, breaking the long silence that had taken over the car.

"What?" he asked, confused.

"That was hot. You sticking up for me. Pushing me beside you when Warren had his panties in a twist."

"Panties in a twist? Katrina, the man looked like he was going to hit you."

"I don't think he'd have the balls to," I said.

"That wasn't something I was willing to gamble on." Something fluttered in my belly, but I pushed it down. "Next time, can you please

try not to poke a clearly unstable, drunk man when we're at a company party?"

"I'll do my best," I said.

"Why do I feel like your best is absolutely not going to be enough?" I smiled but let silence hang between us, my mind moving over the night and trying to decide how to bring up the next topic.

"I think he's cheating on your sister," I said with a sigh finally.

Theo didn't respond to my accusation; instead, he kept his eyes straight forward on the road, his fingers gripping the wheel tightly.

"Did you hear me, Theo?"

"I heard you."

"And you have nothing to say about it?" I watched him, somehow even more handsome with lights from oncoming cars bouncing off his face.

"When I first found out Savannah and Warren were dating a few months ago, I had lunch with her. Told her I had some hesitation, because he isn't known to be the most . . . loyal partner. I've known him since college, and anytime he's dated a woman, he's always had at least one more 'on deck.'"

I already knew where this was going based on the look on his face and my conversation with her last week, but I asked anyway.

"And?"

"And she told me this was different, that Warren was ready to settle down. When I pushed it, she left lunch and didn't talk to me for about a week. She really likes him and doesn't want to hear about anything negative. She's living in a bit of an idealist world. Do you know she's had a thing for him since she was in high school?"

"She mentioned that."

"Yeah. Well. To her, him finally deciding to date her is a sign."

"And to you?" I asked.

"I think this is part of some grand plan." He admitted it as if it caused him actual pain to do so. "He'll destroy her." He looked at me then, and it was written all over his face—the worry, the concern, the *panic that his enemy is going to annihilate everything he loves, every-thing he cares about.*

"I know, Theo. I'm not going to let him," I said, even though I had no real plan for how to do that.

"Okay, we can brainstorm that in a few. But is everything else going well? Have you guys kissed again?" Abbie asks, knocking me from my memories. I roll my lips into my teeth, keeping my eyes down. "Oooh, you have something you haven't told me yet, you bitch!" I sigh, knowing there's no fucking not telling her.

"We kissed again. At the party."

"But . . . ?"

"It wasn't for show." Abbie's eyebrows furrow. "There was no one else around. It was in a dark hallway right after I told off Warren for being a dick. I think he was overwhelmed." I pause before speaking, my mind still reeling from that kiss. I haven't been able to decode it yet, to understand what it meant, to pinpoint and explain why it happened or what it meant. And at work on Monday and today, it was back to business, nothing out of the norm.

"It wasn't for show," she says, her words slow and deliberate.

"But it wasn't . . . It wasn't a big deal. I think he got caught up in the moment," I justify.

A long pause spans between us as she stares at me before she finally speaks.

"You've got that look," she says, her brow furrowing.

"What look?"

"That . . . conflicted look. The one you had when we started the scheme with Damien and things started to get real for me. The one you gave Cami when she said it was just casual with Zach, but we knew there was no way in hell she was going to keep shit casual with that man. The look you gave me when we found out Liv was going to marry that asshole. You have something to say but don't know if you should."

God, Abbie is so much more insightful than anyone ever gives her credit for.

Except maybe Damien Martinez. I think he knows if she put her mind to it, she could save world hunger and convince countries that have been feuding for centuries to get along.

But this is eating at me, and I know if I'm going to admit my feelings to anyone, Abbie is a good ear.

I slump in my chair and sigh before putting my head in my hands.

"I'm starting to feel . . . confused." Abbie waits before reaching out, grabbing my hand, and forcing me to look at her.

"Okay. What do you mean you're confused?"

"I'm just . . . That's it. I'm confused. About Theo. About this whole mess and if I'm making the right decision. Abbie, I love this job. I love working with Theo. But now, things are starting to get, well . . . confusing. I like this new version of us. I like it because even though it's slightly different, it's mostly the same." I pause, and she nods like a therapist taking notes and following her normal routine.

"Okay, and what does that mean to you? You're technically engaged now and you're running this whole scheme. Is that not completely different?"

"No, not really. That's the weird part. Most of the time, it's just us. Normal. My boss—my friend—who I fuck with because it's funny. Theo, who pokes back at me because that's our relationship. He's still annoying and grumpy and monotone and way too good for this field, because people in the music industry are fucking vultures, and his moral compass is too well-tuned." I see the way her eyes warm, the way her face softens because I'm not talking about him the way an employee talks about her boss.

I'm talking like a woman who is ridiculously into a man.

"But sometimes?" she prompts.

"Sometimes, I find my mind . . . wandering." I look down at my hands, suddenly shy despite the fact that I'm simply talking with my best friend.

"Wandering," she repeats slowly.

"Yes. In a bad way."

"You're going to have to expand more if you expect me to have any input whatsoever," Abbie says with a smile, prodding me to admit what we both know is happening.

As always, somehow, she knows I need to say all of this out loud.

I could say my mind was wandering because I wanted to kiss him. And I want him to kiss me, want to do a lot more than just that. I want to spend time with him outside of work, but also outside of this fake engagement stuff. I find myself staring at his mother's ring much too often, and even though Warren was there, I enjoyed Sunday dinner with Jeff, Judy, and Savannah. I could tell her how I can picture lunches with his sister, coming back to him and poking fun at him with her, watching him smile warmly at me while I do.

Those are just a few of the dangerous paths my mind has wandered down recently.

But I don't say any of that. Instead, I say, "He . . . likes my laugh." Abbie snorts out a laugh, and I can only assume it's because she saw that entire soliloquy in my mind without me even looking at her but is letting me have the lie all the same.

"Of course he does. You have a beautiful laugh, Kat." I glare at her.

"I have an insane laugh. Like a deranged clown."

"That's not true," she says. I give her a *be honest* look and she smiles. "Maybe a very happy, jovial clown. Deranged is a bit much. You have to be kinder to yourself." I roll my eyes. "Now, tell me what you really mean by *wandering*, Kat."

"Sometimes, I can picture this not being fake. I can picture us . . . doing more. Being more. Which is *insane* because he's so not my type. Fuck, I think if I brought him here, a dive without any fancy folded napkins and caviar and champagne on the menu, he might have a mental breakdown." Abbie laughs and rolls her eyes.

"You're so full of shit. You make this man sound like he's a robot, but I know damn well you'd never be able to endure him if he was a third as boring as you make him out to seem. And even before this, all you did was talk about him. Theo this, Theo that." I roll my eyes and wave her off.

"That's just because I see him *non-stop*. Literally, all I do is work and go home. Who else am I going to talk to you guys about?" I say in explanation that feels false on my tongue. She gives me a small, sad smile.

"So you're saying you haven't gotten the ick yet?" I shake my head and try to ignore my lunch turning in my belly with nerves.

"But we're not really dating, so that's probably what it is, you know? Just my mind and body going chaotic because we're doing everything but, and it's confusing." I shrug and nod, convincing myself that must be the case.

"So you're saying you think if you did more than just pretend, you'd get the ick?" I nod.

"For sure. You know how it happens. I like them, I date them, I really like them, I fuck them, I like them a little bit longer, and then . . . boom. Icked out." She nods in agreement.

"Well, there's your solution," she says matter-of-factly, and my brow furrows.

"What?"

"You have to fuck him," Abbie says, turning to me and crossing her arms on her chest.

"What?!" I shout, the other diners in the tiny restaurant looking our way, but I can't be bothered with that. My body is frozen with shock.

"Fuck him. Get it out of your system."

"It's not in my system!" She gives me a pitying look and tucks her blonde hair behind her ear.

"Oh, honey, if you really believe that, you're more far gone than Cam and I knew."

"Cami?"

Abbie nods sagely, like she and my other best friend have been having long, in-depth conversations about my nonexistent love life, my boss, and my fake relationship when I'm not around.

"You guys have been talking about me?" I try to leave the hurt out of my words, but Abbie hears it anyway.

"No, honey, no. Not like that. We were just talking about your deal with Theo and how we could help you both out. But then we agreed we think you have a thing for him. We've thought that for a while." My eyes go wide and my mouth opens a bit because this is the first I've heard of this.

"I do not have a thing for him," I lie. Sometimes, I wish Abbie wanted to have kids instead of being the cool aunt purely because she makes the best mom faces. Right now, it's saying, *Come on, honey, don't lie to your mother.*

I lie to my mother all the time, but I never lie to Abbie.

Not for long at least.

"It's recent and only because we're pretending to be engaged. We also spend every single day together. Anyone would start to catch feelings," I defend.

Not Theo, that mean little voice in my head says. At least he knows how to separate reality from performance.

I kick the little voice down a flight of stairs and lock her in the basement.

She's a real pain in my ass.

Abbie gives me a look that tells me she thinks this, too, is a lie.

"No one talks about their boss that much, Kat."

"They do if he's the main person they see every day," I say. "Plus, all of you are all paired up, happy in your lives. I love that for you, but it also means I have a lot of free time. I like my job, so I work."

Her face falls, just like I could have predicted it would. Shit.

"Oh, Kat, we—" I wave my hands in the air, cutting her off to better explain and alleviate the guilt I know she's feeling.

"I know. I don't hold it against you; you all are happy, and I'm thrilled for you. But I'd be lying if I said it wasn't a bummer. If I said I didn't wish I had . . . that." Her hand reaches out and grabs mine, her eyes wide with empathy and kindness, twisting my heart a bit but also reminding me I have good freaking friends.

"I get it, Kat. I do. And you'll find it." I shake my head.

"I don't know, Abbie. I don't know if I will. The ick and . . . well, you know."

"I do. But I also know one day, you'll way up and realize you're on date one hundred and seven and haven't gotten the ick yet."

It's not until I get back to the office that I understand she wasn't talking about some fictional boyfriend in the future.

THIRTY

KAT

Theo is out for the day, and the office, despite nearly everyone being present, feels empty without him there.

Lifeless.

It's alarming, the way I miss him when he's gone. I spent the better part of the morning convincing myself otherwise before I finally had to cave to reality.

It wasn't always like this, was it? It's not rare for him to spend days outside the office, going to in-person meetings across the state and in the city, but now it feels . . .

Different.

It's as I'm walking back to my desk after lunch with Savannah (definitely not a stupid, idiotic way to feel closer to Theo. Definitely not) that I notice Theo's door is cracked just a bit. My belly flips for a single, stupid moment as I think maybe he got back before I remember he texted me less than an hour ago, asking me to email him a file when I got back to the office.

Furthermore, I definitely shut the door before I left. Quietly, I walk to my desk, gently placing my bag on my chair but not stopping to take my coat off before tiptoeing closer to the door.

Through the crack, I see him.

Warren is in Theo's office.

Warren is in Theo's office, the door mostly closed, no one around to see. I watch for a few moments, but he's putting things back, straightening papers as if to hide his misdeeds.

He's on his way out, it seems, so I push open the door, startling him.

"Can I help you with something?" I ask, raising an eyebrow at Warren as he moves to where I'm standing. He puts a hand to his chest like he's been spooked before shaking his head with a smile.

"Oh, it's just you."

"I said, can I help you with something?" Crossing my arms on my chest, I block the exit.

Theo has come to the understanding that Warren is absolutely planning something devious, but I don't think he's all in on the fact that Warren is an evil villain in this story. Fortunately for him, I most definitely am.

"No need to get defensive," he says with a chuckle in a *pipe down, little girl* type of way that makes me want to punch him in the fucking face.

"No, I very much think I need to, since you're snooping in my boss's office while he's not around and I was out on lunch."

"I wasn't snooping. I was just looking for something." I tip my head to the side and furrow my brow as if I'm confused.

"I know you have a fourth-grade understanding of grammar and vocabulary, but snooping is pretty much defined by looking for something. Especially if you're doing it when no one is around and you don't want anyone to know about it."

He steps forward, and I should feel nervous since every single part of my ick has always told me he's the kind of person to get violent given the right circumstances, but I'm feeling righteous right now.

This man truly thinks he can come into this building, act like the world's worst (okay, maybe not worst, but really a shitty) person, and then just . . . get the business? Can step on people who actually deserve it, who actually love this company, and no one's going to stop him?

Fuck. That.

"I know you think you're hot shit because you're fucking Carter, but you have no right to speak to me that way," he says, his eyes flaring.

"Why, because it hurts your brain?" I pout and give him a pitying look. "I can use smaller words if you need."

"Get the fuck out of my way," he says, that temper he normally keeps tightly tied down in the presence of Jeff pulsing.

"Why were you in here?"

"Get out of my way before I make you," he says.

A shiver runs down my spine, but I stiffen it regardless.

"How would you do that?" I ask, my voice low.

"What?" I caught him off guard, and it's clear from his face, from the way his head moves back just a fraction.

"I said, how would you make me get out of your way? That way I can transcribe it perfectly to HR when I tell them you were threatening me while snooping in my boss's office."

"You fucking—" he starts, and for a moment, I think he'll do it. I think he'll hit me.

I hope he does and we can end this charade of pretending Warren is a decent person once and for all.

Unfortunately, we're interrupted. "All good here?" Jeff says, coming over to where we're standing in the doorway. When I turn my head to him, his brow is furrowed, his face concerned.

"Hey, Jeff," Warren says, his smile wide. I glare at him, not even pretending to like him.

I don't; what's the fucking point?

"I'm just trying to figure out what Warren was doing in Theo's office," I say, turning to Jeff with a smile now. "I just got back from my lunch, and Theo never told me he left something for Warren." I turn to my enemy. "In fact, typically, if there's something he needs to give someone, he gives it to me."

Jeff turns to Warren, a look of surprise on his face.

"You were in Theodore's office?"

"I was looking for a note I thought he had left me." Warren gives Jeff a kind smile. "I came here, but unfortunately, Katrina wasn't at her desk as I expected." He looks at me, and that smile goes from warm to absolutely vile. "You'd think if your boss was out for the day, you'd stay at your desk to make sure you can help anyone who might need him." In the corner of my eye, Jeff opens his mouth to speak, but I keep my eyes locked to Warren before parrying back.

"Yeah, well, don't try and think too hard. It might hurt. I was out to lunch with your girlfriend. Weird that you guys didn't talk about that, you know?" I say and smile.

He glares.

"Well, I'm sure you and Theodore don't share everything either," he says.

"Oh, no, we absolutely do." I hope he knows what I mean by my look. "We absolutely do."

"As you should," Jeff says, putting an arm around my shoulders. "You know, Katrina, I keep saying it, but our Theodore is a new man now that he can be open with you. You're really good for him." He smiles and looks around the office, and I can feel the burn of Warren's glare on me. "You're good for this entire place."

"Thanks, Jeff," I say, and then I stare back at Warren. "I can't wait to see the great heights Theo will take Catalyst when he runs this place." Warren glares at me until Jeff squeezes me tight then turns to him. In a flash, his face goes from pure hatred and anger to joy and comradery.

It's scary how quickly he can turn it on and off.

"Now, Warren, do you have a minute? I have a question about the potential artist you put on my desk yesterday." They walk off together, and I move through Theo's office, taking photos before I touch anything, but I don't find anything that looks off or out of place.

I don't leave my desk for the rest of the day until Warren goes home.

THIRTY-ONE

THEO

When I walk into the office early Thursday morning, Katrina is already there, staring at her desk. I watch her from a few feet away as she reaches into the drawer, grabs a *Gansito*, opens the packaging, and takes a bite before sitting in her chair.

When she sees me staring at her, she jumps, putting a hand on her chest.

"Jesus Christ!" she shouts. "You scared the shit out of me!" She takes another bite of her chocolate-covered snack before sighing, her entire body going slack, as if the sugar solved all of her problems.

I smile because I can't not when she's being ridiculously adorable.

I missed seeing her yesterday, more than I should admit, and the knowledge of that fucked with my head all night, leaving me tossing and turning instead of sleeping.

"Why are you here so early?" I ask, walking past her desk and into my office. She follows, leaning in the doorway as I take my coat off and hang it, putting my briefcase on her chair.

"I'm gonna snoop," she says, and I look at her, confused.

My gut drops when I see and read her face.

She's in a mood. A devious, dangerous mood. After working so closely with Katrina for so long, I can read her like a book.

"What do you mean?" I ask cautiously.

I don't know why I bother because I know what she's going to say.

"I'm going to snoop in Warren's office before he gets in."

"Why?"

"Because yesterday, I came back from my lunch and he was snooping in yours. It's only right to return the favor." She smiles wide, takes the last bite, and tosses the wrapper in my garbage.

"What?" I ask, confused since this is the first I've heard of this. She nods.

"Yeah, it was after I came back from lunch with Savannah. I didn't want to bug you while you were with clients, but he was just nosing around your office. Nothing was moved, though make sure you keep an eye out."

"You caught him in my office?"

"Yeah, he was super pissed at me—" My stomach flips with nerves at the idea of an angry Warren in Katrina's presence.

"Did he touch you?" She shakes her head quickly, her loose, dark hair swaying as she does.

"No, Jeff walked up and intervened. It was no big, but I'm feeling . . . inspired now." The quick flash of relief is overtaken by the mischievous smile on her lips.

"Katrina—" I start, but she just smiles, turns back to her desk, and grabs a small black case. "What is that?" She smiles deviously at me.

"A lock pick set."

She says it like someone might say a *grilled cheese sandwich*: unimportant and basic.

"Why do you have a lock pick set?" I ask, exasperated even though the day has barely started.

"To pick locks."

"What kind of locks?"

"Oh, all kinds. I've watched a bunch of YouTube videos. You

never know when it could come in handy." She closes the drawer she grabbed the kit from and turns toward me.

"Katrina, don't be stupid. This is a bad idea. What if you get caught?"

"There's no one here to catch me doing anything. What if we find something? What if he has some crazy master plan right on his desk?" I stare at her with exhaustion.

"Why would he do that?"

"I don't know! Because he's insane?"

"Katrina," I say in warning, trying to show her just how unhinged this is. But as always, she doesn't listen, instead turning toward Warren's office.

I have no choice but to follow her, the strides of my legs eating up the space between us quickly. She continues to ignore me as she walks through his open door.

I guess that's a small help, no fingerprints from her touching his doorknob. Why anyone would be dusting the office for prints, I don't know, but . . .

"Katrina, come on. This is crazy," I say, my eyes flicking between her and the reception area, half expecting Warren to jump out with a *gotcha!* because we tripped some kind of booby trap he set to catch us doing just this.

"You don't have to be here," she says, moving things and putting them back precisely how they were, as if she took a mental photograph.

"I do because you're being fucking reckless."

"You say reckless. I say proactive." She gives me a stunning smile, and I groan as she tries a drawer, finds it locked, and excitedly reaches for the pick kit. She moves smoothly, like this is a well-practiced thing she does often, using two stick-like things and fiddling, her tongue sticking out the side of her mouth as she does before finally, there's a click.

She jumps, clapping excitedly, and slides open the drawer, taking a picture.

CHAPTER THIRTY-ONE   197

"I have to make sure I put things back exactly the same way," she muses to herself before shifting things.

"Katrina, let's just go. You're not going to find anything—" She gasps, and my heart stops. Her entire body goes still as she holds a piece of paper, eyes wide and mouth open. "What?" I ask, moving closer to her now.

"It's a list of your clients."

"My clients?"

"The ones you've suggested and successfully signed."

"Okay . . . ?" I ask, confused. "He's the director of A&R, and he's on the board. Of course, he would have that."

"It's only your clients, Theo." She moves a page and mumbles a curse under her breath, and my gut sinks. Pulling out her phone, she starts taking photos of each page.

"What?"

"It's a report on you, Theo." Her eyes meet mine. "Your clients, your losses. The revenue you've gotten the firm. He has it all outlined."

"And . . ." I'm still not understanding.

"And only you, Theo. There's no one else on this list."

Slowly, I start to get it.

"He's looking for . . . something."

"He's looking for anything," she says. "He's grasping at straws. He knows you're the right choice, that you're a shoo-in. All of this?" She waves at the stack of papers. "Nothing in it puts you in a bad light."

On the page, there are a few sections highlighted, and without looking, I know those are my losses.

"I'm not perfect, Katrina. I've had losses for the company and made bad decisions."

"Everyone does. But I bet if we pull a report on Warren, it will be much worse." Something tells me a similar report will be on my desk by the end of the day.

My eyes stay locked on the papers, though, on a single line of black. Cassandra Key has been crossed out on my list of acquisitions.

Before I can even try to put together what that means, read each of the notes he's written in the margins, I hear it.

The deep laugh of Warren filling the office too loud because he's always putting on a show.

Warren is here.

And we are so fucked.

THIRTY-TWO

KAT

The look on Theo's face would be funny if we weren't moments away from fucking disaster.

"Warren's here," Theo whispers, as if I need him to tell me.

There's no way out without him knowing we were both in here, doing God knows what, and he'll tell Jeff, that much I know. He'll spin it to make us look bad, no matter if it's true or not.

No matter that he did the same fucking thing yesterday.

"Come on," I whisper, putting the items in the drawer back as best I can then reaching for a closet door, praying it's not full. Warren's office is a mirror of Theo's, and while Theo's closet is empty, his neurotic organization ensures he doesn't have any extra stuff, I don't know if that's the same for Warren.

I'm relieved when all that's in the closet is a few boxes of files and a set of old golf clubs collecting dust.

Grabbing Theo's hand, I drag him in, his big, broad body taking up most of the space so our bodies are flush, our breathing heavy and panicked.

"What are we doing, Katrina?" he whispers, but I shake my head, putting a finger to his lips.

We can't speak.

We can't make a fucking move in here. Warren can't find out we're on to him, can't find out we're trying to uncover . . . something.

Anything.

My mind is still reeling with panic and confusion and the realization that we have our first piece of real proof that Warren is actively out to get Theo. Before this, everything was speculation and assumption. Even losing Oliver Porter to Blacknote couldn't be pinned to Warren. But that list? Those notes? As much as he'd like to, I don't think Theo can dismiss them. It won't be enough to convince Jeff of Warren's poor intentions, but it's a start.

I hear Warren's shoes on the floor, hear his laugh again on the phone, hear his chair roll out and him sitting.

He's in the office, and I'm holding my breath. Theo's hands settle on my hips, the tight space not leaving him many options.

"I'm telling you, there's no fucking way he's going to get that job, Travis." Travis? The owner of Blacknote, Travis? "No, I don't care about the fucking bitch he's marrying. We all know it's bullshit, and even though he's a dumb fuck, Jeff won't fall for it." My eyes widen as I realize what we're listening to.

Warren is on a call with our biggest rival and talking about Theo getting the president's position. About me, too, apparently, and our engagement.

Theo's fingers on my hips tighten.

"Everything is still going to plan." My pulse beats.

There is a plan. My eyes widen, and in the dim light, I catch Theo's, his thoughts reflected there.

This is so bad.

"Now, enough about this shit. Tell me about that bitch you were fucking with."

My eyes drift closed as dread fills my chest. This could take a while. Glancing at my watch, I see it's not even 8 yet. At 9, Jessica will be in, and I can send her an SOS text, ask her to call Warren out to the lobby, and we can make a run for it. Unfortunately, that means over an hour in this crowded closet, not making a sound.

An hour of my back against the wall, Theo right in front of me, his body heat seeping through his clothes and mine, heating my skin.

An hour of our breaths mingling, of his hands on my hips. No room to move. Every time I breathe in, my breasts brush against his chest. My hands are on his shoulders so I can keep myself steady, but that means I can feel the taut muscles of his shoulders, the warmth of them.

I no longer worry about what will happen if Warren catches us.

I am suddenly wondering what will happen if I kiss Theo? If we do more than that in this small, enclosed space.

If we kiss outside of the deal, outside of planned events, what happens then?

But then I look up at Theo and all nerves, all panic, all worries wash away.

Because he's looking at me like he would give anything to devour me. In this dark, dim, enclosed space, he looks like a starving man, and I'm the first meal he's seen for days.

And I do something so stupid, so reckless, so unbelievable. I reach up and left touch my ear.

He tracks my every move, and when he sees the small shift, his eyes flare, that fire burning there before I feel a silent rumble in his chest.

The hand on my hips digs in, one moving to my waist and tugging me in closer to him, our bodies plastered to each other as his lips crash into mine.

It's an explosion of heat and lust and desire. He tastes like black coffee and smells like the cologne he wears religiously, the one I bought him for his birthday last year, and, underneath that, clean soap.

And his lips devour mine. They press to mine with control at first, and my quiet gasp of shock has him using the move to his advantage, slipping his tongue into my mouth and tasting me.

My tongue comes and tangles with his, this kiss so much more than anything else we've done so far. My hands move up, gripping the sides of his head as one of his hands moves down to my ass, gripping tightly.

This is feral.

This is pure, unhinged lust and desire. A match striking and setting fire to gasoline we've been pouring over everything with every interaction over the past month or so. Longer if I'm being honest with myself.

Much longer.

The need that's been pooling in my belly, seeping into my veins, is tinder, and Theo is setting fire to it.

He moves, pressing me against the wall silently, and somehow, we both know not to make a single sound as Warren's voice continues to drone in the background, but I don't even process it.

All I can think of are Theo's hands on my body, his lips tasting mine, and the way a silent growl rumbles through his chest. One hand moves up my waist, cupping my breast and thumbing my tight nipple through my thin shirt and unpadded bra, and I buck my hips into him, feeling him hard. My hand starts to move, to even the playing field—

Something clatters to the ground in Warren's office, a mumbled curse coming through the door, and we both freeze, Theo's lips on mine, one hand on my ass, the other frozen on my breast.

"Nah, just dropped my stapler," Warren says. His chair makes a wheeling noise as it moves over the plastic mat beneath his desk. "Hold on, let me open up the file." There are some typing noises before he lets out an irritated curse. "Fuck." My gut drops with the single word.

Did he notice I moved something? Is he going to know we are in here? Maybe something was set up to tip him off to intruders? A booby trap we didn't see?

My mind convinces me that in just a few beats, he'll be opening this door, finding Theo and me in this compromising position, and everything we've been working to protect will go up in flames.

"I forgot my bag in the car. No, no, I'll go get it right now." The sounds of his chair rolling back and then of his footsteps retreating come through the closet.

We hold still.

We don't move until I vaguely hear the office door slam shut.

"Let's go," I whisper. His lips are so close still, mine brush against them when I speak, a sweet memory of what just happened.

What just happened that I'm fully going to ignore.

It was clearly . . . adrenaline. Adrenaline from almost being caught making us lose our minds.

Yes.

That's it.

Simple as that.

I don't even listen to whatever he's going to say before I move my hand to the doorknob, checking to make sure the coast is clear before stepping out. Theo follows me, closing the closet behind us. I'm already halfway to his office when he catches up to me, his fingers wrapping my wrist and pulling me back.

"Katrina, we should—"

"It was adrenaline," I say with a smile I don't feel. "No big."

"I think we should talk about—"

His phone rings in his pocket, loud and obnoxious.

"Good thing that didn't ring three minutes ago," I say with a smile, but he continues to stare at me.

It's an intense stare I've never seen before, and it steals the breath from my lungs.

Possibilities, the optimistic voice in my head whispers. Possibilities are in his eyes.

I shake my head slightly to send her back to the depths of hell.

I need out.

I need out of his gaze that reads past all of my defenses.

"Go. Answer that. I have to use the bathroom anyway." And then I walk toward the bathroom I don't need and away from Theo, trying to figure out how to save the small amount of sanity I have left and how to quash this crush on Theodore Carter I absolutely cannot have.

THIRTY-THREE

KAT

My phone blares out a loud warning, breaking me from my concentration on what I'm working on in Theo's office.

When I grab it to stop the screaming, I take in three things.

One, I missed a text from Jessica an hour ago.

Two, it's nearly 6 pm, and the office is completely empty. This shouldn't be much of a surprise since Catalyst encourages its employees to keep semi-normal hours, but it's *empty* empty. I'm pretty sure Theo and I are the only people left in this building.

And three, there is an alarming warning for a snow squall taking place right now.

"Shit," I say, looking out Theo's large windows and seeing a complete whiteout.

Theo and I have been locked in his office since noon, first quietly crafting an offer for a new talent Theo found but hasn't even mentioned to the board in an effort to ensure Warren can't sabotage it before it's off the ground, then digging into all of Warren's accounts and artists and trying to create a game plan for how to move forward with this plan of revenge and justice.

"What?" Theo asks.

"Snow." He looks out the window and nods, then shrugs.

"Well, it's the season. You never know what you're going to get in New Jersey in March."

"Mmm," I say, watching a thick coat of snow fall from the clouds.

"Is that a problem?" He does that, I've realized. He guesses what I'm thinking when I respond with just a single sound. I'm assuming it's what makes him such a great businessman: being able to read people and the thoughts they don't say out loud.

"I don't drive in the snow. It makes me anxious." Theo looks around the office, the building silent, and before he even says it, I know.

"I think everyone's left for the night."

I nod.

"Jessica told me she was locking us in about an hour ago."

"Snow wasn't in the forecast this morning," he says.

"Like you said, kind of par for the course this time of year." I sigh, knowing even once the whiteout ends, I probably won't feel comfortable leaving for at least another hour or so, until I can see the black of the street. I open the weather app and see I might be even more fucked than I thought. "Shit. It's supposed to snow for three more hours." I groan.

"Do you—" He stops then continues, and I can't help but wonder why he looks . . . suddenly nervous. "Do you have plans tonight?"

"Plans?"

"Like, a date or something. Plans. You seem disappointed you won't be able to get home easily . . ." His voice trails off and his eyes move to the window, like he's clearly avoiding looking at me.

"I . . . Why would I have a date tonight?" I let out a confused laugh. He doesn't meet my eyes when he speaks again, keeping his locked on the road I can barely see now.

"You're beautiful, Katrina. You know that. I'm sure you have a long list of options." His jaw is tight, and I don't know what it is that makes me do it, since in any other situation, his assumption would annoy me more than anything, but I stand from my chair, walk around his desk, and sit on the edge of it before I put a hand on his shoulder.

"Hey," I say, and his eyes finally meet mine. "It's you and me, Theo. I don't have anyone else to spend my nights with for the foreseeable future."

He stares, reading me in a way that makes me want to close my eyes or step away, but I resist the urge, letting him see the truth there.

The truth of the matter is there is no one else, and there won't be until whatever it is we're doing fades away. Until my crush and this impossible attraction to him ends.

Until I stop being useful to him.

The thought makes my belly feel sour.

"You could," he says, stubborn and frustrating as always. "So long as you weren't posting about it or whatever or being obvious, what would I care?" It's strange, seeing him like this, uncomfortable and irritated, especially when I know one way or another, I'm the cause.

I shake my head. "I care, Theo. I care. It's your reputation. My reputation too, really. You're my fiancé. I wouldn't do you like that. I haven't even been vetting at The Ex Files." And there it is: a small smile and a flash of relief in his eyes. Relief I refuse to dig too far into, to let my hopeless romantic get her grimy claws into or else she'll take it as hope, and hope in a situation like this is dangerous.

"No, all I have to do tonight is watch the *telenovelas* I saved and eat junk food."

"Hmm," he says, eyes continuing to decode me in his way. I stand, needing space, and start pacing the office.

"We'll have to raid the fridge. See if anyone left anything good we can eat."

"There are also prepped meals in the freezer and shelf-stable stuff in the kitchen," he says as I walk toward my desk. "We keep it just in case something like this happens. It was something I encouraged Jeff to enact a few years ago, after Sandy."

"Of course you did, Mister Always Prepared, always taking care of his employees." I smile. "Though, I should be fine. I've got my stash." I open the big drawer on my desk and stare in there, noticing just one bag of Cheez-Its, two bags of pretzels, and that, the saddest news of all, I have eaten my entire stash of *Gansitos*.

Stress eating, a result from the constant back and forth with Theo and Warren and Jeff, has caused me to nearly diminish my entire drawer without realizing.

I think longingly about the bag of snacks I bought the other day sitting in a red bag on my kitchen table. I'd meant to bring it this morning but was rushing to get to work early and snoop in stupid Warren's office and completely forgot.

"Goddammit," I say with a grumble. What a time to run out of snacks.

"What?" Theo asks, watching me with worry, leaning in the doorway of his office. "Is something wrong? Do you need something from home? Are you going to be okay?" His alarm and worry would be cute if he wasn't so totally off-limits.

That's the decision I came to after our kiss in Warren's closet this morning. I need to stay as far away from Theo Carter as humanly possible for my heart and mental sanity.

"I'm almost out of snacks," I say with a pout, collapsing in my chair and crossing my arms on my chest.

"What?"

"I'm almost out of snacks." I gesture to the mostly empty drawer. "I have more at home, but I forgot them."

"No, you're not," Theo counters, completely casually, and I glare a him.

"Sorry, boss man, I definitely am. I guess I'll just starve." I groan melodramatically, as if I can't survive three hours without a constant supply.

I'm not actually sure if I can, if I'm being honest.

Some people have girl dinner, a meal of random snacks. I've taken that to the next level by just snaking from 9 to 5. The same way I get bored with people and jobs, I get bored with food, so having a variety throughout the day helps add a bit of a dopamine rush.

"No, you're not. Come," he repeats, going into his office. I follow him, crossing my arms on my chest.

"You know, maybe you should go home. You're clearly way more tired than I realized," I say with a laugh as he moves behind his desk, opening a closet door. The same closet that, in Warren's office, we hid in together.

Nope, nope, nope. Not thinking about that. No way.

"No, you're not out of snacks. I've got more."

"You . . . You have more?" I ask, confused but moving closer to where he's holding the door open.

And then I see it.

Behind that closet door, a door I never check because why would I, is half a dozen boxes filled with . . . snacks.

My snacks, to be specific.

There's a box of pretzels and a box of Cheez-Its and mini bags of Skittles, at least four boxes of *Gansitos* and mango *paletas*, and even a box of De la Rosa candies.

"Why do you have that?" I ask, confused as can be.

Theodore Carter does not eat junk food.

He does not eat Cheez-Its and Skittles and pretzels and Reese's Cups.

He eats plain popped popcorn and drinks protein shakes.

He eats salads and salmon and wild rice.

Brain food, he once told me when I made fun of him.

Instead of answering, he stares at me like I'm the insane one. When he does answer, I'm blown away.

"I have it for you," he says succinctly like it's obvious.

For me.

For me?

"You have an entire closet of snacks for . . . me?" He looks at me, his face as confused as I feel.

"Well, yeah, Katrina. I've had it since . . ." He shrugs as he tries to remember. "July maybe? June?"

I started here in April.

"I saw you were always eating shit out of that drawer. At the time, I thought it was because you were so busy, you didn't feel like you had time to eat." I remember him asking me that once not long after I started working here. He pulled me into his office, all concerned, and asked if I was too busy to eat. I laughed and told him I preferred snacks.

"At the time, I figured it wasn't right for you to have to pay for all these snacks, because I was working you too hard and you were too embarrassed to admit it." He shrugs again.

I remember that conversation, him calling me into his office to ask if I needed more personal time to eat meals and thinking it was weird.

I remember also thinking it was weird when for maybe three weeks straight, anytime I'd pull a new snack out of the drawer, he'd ask me what it was.

"Gansitos," I told him once. *"They're little Mexican snack cakes filled with cream and strawberry. I ate them all the time growing up. Do you want one?"* I thought he was just curious, seeing something he'd never tried before, so I held a package out to him. He'd shaken his head, his hands not even leaving his pockets as he watching, calculating.

"No, I don't like sugar," he'd said. I remember thinking the exchange was weird, the way he was taking in the package, committing it to memory, but now I get it.

He was doing exactly that, committing the brand and the snack to memory so he could buy them, keep them for me in his office. He continues talking, oblivious to the mind-blowing realization I'm coming to.

"Of course, eventually, I figured out you just like snacking instead of eating real meals and you weren't lying when I asked if you were overworked. But I . . . I kept up the habit, I guess." He shrugs like it's no big deal.

But it is.

It's a huge deal to me.

People don't do this for me. Sure, Cami and Abbie do, in their own way. But other than that? Other than my two closest people, women I see as sisters more than friends?

Absolutely not.

"You're a good guy, you know that, Theo Carter?" I ask with a small smile, turning to face him. He's only a few inches from me, the random snack closet behind me now, and if he just leaned in a bit, he would . . .

A text beeps on his cell and he jumps back, walking to his desk to grab and check it.

"Uh, yeah. I just double-checked with Jeff. The roads are a mess. We'll need to stay here until we, uhm... Until they plow." He scratches behind his neck, clearly uncomfortable, before sitting at his desk, avoiding my eyes.

My stomach churns.

Why is it so weird between us now? Is it because we kissed in the closet? With no one watching, no one to catch us? Is it because he has no excuses for why he did it? If so, why didn't he freak out after the engagement party when he kissed me in that hallway? Is he second-guessing things?

Regardless, I sigh and then shake my shoulders out, deciding to revert back to myself. The Katrina who isn't fazed by anything, the one who teases Theo, the one who is a fun time, who doesn't get attached because she can't, so she treats life like a little game.

I walk toward the window behind his desk, carefully avoiding his eyes and him. The squall has stopped, but now snow is slowly falling from the sky in big, fat flakes, the kind that looks slow and peaceful but piles up quickly. It's a picturesque scene of empty roads coated in a thick layer of white and it should calm me, but . . . it doesn't.

"I'm so bored," I say, dying to force myself out of this funk, then sit in my chair, groaning. Theo smiles at me, and it makes my belly flip.

"Ten minutes ago, we were working and you weren't bored."

"Yeah, but ten minutes ago, I didn't realize I was stuck here. Now,

I know I can't leave and have nothing to do." I look at the ceiling. "Want to play a game?"

"A game?" Theo asks, looking skeptical.

"Yeah!" That seems like the perfect way to pass the time, now that I think of it. "Let's play truth or dare." He rolls his eyes.

"Jesus Christ, Katrina, we are grown adults."

"We're grown adults pretending we're getting married. I don't think we're that far above playing a game," I say, raising an eyebrow. "Plus, we can use it to get to know each other better. You know, for the mission."

"The mission?" he asks with a raised eyebrow.

"Warren is literally spending every moment of his life trying to find anything to tear you down or prove this is all bullshit. I'm sure there's shit a fiancé would know about one another that we don't. If we're called out on it, it would be weird, right?"

He sighs, but he doesn't argue, so I keep pushing.

"Come on! What's the worst that could happen?" He looks at me like *do you really need to ask that?* but eventually sighs, sitting back in his desk chair and shrugging.

"Fine. Let's play. Nothing too crazy, though."

"Ah! Look at you, growing. Being open to fun."

"You know, I really don't appreciate your constant assumption and accusation that I don't know how to have fun." I stare at him then give him a fake sad look.

"I am so sorry to tell you, Theo, but we're literally in this mess because you have had such little fun, your boss is worried if he gives you more responsibilities, you'll never recover." He glares at me, and I stand, wandering around the office, thinking aloud. "The only downside is it would be much more fun if we had liquor."

"I have liquor."

I stop and stare at him, then I smile and put a hand on my chest.

"My lord, straight and narrow, always plays by the rules Theodore Carter is drinking on the job? So Warren wasn't pulling that out of his ass, huh?" He rolls his eyes but bends, opening a drawer in his desk and pulling out a fancy bottle of whiskey and two crystal glasses.

"I occasionally have meetings where I need to schmooze people. A drink can help sometimes."

"And you're getting potential clients drunk so you can take advantage of them?" I shake my head with a laugh, but I sit on the edge of his desk all the same. "Pour me a shot, bartender."

"This is not shot whiskey, Katrina."

"It is when you're snowed in with your boss and bored out of your mind." He stares, and I stare back before finally, he sighs, pouring what amounts to two shots into the glasses and handing me one.

I shoot mine back then grab my can of soda off his desk and drink it as a chaser. Theo takes a small sip of his, but when I glare, he sighs and downs it, wincing.

"Alright, Katrina," he says. "Truth or dare?"

"Why do I have to go first?"

"Because I'm your boss and this was your ridiculous idea. Now, truth or dare?"

I could argue it, but I don't, instead contemplating my choices.

The fun answer is never truth, but I'm secretly hoping Theo will also ask for a truth if I go first because I have a million questions I'm dying to ask him.

"Truth," I say, the liquor warming my belly already. The snow continues to fall in the window behind him, and I wonder how long we'll be stuck in here.

"Huh," he says, surprised. "I didn't think you'd go with that."

"Well, I'm just chock-full of surprises, you know?" I smile wide, and he nods.

"That I do know." A moment passes before he nods and asks his question, not nearly long enough for him to think of something, so I wonder how long he's been wondering about this one. "Why aren't you dating anyone for real?" Theo asks, and I stare at him with false shock.

"You couldn't start with an easy one?" I ask, and he smiles.

God, he smiles.

I love it when Theo smiles. It's such a rare occurrence that the look cracks through his grumpy demeanor, but when it does . . . it's magnificent.

"You can skip," he says. "But I think the rule is if you skip, you take a shot. At least, that's how it was in college. I haven't really played since then."

"I'll answer. But I'm gonna need a shot after I spill my guts to you."

"Deal," he says then pours us each another shot. I throw mine back, and he shakes his head with a small smile on his lips, taking a small sip of his.

Sighing, I get into my truth. "So I have this ick factor, you know?" He nods, and I continue. "It makes me notice things, hyperfixate on small, not even really red flags, but things that, if I had to deal with them for years and years, would probably drive me insane."

"Isn't that kind of part of being in a relationship? Taking the good with the bad, balancing out what you can and can't endure for forever?" I nod, suddenly self-conscious because he's right. A man grabbing ice with his hands or calling his mother Mama shouldn't be a dealbreaker in theory. But for me . . .

"My parents divorced after 25 years of being together. They dated for five years before getting married, then they had me two years later. They divorced the summer after I graduated high school, citing irreconcilable differences. It was one of those, *stay together for the kids* type things. They'd been taught their entire lives divorce was out of the cards, but I think once I wasn't in the house, it became impossible to ignore. At some point, they just . . . fell out of love." I shrug.

"That happens all the time, though," he says, his face kind and comforting. I shake my head.

"It does if you don't listen to your gut, to your instincts. My grandparents... I didn't see them too often. They lived in Mexico my whole life, but when I did, I saw two people so wildly in love, it was nearly tangible. My *abuela*, she had the ick factor too, and it took her a while to find my *abuelo*. She told me to always trust my gut, that one day the perfect man would fall into my life and I'd just.... I'd *know*. I'm waiting for that. I refuse to be like my mother, ignoring my *abuela's* advice and having to start over." The breath I release feels heavy, much too heavy for a casual truth-or-dare game, but I continue on. "I don't want that. I don't want to stay together for the kids or be married most of my life and have to start over when I'm 50. I want the kind of love . . ." I sigh, shaking my head because that doesn't matter.

I don't need Theo Carter to know what an incurably hopeless romantic I am, how I calculate forevers and the probability of relationships lasting in a matter of moments, then never stop making those calculations until I find something that might, maybe, possibly, one day ruin our happiness.

"My mom told me when she was just starting to date my dad, when they were only together a few months, she felt it. Something dumb—the way he chewed—was bothering her. But she was so in love that she ignored it, ignored *abuela's* advice. She tells me all the time she wishes she didn't." She, of course, also told me she was happy she had ignored it because she got me at the end of it all, but still, I can always see that hint of regret in her eyes.

And every time I'm with her, I see it when she tells me about her most recent disastrous date as she continues trying to find her someone, even now.

"So I refuse not to heed my own ick factor. If my gut says someone isn't for me, I believe it." I shrug, trying to play it cool. Reaching out, I grab the glass he refilled with more liquor and knock it back, ignoring the sirens in my brain screaming *bad idea!* "Okay, enough about my sob story and indefinite single status. Truth or dare, Theo," I say, changing the subject because that was way too much for a fake fiancé, too much for my boss that I have an undeniable crush on.

"Dare," he says instantly.

My mouth drops open in shock.

"Did you just say dare?"

"Yes."

"You, Theodore Daniel Carter, chose dare."

"Jesus Christ, Katrina, yes. I chose dare. Was that the wrong answer? Is that against the rules?"

I stare for a long minute, trying to decode him and failing.

"No. Not against the rules. Just . . . a shock is all."

"Why?"

"Because it's you." I continue speaking before he can argue or change his answer. "Okay, I dare you to . . ." I think that's the moment the liquor hits my system, making my belly warm and my head just a bit fuzzy and my decisions questionable.

It's the only thing I can think of for why I say what I say next.

"I dare you to take your shirt off."

"What?" he asks, his head snapping back, and I think in any other moment, sans alcohol and the tension that's been between us for weeks and my mind blurred with thoughts of him and being snowed in this office together and whiskey, I would read that gesture and back down.

But I'm an idiot, so I don't.

"I don't actually know if you have a chest under that shirt," I say. "I've only ever seen you in button-downs and suit jackets. Do you have arms under there?" Now that I think of it, it's true. Never a tee shirt or a sweatshirt or anything. I've only ever seen him in those suits and shirts, which are gorgeous, but . . .

His fingers move to his tie, loosening it, and my belly drops to the fucking floor.

"Are you . . . ?" I ask, watching his hands loosen the knot of silk and toss his tie on the carpet, not caring about the material, regardless of the ridiculously expensive brand. "Are you actually doing it?" His hands pause, and again, I regret my words.

"I thought that was how you play truth or dare? You . . . You pick, and I have to do it?" I continue to stare before finally shaking my head.

"No. Yes. No. I mean, yes, that's how you play. You're just . . . you. I didn't think you knew how to play."

"Did you . . ." His hands pause at the first of the buttons. "Did you not actually want me to do this? I'm not really sure what the rules are between . . . with us." He's saying what I'm thinking always, but I shake my head quickly, the world swimming as I do.

"No. No! Please. Please do," I say.

Then he does it.

He fucking smiles again.

He must know what he's doing. Or maybe it's the liquor softening his normally rigid demeanor. Either way, I watch with rapt attention as Theo's deft fingers undo his shirt one button at a time, revealing tan skin, a light dusting of chest hair, small nipples I want to run my tongue over, broad shoulders begging for my fingernails, and strong arms that could definitely hold me up against a wall.

I'm pretty sure I stare long after he's finished putting the shirt gently over his chair and has sat back down, my eyes fixated on everything that is . . . Theo Carter sans shirt. Finally, I shake myself out of it.

"You know, after that? I need another shot," I mumble, pouring the liquor into the crystal glass and downing it, loving the heat pooling in my belly.

Yes, see? The warmth is from the liquor burning. Nothing else. That is all. Definitely not the way Theo's eyes are searing into me or how my body wants to react to how fucking good he looks without a shirt. Couldn't he have a gut? Couldn't he have a giant carpet of chest hair? That's an ick for me, after all. Though, knowing my fucked-up head, it would somehow be flipped to becoming a turn-on, too. The curse of reading one too many Omegaverses or something. Suddenly, I'd be super into dudes covered in hair from head to toe, even though I've dumped more than one guy for it in the past.

But no.

Theo Carter is perfect in every stupid way, with the perfect dusting of chest hair so he doesn't look like a baby seal, but not too much so he toes into Sasquatch territory.

"Truth or dare?" he asks. It could be seconds or hours later. I've lost all concept of time with Theo's exquisite chest in my line of vision.

"Dare," I say with a smile.

I've always been a dare girl, always loved the rush of people giving me a task they think I won't fulfill, only to prove them wrong.

"Tell me a secret about yourself," he says.

My entire body freezes.

One thing about me, the way I live, the way my brain works, the way I verbally vomit everything, I don't have secrets. I can't, not for long. Sooner rather than later, my inability to shut up breaks in and spills it.

"I don't . . . I don't have one," I say with a nervous laugh.

But that's not all the way true, is it? that obnoxious voice asks.

"You don't have a secret?"

"Not unless I'm pretending I'm engaged to my boss in order to make sure he gets the job he deserves counts." Theo lets out a thick, low laugh, and a chill runs through my body, a reminder of the one secret I do have from Theo.

"What about something only your good friends know?"

I wrack my brain, trying to think of something, anything to give him. Finally, I smile.

"When my friend Abbie was dumped by her asshole ex, we did all this crazy shit to get back at him. I bought a couple hundred keys and taped *if found, call* to them, and added his number. We put glitter in the vents of his fancy-ass car, so every time he turned the heat on, it blew out glitter. My friend Cami posted his phone number in a forum and said it was Harry Styles. Shit like that." I shrug, smiling fondly.

"You did all that just because he dumped her?" He looks at me with a concerned, furrowed brow, and I smile.

"And Abbie fucked his boss." His eyes go wider and my smile does the same. "So you know, don't fuck me over."

"Noted. Okay, your turn." My voice feels raspy when I speak again, a result of the way his eyes are burning on me, the way the liquor is warm in my belly.

"Truth or dare?"

"Truth," he says in a near whisper. I'm still sitting on the edge of his desk, my feet swinging as I do, and he leans forward, brushing a loose piece of hair behind my ear. Each millimeter of skin his fingers touches sparks to life, a warm fire that travels to my belly and other places it absolutely should not be.

Or maybe it should.

If this is going to end, no strings attached, why not just go all the way? The ick factor will kick in eventually, right? It's the liquor speaking when I open my mouth. "Are you attracted to me?"

I would say I don't know why I said that, but I do. It's just . . . Theo. It's everything he is, everything we are, pushing me to my breaking point over and over again.

"Yes," he says firmly, solidly. No hesitation in his words.

I blink, shocked, but recover quickly.

"Well, Mr. Carter, I never thought you would actually admit that. I was sure you'd take a shot," I say, trying to keep things playful and fun despite the way my heart is beating, despite the way his eyes have turned dark, searing through me.

"That. That's mine," he says, his voice gravel.

"What?"

"My secret. You told me your secret. That's mine." I shake my head, not understanding. Maybe the liquor is getting to him, too.

"You lost me, boss man."

"The reason I let you call me Theo is because on your first day, you asked if you should call me Theo or Mr. Carter. I knew if you were walking around my office all fucking day calling me Mr. Carter, I'd never get a thing done."

A bolt of desire runs through me, my heart skipping a beat.

"Those words on your lips have an effect on me I still don't quite understand, but every time you say it, I want to fuck you until you're out of my system."

Out of his system implies I'm in his system.

Jesus. Christ.

"I dare you to kiss me," I whisper, something snapping in me.

Fuck being sensical.

Fuck playing this safe.

I want to taste Theodore Carter.

I want to touch his chest and claw my nails into his back, and I want to forget all the reasons this is a bad, bad idea.

For one single night, I want Theo to be mine. Really mine. In all the ways that matter at this moment.

"It's not your turn," he says but stands, moving closer to me, like I'm a magnet and he's metal, pulled to me without choice.

"Fine. Your turn," I whisper, my voice barely audible as he closes the already small gap between us. Desire pours off him, waves of it as he comes closer, his bare chest begging for my hands. I'm dying to know what his skin feels like, what that smattering of hair would feel like under my palms. . .

I'm drunk on something, and if I'm being completely honest, I'm not sure if it's the liquor or Theo, but I don't think I care anymore.

"Truth or dare," he whispers, and he's so close now, standing between my spread legs as I sit on his desk, and I can feel his breath on me.

"Dare," I reply, my body shivering with something very, very far from cold.

"I dare you to let me kiss you," he says then bends his head and presses his lips to mine.

THIRTY-FOUR

KAT

The kiss is so unlike any other we've had from the start. It's all lips and clashing teeth and nips. I moan as his tongue enters my mouth, and it's not low and quiet—it's loud and filled with all of the pent-up emotion I've been failing to beat back.

My hand moves up, touching his abs, his skin, letting the hair feather along my palms just like I daydreamed about not moments ago. They continue up until they're tunneling into the short hair at the back of his neck. He's tall, but sitting on this desk, him standing between my legs, we're almost the same height. His head still tips down, and his shoulders bend as his lips trail to my neck, nipping at my ear. I moan again when I feel his panting breath against my ear.

"This is a bad idea," he says, but his hands start making their way up the back of my shirt, burning a path of lust and need along my skin.

"It's a great idea. Maybe the best idea," I say, my hands moving to his belt, fumbling to try and get more skin to run my hands on. My skirt is hiking with each move of my hips and the next time I shift, my center is brushing against his hard cock. He groans loudly, his fumbling fingers undoing my bra strap beneath my shirt.

"You work for me." He continues his argument, but his actions don't match the words as he undoes the clasp of my bra, one large hand moving to the front, my breast filling his palm. My head tips back with a moan, giving him more access to that spot beneath my ear. He scrapes his teeth against it, and I move my hips, shifting again, and now his cock is grinding into me.

"And I give you one more week before everything you say and do gives me the ick. Might as well capitalize on this attraction while we can." His thumb and forefingers come together to pinch my nipple and I yell, the sound melting into a moan. "But until then, you're driving me crazy. I need you, Theo. I need this. We need this. We need to just . . . get it over with."

It makes sense to me in my liquor and lust-fueled mind.

"Get it out of our systems," he says. It seems like it makes sense to him in his own lust-addled mind.

I don't mention that whenever anyone says something like that in the movies, it's the kiss of death for one and done.

"Exactly."

And then his lips are on mine again, and I remember I'm supposed to be convincing him to fuck me. I decide actions work better than words. You can't misinterpret actions the way you can read too far into words. I lift my arms, cueing him to lift my shirt up and over my head. He takes my hint, always knowing what I want.

Suddenly, this seems like the absolute *best idea I've ever had*. Who else would know what my body craves, would anticipate my needs when I can't speak, than the man who has proven to be an expert at all that is *me*?

When his hands move back to my breasts, he palms them and groans. "Fuck, your tits are even better than I thought." I don't give myself much time to think about the fact that *Theo has thought about my tits*, instead moving my hands back to his belt, trying to remove it. My hands fumble a bit, and I lose concentration as his lips move to my nipple, sucking deep. It's as if it has a direct line to my clit that starts throbbing with need.

Finally, the belt comes undone. His lips move on my nipple as I tug the leather from the metal buckle. Somehow, I'm able to undo the top button of his pants, tearing the fly down as his teeth scrape my sensitive flesh. As his mouth leaves my nipple before he breathes cool air on my wet skin, I sneak my hand into his pants and find him.

He's warm and smooth, thick and so, so hard. He moans against my breast as I grip him, tugging once.

"Fuck, kitten," he says then nips at my nipple. I remember instantly the last time he used that name, the way I thought I liked it then, but now, with my hand in his pants, his mouth on my breast, I like it a fuck of a lot more.

"Theo," I groan, the pet name and the feel of him throbbing in my hand ratcheting up my need as I tug at his cock.

"Yeah, just like that." He moans, his head against my neck as he leans into me. I look at him, his hair a mess from my fingers, his eyes drifting closed, his mouth open, panting hard, and I think I could come like this, watching him and hearing him, giving him pleasure.

"This is so fucking hot." I moan, trying to tighten my thighs to get some kind of relief and forgetting they're wrapped around his hips. It's a reminder to him, too, because his eyes open, and he stands, knocking my hand from his pants. "No," I mewl like a child, but then I'm quieted by the look in his eyes. His hand moves to my jaw, and he presses a hot, wet kiss to my lips before breaking it again.

"If we're doing this, let's at least keep it on theme," Theo says, and I stare at him in confusion but squeal as he lifts me, my legs, still in my stockings and heels and panties, wrapping around his waist as he walks me through the office. I giggle as he peppers kisses to my lips and skin, the feeling spreading fire across my body as his five o'clock shadow scrapes across my neck, the giggles turning into a moan as he sucks beneath my ear.

"Where are we going?" I ask, but it's a useless question because he's turning the knob of Warren's office, flicking the lights on, and placing my ass on the cold wood of Warren's mostly clear desk. It's huge, just like Theo's, with his computer monitor mounted on the wall, a retractable arm moving it to in front of him when he's working. All that's on the desk is Warren's name plaque, a keyboard, mouse, and mousepad.

"What are we—"

"If I'm going to cross the fucking line, Katrina, if I'm going to fuck you like I want to, I'm doing it on his desk. This is the kind of revenge I can get behind," he says.

"What?" I ask, aghast.

Who the fuck is this man?

And why is he turning me on so much?

I don't have much time to think about any of it because then he moves his hands to my thighs, spreading them wide.

And then he falls to his knees, and I moan at the sight.

At the force that is Theodore Carter, Vice President of Catalyst Records, normally all domineering and professional and put together, looking absolutely *feral* and *hungry* and on his knees before me.

"I hate the way he looks at you," he says, trailing a finger from my ankle up my stockings, up the inside of my thigh. The feeling becomes more intense as he touches the spot between my stocking and my panties, his hand on the sensitive skin. "I hate how he stares at your body as if he thinks I don't own it. As if you're not *mine*."

My conscious brain has shut off, and I'm living in a fantasy world where Theo *does* own me, where I am his.

And I really fucking love it here.

"I hate how his eyes trail over your body in your tight skirts, the way his eyes move on your tits, on your ass." He trails a finger up the soaked center of my thong, and my breathing hitches. His blue eyes are hooded with fury and fire when he looks up at me, dark lashes framing them. I wish I could take a picture of this, him on his knees before me, shirtless, his pants undone, my skirt up to my stomach, on our enemy's desk about to . . .

His voice breaks in before I can start to come to terms with what's about to happen between us.

"But I fucking love these." He groans then presses a kiss to the tender skin right above the lace at the top of my inner thigh, between where my leg ends and my pussy begins, then pulls his face back and snaps the elastic against my skin. It sends shockwaves straight to my clit, throbbing with need.

"Fuck, Theo, please," I whisper, my hand moving to his thick hair and twisting it around my fingers. I don't know what I'm begging for —for him to fuck me, to eat me, to just touch me . . . but I'll take all of the above.

"I've wondered about this, you know," he says conversationally, looking at me. Like this, he looks so phenomenal. All hooded eyes and undeniable lust, need written across his face.

"Wondered what?" I ask, shocked the words are able to come from my lips. They're so breathy, basically coming out in pants as I watch his finger dip under the elastic of my thong at my hip, trailing down then back up, each time getting closer and closer to where I need him. Right before he gets to where I'm already soaked, his fingers leave altogether and I mewl in protest.

"If we were together like this, would you be a brat, or would you listen to me?" His fingers dance along the bare skin of my thigh before he dips one under once more, sliding it along the elastic in the same heady taunt.

I moan loudly, already close to the edge and he has barely even touched me.

"If you would be a good girl, use your manners." He continues the torture, this time sliding up and down the elastic along the crotch of my underwear, ghosting over my pussy. "I've jacked off to it more than I care to admit, Katrina."

No one calls me that, *Katrina*. I fought everyone tooth and nail since I was a kid to call me Kat, but he does, and I fucking love it. I love it even more when we're like this, when it sounds like a tease. A *threat*.

"I'll be whatever you want," I say, my voice throaty. "If you want a brat you can punish, I'm yours. If you want me to be your good girl, that's what I am."

It's my specialty, after all. Becoming whatever anyone wants of me. Anticipating it, executing it, shifting.

He stares at me for long moments, and I worry I said something wrong, that I should have been more subtle or sexier or . . . anything, but then he smiles. His fingers leave my underwear and he stands, moving his hands to the stretchy fabric of my skirt at my hips and tugging. I lift my hips to help him tear it down my legs, but then I put my hand back to the desk to steady myself as he stands tall, leaning over me. I almost fall back, but his strong arm moves to my lower back, holding me, supporting me.

"I want you to be mine, Katrina," he says, and my pulse stops. "But if I can't have that, I want you to be you."

I don't have time to think on it, to decode what it could mean, to remind myself he's drunk and speaking out of his ass and that we're just having *fun* because his lips are on mine. He's kissing me like if he doesn't right now, the world might end. My hands move to his neck and I hold him tight, letting my tongue twine with his.

He stands and steps back, taking in my body.

I widen my legs, never ashamed of my curves, of my stretch marks, of my soft places. I've always loved my body, and any man who doesn't?

Well, it's just another relationship-ending ick.

"Feet on either side of the desk, Katrina," he demands. His hand taps the edge of the desk. I move to toe my heel off, but he shakes his head. "Fuck no. You keep those on." My breathing falters, and I'm unable to concentrate on anything as his hand wraps my ankle, making the stiletto heel dig into the edge of Warren's desk. He repeats the move with my second foot before kneeling. My fingers bite into the desk as I look down my body at him, as his finger dips beneath the elastic of my underwear once more.

But instead of teasing me, instead of playing, he tugs it aside and places his mouth on me without a moment of hesitation.

Instantly, his lips circle my swollen, sensitive client and he sucks hard, moaning as he tastes me. I *scream*, my hand slipping and knocking the desk plate to the ground with a clatter before my fingers are in Theo's hair, twining it and holding him against me as he sucks and nips at my clit.

"Jesus, fuck." I moan, my hips bucking to get more. At this rate, with the buildup that feels like it has been going on for *weeks,* it won't take me long. His teeth scratch against me, driving me higher as he slides two fingers into me easily. I'm so wet, I can hear his fingers working in me, and the sound of them plus the absolutely naughty sounds of his mouth on me send me plummeting toward the edge.

"Fuck, yes, yes. Oh, fuck, I'm going to come." I moan, my eyes drifting shut as the pleasure starts to crest, to build. I'm almost there. A hint of pain in my thigh, Theo's fingers digging into me as a warning as he eats, has me opening my eyes, looking down my body to see him.

His blue eyes are hooded and locked on me, mouth on my cunt, and somehow, even though he's working me and even though he says nothing, I can *feel* the demand, feel him telling me silently to come for him.

And then I *scream*, my voice going hoarse as I come and come and *come* on Theo's face and fingers. When I think I'm done, my body spasming with shocks of pleasure, his fingers crook and my body shakes again, my own fingers gripping tighter in his hair as my hips lift and I fully ride his face until I find it again, his name on my lips.

That one seems to be enough for him, and his tongue goes wide as he licks me from opening to clit once, twice, then cleans his fingers, his eyes locked to me as I try and catch my breath.

When he's done, he fucking *smiles.*

His smiles are rare and breathtaking, but this one is a beast of its own and an image I know I'll imagine for years and years to come, long after this ruse is over, while I make myself come on my fingers as I do.

Nothing will ever fucking top this view.

Never.

"Good?" he asks, and if I wasn't about to fall off this desk, if my pulse wasn't going a million miles a minute, I'd laugh. I'd laugh *hard*. Instead, I grumble something incoherent, and he smiles wider as he stands. One hand slides up my thigh, hooking beneath my knee and helping it touch the ground. He leaves the other foot up, and, *fuck me*, he slides two still-wet fingers inside of me. I moan, my head tipping back, His tongue touches my neck and trails up until his lips are at my ear, his voice a low, turned-on, barely hanging on rumble as he does.

"Now, I'm going to fuck you, Katrina. I'm going to help you off this desk." He crooks his fingers, and my entire body jolts. "I'm going to turn you around." Another slide in and out, his thumb brushing against my oversensitive clit. "I'm going to push you into this desk, and I'm going to come inside of you." I moan low and loud now. "Only thing I gotta know is if I need a condom."

Even with his finger buried in me, I pause in confusion.

"What?"

"I was tested at my last physical. Everything came back negative." *Oh my god, I get it now.* "I want to feel you around my cock, if possible."

I moan both because *I want that*, too, and because his fingers are still fucking me, building me to the top again, the wave begging to crest.

"I want that." I moan.

"Birth control?"

"I'm on the pill, and last time I was tested, everything was clear. I haven't . . . since." I let my eyes drift open and see he's now smiling wolfishly.

He really, really likes this news.

It makes me smile too, one that quickly turns to a pout as he takes his fingers from me. But there's no time to argue when he helps my other leg to the ground, steadies me with his hands on my hips, then turns me until I'm facing the window behind Warren's desk, snow still falling peacefully.

A hand on the nape of my presses. "Bend, baby." I do as he asks and his low, approving rumble meets my ears. "Yes, just like that. Good girl."

My face presses against the cool wood of Warrens's desk, and Theo's hands move up the outsides of my thighs, one tugging my thong to the side again.

"Theo, please." I moan as a finger grazes against where I'm desperate for him.

"Here? This is what you want?" he asks, swiping a finger against where I need him.

"Yes. Please. Fuck me," I beg.

He chuckles.

He fucking laughs while I'm face down on the desk, begging for his cock. The head of him runs up and down my slit before notching into me. I moan as the thick head stretches me and try to buck back to get more of the exquisite feeling.

"Uh-uh, kitten," he says, his voice low, and the word, the endearment, has me both melting and claiming what little of him is inside of me. He groans as I do, and I smile to myself. "You get me when I'm good and ready to give it to you." He slides another inch in, and I groan at the feel. He's so fucking thick, and it's been so long since I've had a man inside of me. I tighten on him again, trying to convince him to slide all the way in.

"Don't play games you won't win, Katrina," he says, pushing in another half-inch.

"You fuck me, we both win, Carter. Now, *fuck me*."

Something about it, probably the use of his surname, snaps something in him, and he does as I demand, slamming in and planting himself deep. We both moan, and my vision goes spotty. One of his hands moves, leaving my hips to grab my hair, twist it around his fist, and tug. I moan again.

I've *always* loved rougher sex, always loved being spanked, getting my hair tugged. Any man who wasn't able to give it to me the way I asked became an *ick*. Never in a million years would I have thought Theo would be able to. But he does, tugging and tilting my head to look at him as he bends a bit, his cock pushing into me farther.

"Now, you listen to me, Katrina. You're a brat in the office, you're a brat in meetings, you're a brat anywhere else, but when my cock is inside of you, you play nice. You be my good little assistant, and you take it how I'm ready to give it to you."

A low, loud moan leaves my lips as my eyes go hooded and hot.

Fuck, he's *perfect*.

"Now, I'm going to fuck you, and I'm going to fuck you hard, and I'm going to watch your ass move as you take me because, honey, I'm telling you now, I've dreamt of nothing more than your ass while I take you from behind for fucking *months*. When you come, you're going to take me with you, and I'm going to fill this tight cunt up with my cum. So much that when you're sitting at your desk tomorrow, being my good little assistant, I'm gonna know it's still dripping out of you."

Again, I moan, but I don't close my eyes, instead looking into his blues that have gone so dark now, they're nearly black as he towers over me.

"Yeah?" he asks, and I realize then, he wants an answer.

"Yeah, Theo. Please," I say, and he smiles, bends low, going *deeper still*, and presses his mouth to mine.

"Fucking perfect," he says against my lips, but before I can over-think that, he lets go of my hair, stands tall, and slides out.

Then he slams back in. A guttural, low moan leaves my lips, and I try to move, to go up onto my arms, to help get him in deeper, but his hand moves to my back, holding me down. "No, you let me fuck you. This is how I want you, Katrina."

I freeze. I *do* work to please him, after all.

"That's my good girl," he says, barely even loud enough for me to hear, as if he's speaking to himself, before he starts fucking me.

Hard.

"God, this fucking ass. Taunting me for months in those tiny, tight fucking skirts. What should I do about that?" He pulls out then slams in again, and I moan deep. His thumb is tugging my thong to the side, his big hand cupping one of my ass cheeks, the cotton pinching my swollen clit with each movement. "God, the way it fucking moves every time I do this." He slides out and in again, and my ass shakes with the rough movement.

"Yes, yes, god."

"Fuck, are you going to come for me again?"

"Yes, please don't stop."

"No fucking way." He groans, his thrusts going harder, deeper, more wild. His hand moves my hair, pushing it to one side as his chest lies on my back, his lips at my ear. As he nips my earlobe, I tighten around him, and he moans deep.

A man moaning? Hot.

Theo moaning because he likes the feel of my pussy clamping down on him? *Stellar.*

"Who's fucking you, Katrina?" His voice is unhinged, gravely, and full of need.

"Oh, fuck." I moan as I spiral toward coming, as it builds in my belly, as he fucks me into the desk, the wood biting at the front of my thighs in a delicious way I hope will leave bruises.

"Who's fucking you, Katrina?"

"You are. Fuck, you are." His hand moves from my hip, dipping into the front of the panties I'm still wearing, pressing on my clit but not moving. "Make me come, please," I beg. But he doesn't. I'm near tears with the need for just a *little bit more,* and he's holding the leash, somehow knowing just how much to press and rub against me without giving me everything as he fucks me near violently.

I fucking love it.

I love how he doesn't let me get my way, that he wants me to submit to him when outside of *this,* I never do.

But I really, really want to come, and I want him to come inside of me as I do.

So, I moan the words I've secretly moaned in the safety of my own bed, writhing with my vibrator.

"Please, come inside me, Mr. Carter."

And there it is.

He loses whatever tight grasp he has on his control, growling as he fucks me with abandon once, twice, three times before pressing hard on my clit and moaning my name *loud* in my ear.

I shatter, coming as I feel him plant deep and start to pulse, filling me with his cum. And then, as he continues to circle my clit, I come again, moaning his name as my body begins to relax finally, spent and content and full of Theo Carter.

We lie like that for long minutes, my chest on the desk, Theo's on my back but not enough to suffocate me, him still deep in me. I let out a delighted, happy sigh of relief, and he chuckles, the sound vibrating through me as he does.

"What?" I say, sleepy but not too sleepy not to be annoyed that he's *inside of me* and laughing.

"Nothing, kitten."

"What, Theo?" I ask, now moving toward even more annoyed. He slides out and I mewl, him standing then helping me up and holding me.

I glare at him.

He smiles.

"A while ago, I wondered if you'd purr like a kitten when you had my cock inside of you. Turns out, when you're full of me and satisfied, you do."

I want to glare, but I can't.

Instead, I smile.

When he smiles back, free and happy and so fucking handsome, I forget that I was ever even annoyed with him at all.

THIRTY-FIVE

KAT

We eat snacks and someone's leftover pizza out of the fridge before I finally yawn, the liquor leaving my body warm and the sex leaving it exhausted. I'm sitting on the couch in the reception in my underwear with Theo's button-down over top. He pulled his slacks back on, throwing on an old tee shirt from his gym bag that smelled a bit like sweat and a lot like Theo.

Strange because usually, that sweat smell gives me the ick, but with Theo, it just feels... like him. Like a part of him I get to have that his normally perfect facade doesn't show the rest of the world.

"Tired?" he asks, standing in front of me and pushing my hair behind my shoulders and looking at me with concern. I nod.

"Do you think the roads are clear?"

"Not sure. Let me check." He stands, and I cuddle deeper into the couch.

"Either way, I'll have to wait a bit until the cabs are back on the road," I say through another yawn. "I'm still a bit tipsy and way too tired to drive."

"No need, I'll drive you home." He walks toward one of the large windows, taking in the darkness outside and the streets below.

"You drank, too," I remind him. He turns to look at me over his shoulder, his broad shoulders flexing beneath the thin tee shirt as he gives me a quizzical look.

"Had one shot two hours ago, sipped on the second one. Promise I'm good to drive." I stare at him. "I'd never put you in danger, Katrina."

He says it like that's why I'm staring at him, like I'm thinking he would ever put me in danger. But I'm just confused by *only one shot*.

He was drunk, just like me two hours ago when I convinced him to cross the line and fuck me on Warren's desk. When I convinced him I wasn't going to fall for him and that adding a physical connection would make our engagement seem more realistic while getting that itch out from under our skin.

He was drunk because there's no world where careful, strategic Theodore Carter would fuck his fake fiancée, his assistant, without being impaired.

Right?

"You're sober?" I ask, baffled. He looks back at me, similar confusion on his face.

"I've been sober all night. I'm a lot bigger than you. That little barely makes an impact."

"Oh," I say, my voice barely a whisper because what the fuck?

"Roads still aren't plowed," he says, turning fully toward me and walking my way. "We might need to stay the night here."

"Stay the night?" I ask, my voice squeaking.

"I mean, we could check in a few hours." I blink at him, so lost, but he just moves to sit next to me, brushing my hair back again. "You're exhausted, though. You should try to get a bit of sleep."

I don't think before I say my next words.

"Will you lie with me?" He looks at me, eyes warm and kind.

"You want me to?"

I nod. "It's chilly." He stares for a beat, two, three, and I think he's going to say no, but he doesn't.

Instead, he moves to the light, hitting the dimmer, and walks over to where I'm lying on the large couch, the back pillows already thrown to the ground for extra room. When he lies down, I leave space between us, suddenly self-conscious. But he just slides his strong arm over my waist, tugging me in close until my face is buried into his chest.

"Sleep, kitten," he whispers into my hair.

And I do as he asks.

THIRTY-SIX

THEO

"What the—" A familiar voice booms through my bedroom, pulling me from sleep.

Strange.

Very, very strange.

"Theodore, are you okay?" The voice is closer now, and slowly, I come back to myself. My arm is around something warm, my entire body against more warmth that is starting to shift. Warmth that makes noise, a garbled, sleepy, irritated noise, but noise all the same.

Like a crack of lightning, it all comes back to me.

Staying late.

The snow.

Whiskey with Katrina.

Truth or dare.

Kissing her.

Fucking her.

Fucking her on Warren's desk.

Staying the night because of the snow.

Cuddling with her.

Jesus fucking Christ.

Slowly, I sit up, noting three alarming things. One, while her ass is covered, the too-big button-down has crept up, showing her perfect legs.

Two, my boss is standing there, a look of concern on his face.

And three, fucking Warren is standing behind him, arms crossed on his chest, a smug smile on his lips.

"Theodore, are you okay?" I sit up, looking around, trying to shake the sleep from my head and focus before this situation gets somehow worse.

"What time is it?" I ask, looking around.

"8:30," Warren says, his voice so fucking douchey, I want to punch him, even this early in the morning. Maybe especially this early in the morning.

"What's going on?" Katrina asks, and then, finally, she opens her eyes. Another reason to hate Warren: I'm missing the first time I get to see what Katrina's eyes look like when she's sleepy and has just woken up. They go wide with panic, and she sits up, looking around.

"It's fine," I say, my voice calmer than I feel as I tuck a piece of her thick hair behind her ear. "It's fine. The snow, remember? We couldn't leave. We stayed here. I just forgot to set an alarm." Truth be told, I didn't set an alarm because I never sleep in. I barely get more than three hours in a single span without waking. My nights are always spent tossing and turning, waking multiple times. It's been that way for as long as I can remember. Except . . . this time, apparently.

Katrina looks around, taking in Jeff, then Warren, then the couch we slept on, then her attire.

"Oh, shit," she whispers then moves to sit behind me, trying to cover herself from the intruders' eyes. I take note of how her voice is raspy when she first wakes, similar to how it sounded when I was—

"What's going on here?" Warren asks, interrupting my thoughts thankfully. "Not very professional of you two to have a sleepover here." He says it like it was a choice, like it was intentional and we decided it would be a fun time.

Jeff looks at Warren with a strange expression, like he isn't sure why he's acting that way, then to me.

"We didn't intend to stay here," I say, looking at Jeff. "We were staying late to work on a proposal, and the next thing we knew, we were snowed in. I texted you, remember? To ask how the roads were?" Jeff nods, and Katrina adds in more context from behind me.

"It wasn't until we got the alert on my phone that we realized how late it was. Then we had to stay until the roads cleared, but . . . they didn't."

"So we spent the night here instead of risking getting into an accident," I finish explaining.

"Well," Jeff says. "I'm glad you two made the right decision. Lots of accidents happened last night. When the first round of snow melted, it froze and then was covered in more snow. Dangerous conditions. The roads are clear now, though." He looks to me, then to Katrina behind me. "I appreciate you working hard for the company, but you also need rest. I want you two to get home and sleep it off."

On the bright side, Warren looks absolutely feral over the fact Jeff isn't mad we were caught in this precarious position.

"It would probably be nice to sleep in your own beds," Warren says, with that same fucking smirk. "Since you don't normally sleep together, right?"

Jeff looks from Warren to me to Katrina, then back at Warren.

"What are you talking about?"

"Well, they don't live together," Warren says. "And they never spend the night together. I do think that's a bit strange, how they're engaged but not sleeping together."

Jeff's brow furrows in confusion, and I feel that distinct tightening in my chest, panic building and crescendoing.

But as always, even half asleep, Katrina is on and ready to take down Warren. I can't see her face with her behind me, but when she wraps an arm around my middle and puts her chin on my shoulder, I can picture her face.

Serene, a gentle smile but fire in her eyes.

"We actually just moved in together," she says with a smile. "We were waiting until we told everyone, but now that the cat's out of the bag, I'm spending all of my nights at Theo's."

I fight the urge to close my eyes and breathe in defeat, knowing what Warren is going to say, but—

"Strange. I haven't seen your car at our building," he says.

Jeff is watching the volleying, and I jump in to save Katrina before she says something that will ruin everything.

"Remember I told you Warren lives in the same building as I do?" I ask, looking over my shoulder at her. Her face doesn't change, but I can see the panic in her eyes, so familiar with all of her looks, before I turn back to Jeff. "I've been dropping her back off at her place every morning since most of her things are still there. She gets ready and comes in at normal time, that way she doesn't have to get here crazy early with me," I say. Jeff nods and smiles.

"Ah, that makes sense! I don't blame you, Katrina. He gets here so early, always ready to work before anyone else and staying long after." My eyes move to Warren, who looks angry.

Suddenly, I find myself wondering if he knew we'd be here. If he knew he'd find something like this and hoped to get me into trouble.

"Why are you here so early, Jeff?" I ask. "You normally aren't in until 9. Near-retirement hours, you called it." Jeff smiles

"Yeah, well, this one over here asked if we could have an early morning meeting. He's got calls later today, and it was the only time that worked for him." I look at Warren and see I was right. Somehow, he knew we were here and hoped to make me look bad.

But how?

"Anyway, you two head out. Warren, why don't we go into my office, let them have some privacy while they get ready to head home." Warren's jaw clenches, but he nods all the same. "And you let us know if we can help with the move, okay? I know Warren's got a truck. I bet it could all fit in there."

The clench of Warren's jaw says everything I need to know before he and Jeff walk off, leaving Katrina and me to get ready and head out for the day.

And come up with yet another plan.

THIRTY-SEVEN

KAT

It only takes a few minutes to get some form of dressed before I'm sitting in Theo's car at his insistence. Both of our vehicles were buried under at least 6 inches of snow with even more behind from the plows, and to quote Theo, "I'm only shoveling out one."

We drive home in relative silence, but the entire time, Theo holds my hand.

He holds it like it's precious, like he thinks if he lets go, I'll float away. He goes so far as to shift into reverse and drive with his left hand awkwardly.

I'm still in a daze, I think, a layer of sleep and confusion in my mind, blurring everything, adding a golden hue to it, but all I keep thinking over and over is: *he was sober.*

Careful, calculated Theodore Carter fucked me on his rival's desk, and he did it completely sober.

I convinced him, of course. Told him my truth, that in a few weeks, it wouldn't matter, sleeping together wouldn't change things because soon, he'd do something and ruin "us" forever, but still, he did it. He let all of the options and outcomes run through his mind and decided sleeping with me was the right one. The benefits outweighed the risks.

The city feels quiet as we drive, the roads plowed and salted already, but everything in a sound-deafening blanket of snow. It feels almost magical, and a quiet, silly part of my mind tells me the world did it for us, celebrated us in this way because we are magic.

Now *that* is most definitely my hopeless romantic speaking.

"My place," he says, an answer to a question I don't remember asking.

"What?"

"We're going to my place."

"Why are we going to your place?"

"Because you can't stay at your place, not when Warren has a vendetta and you just told everyone you're moving in with me." I cringe, remembering my impulsive declaration.

"Warren always has a vendetta."

"Yeah, but now he thinks you're living in the same building he is or, at the very least, that we're lying about it. He's going to be paying close fucking attention, so you're staying at my place." He turns onto the highway but keeps his eyes straight ahead when he drops his next bomb.

"I don't trust him, and I want you close, just in case." A chill enters my bloodstream, pooling in my stomach. "I want to keep you safe."

"Do you think . . ." I don't want to finish my sentence, to finish what feels like an unhinged, paranoid accusation, but I don't have to.

"Yes," he says, and the single word drives fear through me.

"Why?"

"Why do I think he'd try to hurt you, or why would he try to hurt you?"

My instincts regarding Warren have been the same since the very beginning; I don't trust him. I think there's something incredibly off, a vibe or maybe the way he talks or the way he looks at people, I'm not sure. But he's off.

He's the kind of off that, from the beginning, I did what I could not to be alone with him. Did I actually think he would try to hurt me? No, but I didn't want to give him any kind of opportunity.

But now . . .

"Both?"

"Because he's floundering. I don't know how, but he knew we'd be at the office this morning, thought we'd get caught in some position Jeff would view poorly." That surprised me, and I shifted in my seat to watch him better, light flickering on his face as he glides down the empty roads.

"How would he know?"

"I have no idea, but he did. I could tell from the second I saw him, even half asleep. His face . . . He was waiting for the other shoe to drop. And when it didn't, he got angry. I don't trust that he won't keep tabs on you and report to Jeff if he deems something is off."

"Because he knows something is off," I whisper, dreading the fact that we haven't been able to pull this off as well as I thought.

"He thinks he knows something," Theo says. "And based on today and him fucking with the appointments, he's floundering."

"He's scared," I say, my voice low but confidence growing. "Why else would Warren go through all this trouble? If he knew he had the job in the bag, he'd give us a hard time because he's an ass, but he wouldn't be looking for things. He wouldn't be sneaking around, and he wouldn't be making notes on all of your past work over the years, trying to find something to bring to the board." Theo sighs, turning into a parking garage.

"I don't know. Regardless, I'm keeping you close for the next few days at least. Later, we'll pick up your things so you have more stuff at my place. I don't want you staying there for a bit."

"Theo—" He parks the car and looks at me, and I see it there. Exhaustion. Pleading. Worry.

"Please, Katrina. Please, humor me. I got you into this mess; let me make sure you're safe." The fact that Theo doesn't think I'm safe sits heavy in my gut. That mixed with the look on his face has me sighing. And then I do the only thing I can when he looks like that, when he's begging me to do something.

I nod.

"So, you can stay in my guest room," Theo says as we walk into his penthouse, tossing my bag onto his large leather couch before moving his hands to his dark-blue, nearly black jacket. "If you want."

I don't respond as a shiver rolls through me as I watch his long fingers work on the buttons of his coat.

I should still be panicked. I should be concerned about the implications of this fake relationship escalating. I should be worried about the fact that Warren definitely sees me as a threat now. I should be thinking about how we absolutely crossed a line last night and how to make sure we stay within the safe borders of our fake little relationship moving forward.

Instead, I'm watching his fingers move deftly along black buttons.

Fingers that were in me not long ago.

What is happening to me?

This is Theo Carter.

My boss.

Somehow, in the last two months, I've allowed my brain to become unbearably scrambled. Now, I'm wearing his mother's engagement ring, telling everyone at the office we're to be married, and instead of harboring my secret, quiet crush, I'm letting him eat me out and fuck me on his rival's desk.

And now I'm at his penthouse, ready to move in.

Worse, even though I should be feeling the suffocating edges of it, should feel it creeping in on me, ready to ruin everything, I don't feel the ick coming on.

I don't feel it.

And I've clearly lost any ability to think wisely.

Instead, I say, "Or?"

"Or . . ." Theo turns to me as he tosses his coat on the couch, so unlike the man who is always so clinical, so particular, so calculated. It's like something untethered in him, be it from what happened in the office or his realization of Warren or me being in his home right now, I don't know. But something about Theo has changed.

And I think I like it.

He takes a step closer, his arm reaching out to grab me and pull me in close. "Or you can stay in my room. In my bed."

An intelligent woman would say perfect, grab her bag, and walk to said guest room, leaving, at the very least, a closed door between her and the man she absolutely cannot have.

But I smile.

I smile because I'm not a smart woman. Clearly, I'm a moron.

"Do you want that? Me to spend the night in your bed?" He smiles, but I see the nerves behind his eyes.

"It's all I've been able to think about, Katrina, for better or worse."

"Me sleeping in your bed?" I ask with a squeak.

"Among other things." He dips his head, forehead pressing to mine. "So many other things. So many things I absolutely should not be thinking about."

"I think thinking about those things is exactly what you should be doing, Mr. Carter." I can almost feel the change in the atmosphere, the shift in his attention, in his demeanor as his body stiffens, as the room goes warm.

"Are you sober now?" he asks, his lips brushing mine.

"What?" It feels like that's my response often lately when it's just the two of us, him constantly throwing me off kilter.

"Are you sober?" His breath fans across my lips and face and I shiver. He smiles. "Katrina, are you sober?"

"I, uh . . . ," I start, licking my lips. When my tongue comes out, it gently touches his, and he smiles.

He smiles.

Theodore Carter smiling is a sight to behold, especially when he does it with the look of a wolf finding Granny.

"Yes," I whisper. "Yes, I'm sober." It's been well over twelve hours since I had the last drink, but I don't think that was a question he didn't know the answer to.

Still, when I confirm, his smile somehow widens, and he bends his knees, gripping my thighs before standing, forcing me to wrap my legs around his waist.

"Good," he says and starts walking.

"Good?"

"Yeah, good." He takes a few steps in a direction I can't see. "The second time we do this, I'm making sure you're fully aware of everything that's happening."

"Second time?" I ask, my voice shaking as he walks through a doorway.

"I'm going to lose you soon, right?" he asks, and my gut twists. "You're going to get the ick or whatever?" I nod because I am. I always do. "Then I'm going to enjoy every fucking moment with you while I can." Then I'm on his bed, and his body is crawling up mine, and there are no more words, just actions and feelings.

But late that night, when I'm wrapped up in Theo, wearing his shirt, his heavy arm on my waist, I do have a thought.

And the only one running through my head is: *I'm going to lose you soon, right?*

As if he feels like I'm his right now to have.

I let the idea of being Theo's slide through my veins, leaving golden warmth in its wake until my eyes lose the fight to exhaustion.

THIRTY-EIGHT

THEO

I check my phone once more before setting it to silent as we sit in the Italian restaurant Katrina typically reserves for meetings like this. My number one goal with all artists, current and potential, is to make them feel like they have my undivided attention. Slipping the device into the front pouch of my briefcase, I turn to her.

"Do you know exactly what time we told her to meet us here?" Cassandra is chronically on time, but it's five past one, and she hasn't shown up yet. Katrina nods.

"I believe one, but let me double-check the invite I sent over." She reaches for her purse and starts digging, her movements becoming more and more harried as she looks through her bag, in all the pockets, undoing and redoing zippers.

"Everything okay?"

"I think . . . I think I left my phone at the office," she says incredulously. "I never do that. I could have sworn I threw it in my bag." She looks up at me, her eyes wide, her face pale. "I'm so sorry, Theo. I can run to the office and grab it—I have her cell number saved in there too." I shake my head, then reach into my bag for my phone to check my calendar.

"No need. I'll just look at the invite you sent . . ." The time and location are set correctly, and I note that all three invites have been accepted. One for me, one for Katrina, and one for Cassandra.

"It's not like her to be late," I say, confused. She's up for contract renewal, which is why we set this informal lunch up, but it's more of a formality than anything. She was one of my first finds before I was even in A&R and one of the most loyal artists at Catalyst.

"If I had my phone, I would just call her." Katrina groans. Fuck, she's cute when she's pissed like this. "And you don't save clients in your cell in case you lose it. Which, most of the time, I think is pretty smart, except right now when I think it's wildly stupid." She glares at me as if that is going to change anything as I scroll through my emails.

"Ah, there's the issue," I mumble. In my inbox is an email from Cassandra's assistant, telling us she has to reschedule our lunch due to a last-minute interview. It's not unheard of, but usually we get a heads-up for something like this before we've already left the office. "She has to reschedule. She has a call with a magazine." I sigh, putting my phone back in my bag. "Well, this was a waste." She looks at me, a single eyebrow raised, before unrolling her silverware and putting the napkin in her lap.

"Well, I'm staying for lunch because I've been daydreaming about the antipasto since I made the reservation last week." I smile at her.

"Of course. Use the company card. I guess I'll head back to the office and play catch up." She rolls her eyes, reminding me how I made her eyes roll into her head similarly this morning before she got ready for the day.

Maybe that's the real problem, why I didn't see the email until it was too late: Katrina. Ever since the snowstorm, she's been staying at my place, and even though that night, I convinced myself it would be just one time, we've been acting anything but fake.

And honestly, it's been amazing. I've had girlfriends, of course, but most got on my nerves in just a few overnights. But here Katrina is, covering my bathroom sink with her collection of makeup brushes and lotions and hair products, and I don't fucking care.

Most nights, I go to sleep wrapped around her, thinking I wouldn't mind at all if this never ends, if this fake engagement just . . . continues.

Her ick could be a problem, but I've also started to rationalize that I could overcome it, that we could work through whatever ends up being my ick.

"Jesus Christ, Theo, if you catch up anymore, you're going to be done with work for three months out."

"And . . . ?" I ask.

"And a single lunch won't kill you."

"Of course not, but—"

"We also have things to talk about. Plans. Schemes. Or, you know, we could practice being on a date."

"Practice? I think we practiced pretty well this morning." Her mouth drops open, and her eyes go wide, and fuck, I overstepped. "Not . . . I don't . . . I just meant—" And then she starts cackling, her laugh making heads in the restaurant turn our way.

"God, your face!" She wipes a tear from her eye as she comes down from the hilarity. "I didn't think you had a sex joke in you, my god." She lets out a breath and shakes her head. "Not that kind of practice, you fiend. The kind where you don't act all uptight and grumpy when our clothes are still on."

"I much prefer your clothes off," I grumble, and her lips purse, fighting a smile.

"Yeah, well, on Warren's desk, you went on about how you didn't like him looking at me with clothes on. I think pulling off this fake engagement naked might make you go all caveman." Her eyes go a bit dazed, and now I'm smiling. "Not that I'd mind that part. But you need to figure out how to stop being so uptight when we're pretending. Learn how to hang out with me—with clothes on—and not get all . . . awkward."

"I'm not awkward," I defend, incredibly awkwardly. She gives me a look that says *be honest with yourself, for the love of God.*

I sigh and shake my head. She's right, after all—I am very ahead on my to-do list, and I don't know how to act when it's just Katrina and me outside of work, especially when other people are around.

"Come on," she says suddenly, breaking me from my thoughts, and stands.

"What?"

"We're getting good food." I stare at her, confused and unmoving, as she bends, grabbing her bag and shifting it over her shoulder. "Come on, get up." I don't.

"You just said you wanted the antipasto," I argue.

"Yeah, if we were eating at this stuffy restaurant, I want the antipasto. But if we have no one to impress, I want to watch you hover over a plate of tacos and try not to get *barbacoa* on your shirt."

"Katrina, I don't—"

"Don't care, let's go," she says, talking over me and then reaching to grab *my* briefcase.

"Seriously, we can—" I start, but a waitress comes over before I can finish my thought.

"Hello! I'm Bella. I'll be your server today. Are you waiting for another?" she asks, staring at the empty seat and the seat Katrina just vacated.

"Unfortunately, something came up, and we have to head out. So sorry!" Katrina says with a bright smile, reaching over to grab my hand, twining our fingers together, and tugging me up. "Come on, babe." I have no choice but to stand and follow her out the door.

"So you... come here often?" I ask as we sit at a small table in the corner, a full feast laid out in front of us. We walked in and the man at the register greeted Katrina by name she rattled off a long list of items to order, not even bothering to ask me what I wanted.

"Oh, totally. It's my favorite. My dad used to take me here when I would get out of school early and we'd eat so much, we wouldn't be hungry for dinner. It would piss my mom off so much." She reaches across the table grabbing a taco topped with chopped meat, cilantro and onion, squeezing a wedge of lime on top and taking a large bite. "Now I come with Abbie and we eat until we can barely move."

"I didn't even know this place was here," I say, staring at the options and overwhelmed.

"That's because you're boring and live your life like a little robot. If it doesn't fit into your perfect little schedule, you don't do it." I don't bother to argue, because she's not wrong. Most days, I even eat the same three meals to avoid having to think about it. "This one," she says, grabbing a taco and placing it on a white paper plate for me. "*Al pastor*. Pork and pineapple. On top is cilantro and onion." I take the plate with a *thanks* before putting it down on the small cleared spot in front of me.

She watches me intently as I stand, removing my suit jacket, undoing the buttons of my shirt at my wrists, and carefully rolling them to my elbows before sitting again. I flip my tie over my shoulder before lifting the taco and taking a bite.

It's fucking *amazing*.

"Holy fuck," I say, my mouth still full. Instantly, Katrina's full laugh fills the restaurant, and once I swallow, I smile at her.

"See, I knew you'd love it here. Sometimes you need to get out of your little predictable habits, Mr. Carter." I think I would do absolutely anything if she asked me to do while calling me *Mr. Carter*. "A date where we're just us is absolutely what we needed." Then she smiles at me, reaching across the table to push my hair back, even though I know nothing is out of place, before cupping my jaw. I freeze in place, way too many emotions and thoughts swirling in my mind.

She, of course, sees the battle in my eyes and laughs.

"My god, Theo. See, we really do need to do this. A date together where we can work out the uncomfortable kinks. You'd think I was ripping off each fingernail one by one by making you have a basic lunch with me."

I don't tell her that I froze because the feeling of her warm palm on my cheek sent a shockwave through me. I froze because, not for the first time, I realized *I like this*, being with her out in the open, with no expectations or games between us.

Instead, I nod like an idiot. "You're right. This is good. This is... we needed to do this." She beams at me, the shine of her smile burning away any nerves or anxieties or second thoughts before she puts her elbows to the table, propping her chin in her hands and looking at me expectantly.

"There you go! Now, tell me your most embarrassing childhood memory," she says with a bat of her eyes.

I laugh and shake my head before taking another bite of the taco and tell her about a time I threw up down a flight of stairs in middle school, and she tells me about a time when she told a boy she liked him, but didn't realize her dress was tucked into her underwear.

The hour goes like that, great food, funny stories, getting to know each other. Gentle touches and small smiles.

A real date.

For a moment, I wonder what it would be like if this was actually our life. If I could convince her to keep this up. If we took our lunch together, headed here for a quick meal, and spent an hour breaking out of the monotony. What would it be like to walk into work together every day and leave at the same time, to head home together? To have these inside jokes outside of work, to walk into my lonely penthouse to her laugh filling up the space?

And never once do I check my phone through the entire date.

THIRTY-NINE

THEO

I'm smiling down at Katrina as she laughs when we walk back into the office, but the joy and warmth from our date fades to ice instantly, the feel of the place just . . . off. Jeff is on us before we even walk past reception, his face a mask of anger and disappointment. Katrina's hand slips into mine and squeezes tight.

"Where the fuck have you been?" he asks, his voice low as he glares at me. All three of us continue walking toward my office slowly.

"What?" I ask then look to Katrina, who is as equally confused as I am.

"Where the fuck have you been?"

"We . . . We were at lunch. We had a meeting but it was a no-show," I say.

"You had a meeting here," he says. "At the fucking office."

My blood runs cold in my veins.

"This is your client. Warren had to step in and keep her happy."

"She canceled our meeting at Trattoria Seven," I say, my mind reeling.

"She showed us *your* email asking her to meet you at the office."

"What?"

"What's going on?"

"We almost lost her."

"What?" I ask, frustrated. Cassandra was one of the very first clients I suggested Jeff sign on when she was just fifteen and playing in small cafés across the Southeast. When I came to Catalyst full-time, she became my first personal client, and I was under the impression today's meeting was more of a formality.

"She got an offer from Blacknote, better figures, better promises. You know how it goes over there. She was intent on talking to you today to see how things could work." I shake my head, trying to piece together this new information.

"I don't understand. We got an email from her assistant saying she needed to cancel."

"Well, she's here."

"That makes no sense—" Just then, Warren walks out of his office, a wide, mean smile on his lips as he readjusts his jacket. In the conference room, Cassandra meets my eyes and she gives me a small wave and a smile.

She doesn't look angry or put off or like she's about to run off to Blacknote, which should be a relief.

But I can't stare at her long, as my eyes are stuck on Warren and that look on his face.

That look like he won another round. It all clicks into place.

"Don't worry, Theo," Warren says with a shit-eating grin I'd really like to punch off his face. "I took good care of her for you. She's signing another contract with us." My jaw goes tight, dread swirling in my stomach, but I keep my eyes cold when I speak.

"I'd like to see the contract before she signs, make sure it still benefits her and us," I say, and a hint of irritation flares on his face.

Instantly, I know something in that contract will either hurt Cassandra or fuck me over, benefitting Warren. "You almost fucked this account beyond repair, and now you're questioning me?"

"Warren, that's pretty standard—"

"He should be fired for this bullshit," Warren starts, cutting Jeff off. "He's fucking up left and right and we're all stuck here cleaning up the messes." Jeff's face is confused and a bit angry at the accusation and for a split second, I think it's a strange decision. But then Mark Adams, one of the board members, walks past slowly, drawn brows focused on our little group, and I know.

Somehow, I know this is another setup to prove my incompetence to the board. Somehow, he fucked with the meeting, reached out to Cassandra and changed the location, and we were none the wiser.

Before I can even think of the why, Katrina telling me he was in my office a few weeks back comes to mind, and I fight a groan.

"That isn't your—" Jeff starts, irritation on his face, which at the very least is a tiny win, but Katrina cuts him off. She puts a hand to my arm, her eyes wide and doelike in a way I've never seen.

It makes me uneasy instantly.

"You know, Theo, there's a chance I . . ." She pauses, looking at Jeff with those big eyes, and swallows, biting her lip before continuing, "There's a chance I got tricked. Someone fucked with our system, a bot or something. Who knows, maybe it was Blacknote trying to fuck with you. I'm such a ditz." She blinks a few times and then I'm stunned when her eyes start to water and she curls her lips into her mouth. I turn to her just as a tear falls, using my thumb to brush it away and cupping her cheek with my hand.

"No, no, Katrina. It's fine. It was a mistake, no big deal. Cassandra is here and she's staying with Catalyst. No harm, no foul."

"I'm so, so sorry, Theo. I really didn't mean to mess anything up." She turns back to Jeff, and I drop my hand, putting it to her waist and tugging her in close. "And I'm sorry to you, Jeff. It was a careless mistake and it's all my fault."

Except Katrina doesn't make careless mistakes. Not when it comes to work, at least. Finally, she turns to Warren, and her emotions shift again. "Thank you so much for handling this for us. I'm such a scatterbrain sometimes." She stuns me when a goofy frown comes over her face and her finger moves to her hair, twirling a lock there.

What in the fuck is happening?

But it works, somehow, when Jeff's face loses the last bit of irritation and he reaches out for Katrina, pulling her in for a hug.

"No problem at all, my girl. Don't beat yourself up over it, okay? Mistakes happen and you and Theo are invaluable to this team. Hell, we wouldn't even have Cassandra if it wasn't for Theo all those years ago." He rubs her back like she's his daughter he accidentally upset, and she hugs him back, but from this angle, I can see the look of pure hatred on her face directed at Warren. His mirrors the same vehemence, and it's an interesting silent battle to watch. Finally, Jeff breaks the hug, and again, Katrina's face morphs into sadness, but it's a sadness that's been comforted.

God, she's so fucking good.

"Now, Theodore, you make sure your girl is settled and not upset, then come meet me in the conference room with Cassandra. Warren, thank you for your help, but this is Theo's account. We've got it from here."

Warren's jaw is so tight, I wonder if he'll break a tooth.

"Got it, Jeff," he says with a small nod.

Jeff leaves first, headed toward the conference room where Cassandra sits, and Warren turns to Katrina and me. With a quick glance around, I can see no eyes are on us anymore, the entertainment for the afternoon gone. Warren's face is smug and evil, but anger brews beneath it, probably because his latest scheme didn't work the way he thought it would.

But he doesn't say a single word, instead just smiles, reaches into his pocket, and grabs a phone that he tosses on Katrina's desk before walking in the direction of the conference room.

I don't have to see the pretty lilac case she has to know Warren just pulled Katrina's cell from his pocket.

FORTY

KAT

The door to Theo's office clicks behind us, and he moves almost robotically, closing the blinds swiftly as I grab my chair and position it in front of his desk.

My pulse is pounding, and not because I'm in a room alone with Theo.

Because for the first time, we have solid, indisputable evidence that Warren is out to fuck with Catalyst. Warren is working not only to delegitimize Theo, but he's trying to fuck with his career. It seems he doesn't even care if he fucks over the label in the process.

"What was that?" he asks in a low, urgent whisper.

"We got played," I say, my voice equally low.

"What was with the silly little girl game?" I tip my head to the side, confused. "The finger twirling, the I'm a little ditzy bullshit. That's not you, and that was not your fault. He fucked with our appointment and stole your phone, Katrina."

"It was the only thing that made sense. It took the pressure and the blame off of you and put it onto me. Then, if Warren wanted to keep attacking in front of Jeff to prove his point, he'd be attacking a woman who was near tears, hugging and being comforted by the fucking president of the company. Not a great look for him."

Theo sighs, opens his mouth like he wants to argue, and then finally, he sits, running a hand through his hair.

"Warren texted her from your phone. Asked if we could meet at the office instead, didn't he?" I nod. When Jeff and Theo went to the meeting room to talk to Cassandra, I dove into my messages, finding a text I absolutely never sent telling her to meet us at the office.

"He probably grabbed it from my bag when I was using the bathroom before we left." He shakes his head then angrily pounds his fist into his desk.

"Goddammit."

"He's playing dirty now, but he's not being smart about it. He probably saw the lunch in your calendar when he snuck in here. I confronted him, and Jeff saw it happen. Maybe we should—"

"No," Theo says, his voice strong, his eyes cold as flint. "No, we can't bring Jeff into this. That's what he wants."

"That's what he wants?" Theo leans forward and jiggles his mouse, bringing his computer to life and typing in his password.

"Unfortunately, he's smarter than he seems." I scoff out a laugh, but Theo looks at me and the pure anger on his face has any humor melting away. "He's got some kind of plan. There's something up his sleeve. I just don't know what."

"We have enough evidence to show Jeff he's fucking with us, fucking with Catalyst. You and I both know he's leaking artists to Blacknote. We should—" He shakes his head again.

"He's good at what he does: manipulating. He knows what people want to hear, knows how to shift the narrative to make himself look like a victim. He's three steps ahead of us, Katrina, and we're back here playing fucking tic-tac-toe." His fingers move on his keyboard for a minute or two as we sit in silence before his hand slams into his desk, and a noise of frustration leaves his chest.

"He logged in at one twenty that day. It wasn't me because I was in New York. No access."

"I came back at one twenty-five," I say in a whisper. I'd taken a mental note of it after I saw Warren in the office. "Theo, if we show Jeff—" There has to be a way to prove Warren is being malicious, that he's bad for the company and he's not playing fair.

But Theo shakes his head, his eyes going dark and his voice going firm, his shoulders straightening in a way that is both a turn-on and sends a shiver down my spine.

"No. No, this is between Warren and me." He sighs, his head tipping back as he thinks. I watch when everything changes, when his body goes stiff, his shoulders roll back, and when he looks at me, there is steel in his eyes; he's ready to fight.

He stands and starts pacing his office, looking like a caged animal as he runs a hand through his hair. "I've been wanting to play it clean and honest." I raise an eyebrow at him, even in this tense moment able to poke a bit of fun at him. He rolls his eyes. "Fine, mostly honest. I wanted to get this job on my own merit—"

"And someone, maybe an incredibly gorgeous, super smart assistant of yours, told you it wasn't going to work and we need to be on the offensive. I've been saying since the start we need to make him look bad." He stops in front of me, leaning on his desk with his arms crossed on his chest and glaring down at me.

"Is this really the time, Katrina?"

"To remind you how smart, sexy, knowledgeable, and valuable I am? Always." He glares at me and even though I shouldn't, I let a grin stretch wide on my face.

"There's something more we don't know," he says, frustrated. "There's something we don't see. Why does he want the position so badly? It's not much of a pay increase, and it's more work. Sure, there's power in there, but not much more than being the director of A&R." I shrug.

"Maybe he just really hates you. Maybe he just wants you to lose." He sighs.

"Maybe. But . . ." He growls a frustrated noise that kind of turns me on, even though this is neither the time nor the place. "I just know there's something more. I feel it in my gut. There's a piece of this I don't understand, and if I don't get it before the vote, he's going to win and destroy Catalyst." A long, defeated breath leaves him. "We need a plan. We need . . . something. More than just being on the defense and you doing your dumb shit to piss him off."

A wide smile spreads on my lips.

Now *this*? This I can do. This is my specialty.

"Now you're speaking my language, boss man. Where should we start?"

When he looks at me again, he seems . . . nervous. I smile wider. "What are you thinking?" he asks cautiously.

Smart man, if we're being honest. I lean forward with excitement.

"We should break into his office again and bug it. I'm sure he's not nearly at stealthy as he seems with whatever weird ass plan he has going on." He looks at me like I'm insane. "Stupid shit isn't working. Sure, sending sex toys to the office from him is funny as fuck, but it's not enough. You say he has some grand scheme, so we need to figure out what it is."

"You want to . . ." He blinks at me. "You want to break into his office and plant a listening device?"

"New Jersey is a one-party consent state," I say. "I asked Andre." He opens his mouth and closes it, then opens and closes it again like he can't quite decide on what question he wants to ask.

"Andre?"

"My friend Liv's boyfriend. He's an FBI agent."

"And why are we planting this device?"

"Because he's planning something. I know our plan was just to make it so you get the job, and then you finally let me do some dumb shit—watching him get the wrong lunch order every day was really fun until he yelled at Janet that one time, you know—but I think we need a backup plan. Every time he looks at me, he has on a smile like he can't wait to rub something in my face. I want dirt on him." I smile, even though I feel sick to my stomach. "I want evidence that he's an asshole and that he's planning to fuck over Catalyst, and I want to get it by bugging his office or snooping in it." I let silence fill the space between us, allowing him time to digest and understand what I mean.

"I do think Warren has something we don't know planned, one last Hail Mary trick to try and get your job, and I know whatever it is has a chance of winning. He's been floundering, but something changed recently. And since we don't have anything other than a strange hunch that he's not dating Sav with the best intentions and the fact that he's an ass and none of the employees like him, I want more." Theo keeps staring at me, whether it's because he's contemplating or because he's so taken aback, he has no idea what to say, I'm not sure. Either way, I decide to put it all on the table while we're here.

"I also want to put a tracker on his car. That one's less legal, but could give us some really interesting insight."

I expect it then, of course.

His hesitance, his reluctance to jump in on my chaos. But I still get a bit of a dip of disappointment in my belly when he speaks.

"I don't know, Katrina," he says, and my stomach sinks further. "Doesn't it seem a bit . . . extreme?" I stare at him, the tiny shred of hope I felt when I decided it was time it get serious flickering like a birthday candle, the hope that he would somehow miraculously pass this test I set for him.

It's for the best, I tell myself. *If he's not into your brand of chaos, this will never work. If he completely brushes you off, ignores your ideas, or thinks you're insane, you'll get the ick.*

And what perfect timing, considering over the past weeks, I've started to like Theodore Carter.

Way, way more than I should for a fake relationship and much, much more than I should, considering we're talking about my boss.

I open my mouth to speak, but he keeps talking instead.

"We should start smaller," he says, his face considering, and my belly flips, that ember of hope lighting again. "I have access to the office call logs, and he uses a company phone. I can pull that report, send it to you, and you can do some digging." I stare at him, disbelieving and overwhelmed.

"You're not . . . You're not arguing?" His brow furrows.

"Why would I argue with you?"

"Uh, because I'm insane and want to put a tracker on the car of your rival?" He raises a brow and tips his head a bit in question.

"The rival who snuck into my office and attempted to sabotage my career to make himself look better? The one who is clearly manipulating my sister, who is too in love with him to realize?" I cringe. "The one who is trying to take over the business that is rightfully mine?" This time, I smile because I love it when he gets all righteous when he admits out loud that he deserves this company instead of acting chivalrous and modest. My hands go to my hips, and I give him a casual smile, even though my heart is beating out of my chest with his trust, with this new acceptance I didn't expect.

"So, you're not going to tell me that's too far and I need to scale it back?" I ask with a smile. He moves around the desk, walking toward me and pulling me up and into his arms, a reassurance I didn't realize I needed.

Because this man, this fake relationship, my boss, understands me better than almost anyone in my life does or has. He didn't hear my chaos and instantly accuse me of going too far or being crazy. He didn't tell me my brand of justice is too harsh or that I am too much.

And I'm not sure what to do with another failed attempt at getting the ick.

I'm also not sure what to do when I feel him press his lips into my hair and whisper, "I've learned to trust your brand of crazy."

FORTY-ONE

THEO

"Fuck yes, Katrina." I groan, taking her thick, dark hair into my hand and gripping tight as her mouth works me. "That's it, baby. God."

She's a fucking sight, naked on her knees before me, my cock in her mouth, wearing nothing but those fucking shoes she wore to the office today, the shoes that, despite it being the day from hell, I never once stopped thinking about digging into my back while I was cock deep in her once we were home.

Her perfect makeup is smudged a bit on her left eye, probably because she's already come twice, once on my hand, once on my face, and now she's taking me down her throat with such vigor, such demand, I wonder if she's getting off on this more than I am.

"You look so pretty like this, on your knees, taking me." Again, her eyes flare, her tongue going flat along the underside of my cock, and I have to fight the urge to close my eyes.

I want to imprint this image to memory—not that I need to, of course.

No, I don't need this memory to keep me warm at night because I'm going to have it plenty more times in the future. That first morning I saw her sleeping in my bed, curled up in my sheets after I woke up before her to work out, I knew.

I'm going to find a way to keep Katrina Delgado for real.

My hand tugs on her hair, guiding her along my hard cock, and she moans, her eyes drifting shut.

Jesus fucking Christ.

"Shit, you're already ready for another, aren't you, kitten? Purring on my cock while you suck me off." Her eyes open, and there's a new spark of desire there. Despite the pleasure coursing through my body, I smile. "Finger your pussy, baby. Suck me off, ride your fingers, get yourself close."

She moans around me, and I buck my hips without thinking, pushing farther down her throat, but she takes it, her eyes going lazy as she does, as her hips start to move. She's doing as she was told, sliding her fingers into her pussy and riding while she sucks me off.

The vision is magnificent. Her full tits sway gently as she moves, her eyes drooping with pleasure, her swollen, pink lips wrapped around me. Small sounds start to come from her, moans muffled by my dick, and her eyes open a bit wider.

She's close.

Good, because I've been close for some time. I slide out of her mouth, and she moans her disapproval. I can't help but smile before tipping my head to the bed.

"You're gonna ride me until you find it."

Another moan leaves her lips, but it's one full of pleasure and excitement, and she eagerly moves to her high heels, scrambling to follow me as I lie on my big bed, the sheets already mussed from our earlier behavior. I prop myself on some pillows, not willing to miss the show, and stroke my cock as she climbs up, straddling my lap.

"Stop," I say as she tries to reach for me, to position me.

"Theo—"

Her argument dies on her lips as my free hand finds her pussy, soaking wet, and I slide two fingers inside of her. "That's it, Katrina. Ride my fingers." Her eyes drift shut as she moans, and her hips start to buck as she flies closer to the edge. I pump my cock as I watch, feeling my balls tighten. It's been a day of torture, of wanting her, of dying to be deep inside of her.

Like every fucking day, really.

"Theo, I'm gonna—" she starts, her eyes snapping open, and instantly, I remove my fingers. "No! Fuck you." She groans, but I just smile, my hands moving to her hips.

"Put me inside, kitten." She sighs, but does as I ask, her head falling between us like a curtain, but I still see it. Her small hand, tipped in light purple, wraps around my thick cock. She slides the head over her slit, getting it slick and moaning as she does. She teases herself this way, rubbing it over her clit, her hips bucking. "Katrina," I say in warning, but I don't have to say anything more because she's slipping the head to her entrance and sliding down until her ass is on my hips.

A low, satisfied moan leaves her lips as she settles there, getting used to me. My fingertips dig into her hips, but then I move them, putting my hands behind my head to watch the show.

"Ride," I say, the single word sparking irritation in her eyes. She opens her mouth to argue, probably to give me shit as she's wont to do, but I buck my hips, sliding deeper and distracting her.

"Fuck you," she grits out but leans back a bit, letting the head of my cock graze her swollen G-spot, lifting her hips slightly and dropping them back down.

"That's what I'm trying to get you to do," I say. There's humor in my words, but barely because the feel of her cunt sliding up and down on my cock is too fucking much.

Finally, she drops any illusion of being annoyed or wanting to argue with me.

"Oh, god, fuck." She moans then lifts until the head almost slips out and slams back down. "God, you feel so good. Too fucking good, Theo."

I love that she calls me that, but when she's like this, unhinged and falling apart, I love it that much more. When she's like this, she's all fucking mine.

"That's it, baby. Do whatever feels good."

She leans back farther, one hand moving to the bed and the other to her clit. A fucking vision, her thick hips spread over mine, her tits bouncing with each thrust, her hand working herself fast as she tries to get herself there. One of my hands moves, rolling her nipple between thumb and forefinger.

"More," she moans. I know what she needs, so I start to buck my hips in time with hers to get that much deeper, the way she likes, the way she needs. Sweet, silly Katrina likes it rough. I pull her nipple as she slams on me.

"Come on, Katrina. I'm gonna fill you once you come. Come on, baby."

"Fuck, fuck, fuck." She moans, and with the next roll of her clit, I pinch harder, near painfully, and that does it. She screams as she shatters, her back arching, her fingers still working fervently on her clit as she convulses. I thrust up until most of her weight is on my hips rather than the bed and groan loud, my cock twitching and filling her as I come alongside her.

"So what are we on now?" I ask, running a hand through her hair after we've both cleaned up and gotten ready for bed. She's cuddled into my side in her sweet little pajamas, a loose cami with no bra and a pair of sleep shorts. The first time I saw her walking around my place in them, I threw her to my couch and proceeded to fuck her over the arm with those shorts around her ankles.

It seems I have a thing for fucking Katrina with her clothes still on.

She hasn't argued about it, at least.

"Hmm?" she asks sleepily, her eyes closed, her head on my chest.

"What number date are we on? Four? Five? Not sure what counts." Her body goes tight.

"What?"

"I'm not sure which dates count. We've got the dinner through The Ex Files, then Jeff's dinner. The engagement party. Lunch today. Does getting snowed in count?"

I'd count that for the rest of my life, forever grateful for the random snowstorm that changed everything.

"I . . ." She pauses, shifting, but I put my arm around her shoulders, making it so she can't move. "I don't know."

"You don't know if it counts?" She shrugs against my shoulder.

"I've never done this fake dating thing. Do the dates start counting before or after it got . . . real?" She whispers that last word, and I don't bother to fight the smile that spreads on my lips.

God, she's so fucking playing herself.

This has been real since the fucking beginning. Since the day she walked into my office for an interview. We've always been endgame. I've just been too stupid to see it, and she's been too scared.

When I don't speak, she does, and I know she still feels that way.

"It's gonna happen, Theo," she says. "The ick is gonna come."

"Mhmm," I respond, not convinced, rubbing my hand up and down her back soothingly.

"I'm serious." She tries to push up off my chest, but I keep my arm wrapped around her, not letting her.

"That's fine, Kat," I whisper. "That's fine. We'll always be us." Slowly, her body loosens, her shoulders losing their tension before finally, long minutes later, she falls asleep there, her soft breathing the only sound in the room.

That was a calm to her panic: my reassurance we'd always be us.

But what I didn't tell her was that I meant we're not going back. We're always going to be this new, beautiful version of us.

She might be the mistress of revenge, but I'm an expert at mergers and acquisitions.

FORTY-TWO

KAT

"Hey," Theo says from behind me, and when I turn to look at him, his head is sticking out of his office, something that looks like nerves written across his face.

Weird because I've never actually seen Theo Carter nervous, except for when we were driving to Jeff's for that first meeting, and that was an extenuating circumstance.

It's endearing. Adorable, even.

"What's up, boss man?"

The last week or so has been baffling in the best way yet. Every day, I wake up in Theo's bed and get ready while he works in his study. Then, we have breakfast together before he drives both of us into the office. We walk in hand in hand, he gives me a small kiss on my lips, and we go on about our day. At first, I thought the kiss was just in case Warren or Jeff saw, another check in the "convince everyone I'm actually marrying my assistant" column, but then I noticed he would still bend down, tuck my hair behind my ear, and press his lips to mine when we were the first ones here.

My confusion level has been at an all-time high, and my panic about not getting the ick yet is even higher.

All my mind keeps wondering is what happens if it never comes? What happens if, for the first time in my life, I actually like someone?

You'll fuck it all up, my common sense tells me. *Good fucking job, Katrina. You finally find a job you don't get bored with at a company you love and under a boss you respect, and you fuck that up with a fake relationship and then blur the lines even more with a messy friends-with-benefits thing.*

"Saturday, I know you have brunch with your friends, but Sunday, would you want to, uh." He pauses, nerves on his face getting more intense, more noticeable. "Go out with me?"

"Go out with you?"

"Yeah," he says then bites his lip.

"Like a . . . Like a date?" I ask with a smile.

That is definitely not butterflies in my stomach. Nope. Absolutely not.

"Yeah, I guess. Do you have plans on Sunday?"

"None other than sitting on your couch and vegging out."

"Oh, well, if you don't—" Now he's blushing, his cheeks turning a pink I've never seen. I put him out of his misery.

"I mean, I have nothing planned, and I'd love to . . . go out with you." A beat passes before he smiles, and it fills the room with sunshine and happiness.

"Okay. Good. Sounds . . . good." He nods wide, like he's confirming it before going back into his office. I fight a laugh as I shake my head and turn back to face my monitor.

Five minutes later, when the smile is still playing on my lips, I send a prayer up to whatever god is listening I get the ick.

And soon.

FORTY-THREE

KAT

I barely make it through two minutes of brunch with my friends before I blurt it out.

"I fucked my boss."

Cami stops taking off her jacket, and Liv looks at me with wide, shocked eyes.

Abbie starts a slow clap.

"About fucking time," she says with a big, gorgeous smile.

"I'm sorry. Did you say you fucked your boss?" Cami asks once she sits, her face not even a little impressed.

"Didn't you say this was a fake thing?" Liv asks, confused.

I bury my face in my hands and groan.

Abbie's hand moves, rubbing my back. "Don't worry, we've all been there, Kat." Her voice is low and consoling.

"We have?" Liv asks, and when I look up again, her eyes are moving from Abbie to Cami to me. "You've all fucked your bosses?"

"Well, no, but this is what we do, Liv," Cami says, rolling her eyes, exhaustion in her words. She loves Olivia Anderson, probably more than she loves Abbie and me, if only because Liv is her partner's daughter, but it's in a motherly way, where everything she does is met with just a hint of "dear god."

"You fuck your boss?" Liv repeats, aghast.

"Jesus Christ, Liv, no. You commiserate with friends and make them feel like they didn't just make a wildly stupid decision," Cami says then looks at me, an eyebrow raised. "For the record, that's a wildly stupid mistake you made."

"I know! I know," I say. "But it just . . . happened!"

"Oh, you just fell on his dick?" Cami asks. She's softened a lot since getting with Zack, but she's still Cami, after all.

"I also moved in with him," I add casually.

"What in the actual fuck is happening, Kat?" Cami asks.

"You moved in with him?" Even Abbie sounds taken aback. Liv is watching like this is a tennis match, her head moving from left to right.

I probably should have filled Abbie and Cami in a week ago when everything went down, but I . . . I couldn't do it. I couldn't bear to hear them confirm my own fears.

"How did we jump from a silly little fake engagement with your boss so he gets a job to you living with him and fucking him?"

"In my defense, we got drunk during that snowstorm and were stuck in the office. We woke up to his boss and that fuckwad Warren finding us on the couch, and Warren started going on about how we don't live together. I kind of . . . panicked because he's a creep and apparently lives in the same building. He's been taking note of whether my car is in the lot or not."

"What?!" Abbie and Cami yell at the same time.

"Why is this the first time I've heard about this?" Abbie asks.

"Why is he keeping track of where your car is parked? That sounds alarming, Kat," Cami says.

"That's not normal. Do you want Andre to look into this?" Liv asks. I sigh.

"Honestly, I'm still processing all of it myself," I say, looking at

Abbie. "And I have no idea, but it made Theo uncomfortable, so we decided it was better for me to just . . . stay at his place."

"Can we back up and hear the whole story?" Abbie asks. "I know I told you to fuck him the last time we had lunch, but my god. I didn't think you'd actually do it." I sigh but do as she asks.

I tell them about snooping in Warren's office and getting stuck in the closet, about making out with Theo and the palpable sexual tension. I tell them about getting distracted, about the alert, and everyone having already left the office. I fill them in on whiskey and truth or dare and Theo fucking me on Warren's desk and *"I'm sober."* Finally, I tell them about the morning after, about Theo saying I need to stay at his place and us deciding to enjoy this before I get the ick.

When I'm done, all three sit there slack-jawed and wide-eyed before I put the final nail in the coffin.

"He's been stocking my snacks."

"What?" Liv asks, but Abbie and Cami know. Abbie's eyes go soft, and Cami's shoulders drop in defeat.

"I have this snack drawer. He's been restocking it without me knowing. In his office, there's an entire closet of bulk snack boxes. And not just generic stuff. The things he knows I like, *Gansitos* and Vero *paletas*." I shrug. "He said he's had it for months. When I first started working there, he noticed I was snacking all the time, as I do, and he thought it was because I was so overworked, I had no time for meals. He felt guilty, so he bought a bunch of snacks and stuff."

"You didn't notice your drawer was never empty?" Cami asks. It's a fair question.

"I don't know. I wasn't really paying attention. I don't think he stocks it to the top, just throws a few things in there once in a while. I add things all the time. I just bought a lifetime supply of Reese's eggs. Granted, I'm down to like, five, but whatever."

"Valid," Livi says. "Remember the time I gave up Reese's eggs for dickwad?" I look at her.

"Yeah, and then you fucked his FBI agent, who you were fake

dating, so you, of all people, should understand how I got into this mess," I tease.

"Also valid," she responds with a dreamy smile.

"I'm assuming you don't have the ick yet," Abbie says, grabbing bread from the basket and slathering it with butter before taking a large bite.

I groan, collapsing with my head on the table, dishes making clinking noises as I do.

"Hey! Watch it! My drink!" Cami shouts, and I lift my head to glare at her, holding her precious Aperol spritz like it's a child she needs to care for.

"So, are you cured?" Liv asks. We all look at her. "This has never happened before, right?"

"Yes, this is in fact . . . uncharted territory. But I'm not cured."

"How do you know?" Liv asks.

"Because it's not an illness," Abbie answers with a motherly, disappointed look directed at me.

"Oh, it definitely is," I defend.

"Having a really great gut instinct is not an illness, Kat. Some people would kill for your ability."

"Oh, yeah, it's just wonderful never having a serious relationship because I randomly stop liking even the best guys for basically no reason."

"You've saved yourself from wasting too much of your time on people not worth the effort. You've saved yourself from so much heartbreak, Kat." I don't mention the amount of heartbreak my ick has caused, of how many times I've cried when it settled in, of how I felt resigned to live alone forever.

But they all know. I can tell from the soft looks all three of them give me and each other. Thankfully, the waitress comes and takes our brunch orders, offering me a bit of a break from the third degree.

The break, of course, doesn't last long. "So what are you going to do about it?" Abbie asks as soon as the server walks off.

"What do you mean?"

"What are you going to do about not getting the ick yet? You work together and you apparently live together. You're fucking. How many dates have you been on?"

"Five," I mumble under my breath.

"Two away," Liv says, as if I can't do math. I glare at her.

"So? What are you going to do?" Abbie repeats while Cami stares at me, reading me. I want to hide from them both.

"I . . . I don't know. I haven't really thought about it." That's a lie. The looming possibility of getting the ick is all I've been able to think about for the last few weeks, if I'm being honest.

"Can you, like, induce it?" Liv asks with genuine curiosity in her words.

"What do you mean?"

"Like . . . can you make yourself get the ick? Or speed the process along?" I think about it.

"I don't know," I say honestly. "I've never had the need to. It's not usually a perk of my stunning personality, having to force myself to get what comes naturally."

"When are you guys doing something next?"

"He asked me out yesterday," I admit. "He's taking me on a date." Abbie and Cami exchange a look I refuse to decode, even though I don't have to.

"A date?" Abbie asks. I nod, my eyes moving to my plate.

"What kind of date? What's the event?" Cami asks. I mumble my answer under my breath.

"What?"

"I said, it's just a date. No . . ." I pause, taking a deep breath. "No event. He's just . . . taking me out."

I know what their faces are going to show before I even look up—it's what's been going through my mind the whole time.

"So it's a date just for . . . you guys?" I shrug.

"I guess." I keep my eyes down, not wanting to see the looks they're exchanging.

"Okay, so, you should try to get the ick," Abbie says, clapping her hands. When I do finally raise my head, her face is glowing as always, but her eyes are determined. It's the same look she gets when she's ready to scheme, when she's ready to tackle a task, be it clearing out my closet and helping me find my "brand" or thinking of a list of ways to fuck with her douchey ex.

"What?" I ask, but she ignores me.

"Who has a pen? Paper?"

"Me!" Liv says, raising her hand and then digging in her too-full bag. She hands Abbie a spiral-bound notebook and a pen. Abbie takes it with a smile before making space next to her plate, clicking the pen, and finding a clear page.

"We're going to make you get the ick," she says with a wide smile. "We're going to make a list of things that have been deal breakers for you in the past. Big and small, all of them. Then you can test him." I take in her words and let them sink in.

It's . . . It's not a bad idea.

"And what happens if she doesn't?" Liv asks. "What happens if she tries all these things and still doesn't get the ick?" I scoff.

"That won't happen, trust me."

"But what if?" she asks again. I don't answer. I don't know. That's never been an option for me. Abbie looks at all of us, a wide, happy smile on her lips before she answers.

"Then he's her person."

I refuse to acknowledge the kernel of hope those words ignite in my chest.

FORTY-FOUR

KAT

"You talked to your sister, I see," I say as Theo's hand engulfs mine and he leads me through a gravel parking lot and to a small building on the property of the farm he brought me to. It doesn't look like much, just a few cars in an ugly parking lot and a small shack with hand-painted signs. Definitely not somewhere I'd think Theo Carter of the designer clothes and penthouse apartment would visit.

But beyond all of that are fields.

As far as the eye can see, there's nothing but tulips. Hundreds of thousands cover the ground. There are reds and yellows and a bit of green, pink and white and even purple, and when a gentle breeze blows, from this far out, it looks like wind on a lake, the entire field moving in sync.

"Lately, all my sister wants to talk to me about is you," he replies, and I look up at him as we walk, smiling. I never notice how tall, how big Theo is until we're standing like this, him next to me, and I realize I have to actually look up at him to see him, but I like it. I like feeling small and delicate.

I also get the rare image of Theo in something other than a suit and dress shirt. Today, he's in a tightly-fitted Henley, the material clinging to his muscles normally hidden under his work clothes, and a pair of casual khaki jeans. He almost looks . . . normal. Definitely much less like the music media mogul most know him as. And even though I've seen him around his apartment in casual clothes, seeing it out in public feels . . . different. Somehow more intimate. Like I get this version of him that he doesn't give to just anyone.

"What do you normally talk about?" I ask. "When you're not gossiping about me."

There's a beat before he answers, confusion in his words.

"I'm not sure actually." He laughs. "I guess I always just let her talk and don't contribute much. She likes it that way."

"So, your normal routine," I say with a laugh, and he nods as we walk, *Tour the Tulips!* written in big, red, hand-painted letters on a large wooden sign.

The nosy part of me is dying to know what that means, if he normally says nothing and now something has changed, and he's talking to his sister more. Is he simply replying to her questions and needling? Is he talking about me willingly? What is he saying? Is it all part of the game we're playing?

Theo greets the man at the counter, buying two passes for admittance while I look around the cute shop and try not to get lost in my head and overthink, well, everything, as I tend to do.

"Come on," he says, grabbing my hand and tugging me toward the back entrance, where the fields are. I have no choice but to do what I always do, one way or another, and trust Theo blindly.

We're standing in the middle of a field, my mind blown by the beauty, my hand dipping to run across the tips of the barely open blooms, when I force myself to speak. We've wandered for almost an hour in silence. A comfortable silence, but I'd be lying if I said it was a normal one.

"My *abuela*, she loved tulips," I say as I look out over the flowers.

I feel his eyes on me, burning, but don't turn to look at him. "They don't grow in Mexico, it doesn't get cold enough for long enough there, so we'd send her pre-frozen bulbs when we could find them. Her entire home in Michoacán was covered in photos and paintings and statues of tulips." I smile, remembering the yearly childhood trips with my mom I'd look forward to all year, spending a month in the summer visiting her parents. "She was an amazing gardener, with pots on every surface with plants and flowers, raised beds in her little yard growing different vegetables. Peppers and tomatoes and tomatillos. She'd try to teach me every summer, but I swear, everything I touched died." Sighing, I let the memories I usually keep behind a wall seep in. "She passed away when I was twenty-five, but I see tulips, and they always make me think of her." A new moment of silence passes, and I wonder if this will be it, if we'll lapse back into quiet, but then Theo speaks.

"My mom loved it here," he says, his voice low and gravelly. It makes me stand straight and turn toward him—his words and the way he says them—my eyes moving to him. He's standing a few feet away, his hands in his pockets, looking around the fields.

And he's vehemently avoiding my eyes.

"Yeah?" I ask, not trying to say too much or stop him from talking, but wanting to encourage this small share all the same. He nods.

"Tulips were her favorite flowers. Everything in our house growing up was tulips. Curtains and art and plates with tiny tulips on the edges." I stare out across the fields, same as him, giving him space to speak if he wants to.

Something about this moment feels sacred, like he's sharing a secret he's kept safe his whole life with me.

"My parents got engaged here," he continues, his words a mere whisper. "My dad knew Mom loved tulips, and when he got the okay from my grandfather to marry her, he waited a full nine months until it was tulip season, until he could bring her here." A small chuckle escapes as he shakes his head. "My dad always said it pissed my mom off. She was ready to get married, and they had the talk, and then . . .

nothing. My mom used to joke that she was this close"—he pinches his fingers together, but doesn't look at me—"to giving him an ultimatum. But she held out hope, and good thing she did, because he got to propose here."

Again, I give him time to stand there and come to terms with what he's saying, what he's sharing, and decide if he wants to tell me more.

"I wasn't sure why I brought you here," he says, finally looking at me.

"I'm glad you did," I whisper, but he continues speaking as if I didn't say a word, taking two steps closer to me.

"But now that I'm here, I get it. I get it. She's here," he says, the words traveling on the wind and wrapping around me, squeezing tight.

"Your mom?" I whisper. He nods, but isn't looking at me again, instead gazing over the fields, lost in thought.

"You'll never meet her, not really. But I thought if I brought you here, she could meet you."

"I wish I could have," I whisper. "Met her."

The lump in my throat doesn't ease as he grips my hand or as he moves me, turning me until we're facing each other.

It doesn't ease as an arm wraps around my waist or when my arms loop around his neck.

It only lessens when my eyes drift close, when his lips move to mine, and the first tear falls as a strong, temperamental spring wind whips around us, seeming to come from all angles at once and whipping my hair up with it.

"I think that means she likes you," he whispers when he breaks the kiss, but he doesn't say anything else as his thumb grazes over my cheek, wiping the tear away.

And even if it's silly, even if it's just in my head, I can't help but hope he's right.

🌷

I wander around the small farm store decked out in treats and snacks and fertilizers and loads and loads of tulips, while Theo runs off to use the bathroom and grab a drink.

Today has been amazing. We wandered the fields for what felt like an eternity, barely speaking as we did, but not in a bad way. In a comfortable way. The way a couple does when they know everything about each other. When they talk openly and honestly and comfortably enough that there's nothing left to say.

The kind of people who don't need words to speak to one another.

And it scared the fuck out of me.

Because every moment I spend with Theo, I feel good, happy. I feel . . . like I'm home.

All my life, I've been searching for that moment, that person we hear about from the second we can understand relationships. The one. The love of your life. The person with whom you feel an unbreakable bond and a kinship. The person who holds tight to the other end of the invisible string tying you together.

I've watched Abbie and Cami and Livi find it. Watched them discover their other halves were close. I've seen how when they're together, their bodies lean closer to each other, like magnets constantly pulled together.

And I'd be lying if I said I didn't envy it, wasn't desperate to find that myself.

And here I am, in the single situation I've gotten myself into where I can't have that with someone, and I feel it.

The tug in my belly. Is it that golden thread tying me to someone? To him?

And for the first time in my fucking life, I'm not getting the ick.

I don't even sense that it's near.

Normally, if I'm liking a guy and we're on date four or five, I start to notice things. Small moments that aren't a fully blown ick, things I tell myself to ignore, tell myself they're not too big of a deal, that I can live with a man who likes to wear socks and sandals or who doesn't ever want a pet. But then something happens, and it cements they just aren't for me.

But with Theo, I don't have even the smallest hint of the ick.

Nothing.

Abbie's warning words from when I first filled them in on this scheme come back to haunt me. *What if you don't get the ick?* I was so sure I would and we could move on once this was over.

And here I am, more confused than ever before.

Long minutes later, I feel his warm hand on the small of my back.

"You good?" he asks, his voice low and rumbly, for my ears only.

I nod and turn to look at him, shocked to see a big bouquet of red tulips in his hands.

"Uh, yeah. Yeah. I was just looking around." His hand reaches back toward his pocket.

"You want anything? I've got it," he starts, but I shake my head and laugh.

"God, you're good, Theo. You don't need to spend more money on me. We're good."

"These are for you," he says, handing me the bouquet. Again, that strange mix of joy and dread slinks through my veins. I take them with a smile and a whispered thank you then look toward the door, a dark, menacing sky visible through the glass. "We should head back. It's about to pour." Wordlessly, he reaches for my hand, walking me out toward the car.

We're in the gravel parking lot, all of the other visitors already long gone, probably because they, unlike us, looked at the weather report before making a trek to the middle of nowhere, when the rain starts.

It's not just a cute little spring sprinkle. It's a full-on downpour, the sky opening and dumping what feels like gallons upon gallons on us. Almost instantly, my clothes are drenched. Theo's hand in mine tugs as he tries to rush me to his car, but I stop.

I stand there, one arm out, smiling to the sky as water falls on my face. There's no saving my makeup, my hair, or my outfit, so why not enjoy the cool rain, the roll of thunder, and the way the fields of tulips in the distance dance.

This is it, I think. *My chance to get the ick.*

Someone who can't be spontaneous with me is definitely an ick for me, and Theodore Carter is the least spontaneous person I know. I think the time he told Jeff he was getting married without even a woman in mind was the first and only time he moved on any impulse.

And maybe that night in the office when it snowed. But I'm ignoring that for now.

"What are you doing, Katrina?" he asks, almost shouting over the sound of the falling rain.

"Dance with me!" I shout back, holding my arms out.

"What?"

"Dance with me! In the rain!" A million looks cross his face, and I know. I know this is the moment it's going to happen. He's going to say no and run to the car, and I'm going to get the ick.

I'm going to be safe, and we can salvage this fake relationship and our working relationship, and we'll be fine.

"Dance with you?" he asks, taking a step closer, like he can't hear me. I smile and nod, pulling my hand from his and beginning to twirl in the empty parking lot. For a split second, I let my mind contemplate how we were so distracted in the fields not to notice everyone leaving or the dark clouds rolling in.

It's better than anticipating the disappointment that's going to come when Theo laughs at my request and tells me to get into the car.

But as seems to be his way, Theo surprises me.

His warm arm wraps my waist, my shirt already soaked and clinging to my skin, and he pulls me close until I'm flush against his body. He grabs the flowers and tosses them to the ground, something that should upset me, but I can't be bothered in this moment. It's much too magical.

My heart pounds as I take in every single sensation.

The cool spring rain on my skin.

The comforting warmth of his body on mine.

The gravel under my feet.

But mostly, the way his blue eyes are staring into mine, warmth seeping into them.

His body begins to sway, mine moving with him as my arms move up, wrapping around his shoulders, and then we're dancing in the rain together in the parking lot of the tulip farm where his parents fell in love. His head dips, pressing into the place between my neck and shoulder, and one of my hands slides up, touching and twirling his hair.

"I didn't think you'd do it," I whisper as he dances in small circles with me, the rain soaking us to the bone. I should probably feel cold, but all I can feel is the warmth of his body.

"Dance with you?" he asks. He starts to lift his head, but I can't let him do that. I can't. I can't look at him now when he's passing any and every test I give him, when I'm not getting that ick I need to get.

When I might see thoughts and emotions and actions in his eyes that I'm not ready to see. My hand on his neck holds him, pressing a gentle request to stay just like this.

Instead, I nod into his chest.

"I don't know if there's anything I wouldn't do if you asked me, Kat," he says, using that nickname he rarely does.

I don't say anything else, but I am incredibly grateful for the pouring rain that masks the tears running down my cheeks as I realize how deeply screwed I am.

When we get home and I log on to my computer, only one thing is on my mind as I search tulip flower color meaning.

And when I see the results, the mix of panic and joy surges once more.

Love.

FORTY-FIVE

KAT

Good luck. Call me if you need me.

That's what the note on the bouquet of flowers sitting in the kitchen at 8 am this morning read.

A note in Theo's handwriting, the masculine script strangely neat, dark black lines on thick cream cardstock.

Red tulips, in case you were wondering.

He left early in the morning, before the sun was up, needing to drive to the city to meet up with a potential artist. When he did, he leaned over my body, pressed a kiss to my temple, and lifted the warm duvet up to cover my exposed shoulder.

It sends me spiraling, and by the time I arrive at the hotel for the charity luncheon Judy is hosting, I'm on edge.

Because what the fuck am I doing? Abbie and Cami were right— this is going on for too long, and it's getting too close, and things are getting messy.

So fucking messy.

And that mess only escalates when I'm seated at a table with

Savannah and Melody across from me. From what Sav told me when we saw the seating chart, except for Whitney, who is a board member at Catalyst, all of the other women are Melody's friends, all catty bitches Savannah can't stand but plays nice with because, as she said, *that's what you do.*

And shit hits the fan before lunch is even served.

"So, Katrina, how is the wedding planning going?" Whitney asks with a kind smile, leaning across the table to catch my eye. I smile back at her, grateful for the opportunity to continue Theo's mission, to keep trying to convince them we're real.

"Oh, you know, we're just enjoying this time being engaged and out in the open right now. We spent so long keeping things quiet."

"Yeah, why did you keep things so quiet for so long?" Charity, one of Melody's bitchy friends, asks. Her smug smile makes me want to give a bitchy reply, but instead, I take a deep breath through my nose and smile at her.

"Well, you know. I'm his assistant and I really like my job. We wanted to keep things professional in case it didn't work out, that way it wouldn't make things weird. Thankfully, it did," I explain with a forced smile.

"Well, either way, I'm glad. He seems so happy when he's around you," Savannah says. "Honestly, I can't believe I didn't see it earlier. You two always worked like such a well-oiled machine. I just know you are going to make it for the long haul," Whitney agrees.

Before I can even mentally celebrate this small win, Melody's big, stupid mouth opens.

"I just can't imagine being with him forever," Melody says loudly, grabbing everyone's attention. I start to speak, but Savannah reaches out, grabbing my hand and squeezing. It seems she understands I'm about to rip her a new one and is trying to hold me to reality. I wonder if her brother told her I'm not a fan of Melody and asked her to keep an eye on me. It would be a very Theo thing to do.

"He's just so . . . closed off, you know?" Bianca, another one of Melody's friends, asks, and my fingers slowly fold in on themselves.

Don't punch rich bitches at a company event, Katrina, I can almost hear Theo saying in my head. *It's not worth it.*

"I don't," I say with a near-painful smile. I grip Savannah's hand harder and she coughs out a laugh.

"He's just . . . His face is always so angry looking," Melody says with a snotty smile. "It's not cute."

I snap.

"Well, just for your information, your resting bitch face isn't exactly attractive, you know? At least Theo's grumpy face is hot as fuck." I shrug and smile, watching her turn red. "Just because you don't have two whole brain cells to rub together to read people's emotions or the fucking room, doesn't mean someone is angry." Melody opens her mouth as if she wants to snap back at me before she closes it and smiles.

I know that can't mean anything good. She's going in for the kill.

"When he was with me, he was anything but closed off," Melody says, a twinkle in her eyes. It's a lie, but it doesn't stop inquisitive eyes from moving from her and then to me, including Whitney's.

"Melody, drop it. You sound stupid." Savannah groans, but Melody ignores her.

"Did you know we dated?" she asks one of the listening ears. "Last May. Which is so strange because now, suddenly, he's marrying . . . her." I roll my eyes, turning to Whitney with an exasperated look.

"Our Melody is leaving out that it was just one dinner, and Theo dropped her off at home right after." I know this is a fact now. Theo and I gave each other a full rundown of who and what we were involved with during the time we had, supposedly, been dating. "And like I told you, that was the catalyst to us finally getting together." I turn to Whitney fully now and smile wide. "I saw that meeting on his calendar and gosh, I don't know. Something snapped in me. I risked it all and told Theo how I felt, because I was just sick to my stomach about him dating someone. Thankfully, he felt the same. In fact, if I remember correctly, he only went on that date as a favor to your father, Melody." I cover my mouth, and my eyes go wide. "Oops, I probably wasn't supposed to tell you that."

She grinds her teeth.

"Must be a bummer, being so . . . obnoxious your daddy has to get you dates. And then not being able to land the second one on your own? Eek." I give her a falsely sympathetic look.

"Like he'll be with you for long. We all know this is a crock of shit and he's just waiting for the moment he can dump your ass," Melody snaps.

"Drop it, Melody. Jealousy is not a good look on you," Savannah says, boredom in her voice, but I see it there—the irritation brewing on her face. "We all know you've been up his ass for years, trying to land a rich man. You tried; you failed. Don't be so pissy because you're bitter and Teddy ended up with someone better than you."

Unfortunately, when I look at Melody, I see the malice curling there in her eyes, a snake ready to strike. Her smile spreads like an oil slick, devious and dangerous.

"Did you know I also dated Warren for a bit there? Much more than one date . . ." The smile spreads further, and she looks at her nails like this entire conversation is inconsequential to her.

"I thought it was a bit strange when you started dating him. He always told me you weren't his style. Too young, too naive." She shrugs. "I guess he's lowering his standards, just like your brother."

That's when the luncheon turns into a brawl.

"Katrina," his voice says, smooth and expectant, and I wonder if Theo's heard yet, if news has already traveled his way. "To what do I owe the honor of hearing your voice on the phone?" There's noise in the background, cars bustling and people shouting, and I can almost picture his scowl, the way he'd probably cover one ear to hear better, the way he'd bend his head down a bit, trying to concentrate.

"I went to Judy's luncheon today," I say, leaving it at that.

"I know that. I'm wondering why you're calling me and not there still." Without even seeing him, I know he checks his watch, taking in the time. "It ends at 3, and it's not even 1."

I ignore the way he knows what time this dumb lunch ends, the fact that he cares about where I am and when I'll be done, because that will continue the spiral of my mind going places I don't have the wherewithal to go.

Instead, I move back toward my goal of getting the ick.

The fact that it hasn't happened yet fills me with dread any time I think of it. When it finally happens, I think this time, it's going to hurt. It's not going to be the easy, vague relief mixed with mild disappointment it usually is.

It's going to be losing this . . . thing we've been pretending to build that, at some point, started to feel a lot less fake and a whole lot more real.

At night, when the room is quiet and my thoughts get too loud right before I fall asleep tucked into him, the fucked-up part of my mind that loves to stir the pot wonders if it ever was fake.

But my mission to get the ick comes to life again—a man who can't handle that I might do dumb shit, might get into an argument at a charity lunch, might accidentally incite his sister into getting into a fight simply isn't for me. A man who can't understand that I am chaos personified, that I take action and then think, will never work for me.

Which means Theodore Carter is not for me.

Theo likes predictability. He likes when things go according to his well-thought-out plans, when they move along smoothly and without hiccups. He's going to be annoyed, furious, even, that I did this, that I'm associated with him, which means this reflects poorly on him.

And that will be an ick.

In a way, I have to wonder if that's why I did it, why I didn't stop the fight when I saw things going badly.

"Savannah got into a fight so it ended early."

There's a long pause before Theo speaks.

"I'm sorry?"

"I said, Savannah got into a fight so it ended early," I repeat. There's another stretch of silence, and I fill it in. "Well, I guess it wasn't a full-blown fight, but it got close." Another pause and more silence. "I stopped her before there was any real damage if that helps at all."

And I did. While she got one good punch at Melody's face (though, I noted with disappointment, not on her shitty fake nose), it degraded into a catfight of the hair-pulling and slapping variety before I stepped in and tugged Savannah off her.

There's a deep breath before he finally speaks, exhaustion in his words, and hearing them makes me smile. I'm not sure what that says about me, but I'm assuming nothing great.

"I'll be home in an hour."

FORTY-SIX

KAT

"So, you're telling me Melody implied Warren was lowering his standards to be with Savannah and my sister just . . . lunged at her?" I nod and smile, pulling another long string of noodles from the white takeout container Theo grabbed on his way home.

Home.

God.

Why does that feel so good?

"Melody is a piece of work," I say. "She was acting all weird and sweet to me until we sat down, and then bam, she started telling Whitney all about how she doesn't believe we're actually together. It felt very . . . familiar, you know? Like the time Warren cornered me in the break room."

"So you think they're working together?"

"I don't know. I mean, he wasn't even there. But it does kind of lean into my idea that they're together somehow. She was definitely trying to make me look bad. Even once I got Savannah off her, she was screaming to Judy that this was all my fault and that I was going to ruin everything if I married you." Again, Theo hums.

"Well, if it helps, Jeff called right after I got off the phone with you to fill me in, and he couldn't stop laughing. Told me you were a feisty one and I'd better make sure not to piss you off." I sit back with my mouth open.

"I didn't even fight! Your sister did!" That smile I love so much slides across his face, and I can't help but return it.

"Yeah, but my sister gave you the stamp of approval, which means in Jeff's eyes, you two are forever in cahoots."

"Did you just say *in cahoots*?" He pauses and stares at me, confused.

"Yes . . . ?"

"God, you're so old." That makes him roll his eyes and toss a wrapped fortune cookie at me. I giggle and return the favor, and we settle into a comfortable silence as we eat, but something is still weighing on me.

"So are you . . ." I pause, taking a sip of my soda and avoiding his eyes. "Are you mad?"

"Am I mad?" he asks, and I nod. "About what?"

"That Savannah got into a fight. That I kind of incited said fight. That I didn't stop it before she got a good hit in." I'm rambling as I pick at a napkin, making tiny bits of confetti from it. His hands reach out, grabbing mine and stopping my destruction.

"Kat, look at me." I do because he used my nickname, the one he never used to use, but now occasionally does, and it still throws me off. "Why would I be mad?"

"I mean, there are a million reasons," I say, pausing.

"Tell me all of them." I look up and see his face is serious, and I give him an exasperated look.

"Come on, Theo. There are a million. Maybe because I got into a fight with Ray Harmon's daughter? Or that I fucked up Judy's lunch? My entire mission is to make this"—I wave a hand between us—"believable, and instead, I started a riot!"

A small smile forms on his lips .

"And?"

"And? And I fucked that up! I couldn't handle my emotions and I let Melody win. I wanted to bait her because she was being a bitch and trying to make me feel like shit and it worked. I did feel like shit, thinking about her being with you and telling everyone we were fake." I pause, realizing I slipped, possibly revealing my feelings are becoming anything but fake. I keep talking to cover. "Because I didn't want to fuck up our plan. Of course."

He smiles, the kind of smile that is almost like he knows something I don't.

"Of course," he says with playfulness in his words, then he stands, grabbing trash from the table and walking toward the garbage can beneath the sink.

"But . . . you're not mad." He shakes his head, walking back toward me. "How?"

"How?"

"How are you not mad? This is . . . This is everything you wanted to avoid. Drama, chaos, mess . . ."

"I've come to learn that if I want you, I have to take all of you, Katrina. And I like every bit of you. You are chaos, and somehow, when you're around, I like a little bit of chaos." He puts a hand out for me to grab and tugs, lifting me until I'm flush against him.

"You like me," I whisper.

"I do, Kat." And then he kisses me, and I forget all of the reasons I wanted him not to like that. I forget my icks and I forget Melody and I forget this scheme of ours, and there's just Theo, kissing me in his penthouse on a Saturday night over Chinese.

His lips trail down my neck and his hands move down to my ass before he hoists me up, forcing me to wrap my legs around his hips.

"I'm just glad you didn't get a shot in. You'd cause some damage, and I'd rather not have to visit you in prison. Conjugal visits don't sound that fun, in my opinion," he says as he starts to move, to walk me to the bedroom as he peppers my neck with kisses. I smile and shrug.

"I don't know. It could be a fun little role-play situation," I say, attempting to ignore the idea of conjugal visits with Theo. His fingers dig into my hips, and I giggle at the raw heat in his eyes.

"The amount I like to fuck you, I don't think the DOJ would allow."

FORTY-SEVEN

THEO

Katrina is quiet the entire drive to the hotel where the annual gala takes place the following Saturday, and I don't like it.

It's so far off what I have grown to expect from her, it makes me uneasy. But she packed up her overnight bag in near silence, walked down the stairs from my penthouse to the car holding it and a dress bag despite me insisting I do it for her, and then stared out the window the entire drive.

"Okay," I say once we get into our hotel room, Katrina throwing her bags onto the bed, keeping her back to me. "What's going on?"

I booked the room months earlier, when Katrina and I first started this game, so there are two queen beds, though I only plan to use one of them. I can already see her trying to distance herself, though, to claim one bed as "hers."

She thinks this will be over as soon as the vote is.

But she's wrong. So damn wrong.

This is us now, whether or not she gets some kind of mythical ick.

"What?" she asks, not even turning to look at me, instead rifling through her bag, but not actually grabbing anything.

I move, leaning against the wall facing her, crossing my arms on my chest. "I'm not playing this game, Katrina. What's going on?"

"Nothing, I'm just looking for my—" I cut her off, walking toward her and grabbing her wrist, turning her body to face mine, and putting my hands on her jaw. As I hold her face, forcing her to look at me, she moves her own hands on instinct, looping them around my neck.

God, she's so fucking gone and she doesn't even know it. Or doesn't want to admit it, at the very least.

Before I get into my question, I shift her even closer, tipping her head up a bit to press my lips to hers, the warmth of her sliding through my veins as I do.

It's what she does to me. She warms me, soothes me. When I'm stressed or overwhelmed and feeling lost, all I have to do is look at her, touch her, remind myself she's real, and it eases. When I pull back from the kiss, her eyes are hooded, but I can see it still.

I do the same to her.

And that... *That* is why this isn't going to end. I'll be damned if I give that up or if I let her give that up for herself. We both need this, need each other.

"What's wrong, Katrina?" I whisper, my breath and lips brushing against hers. Her arms tighten around my neck and her eyes close fully, like she's still fighting it. Quickly, I move us so I'm sitting on the bed she was standing in front of, lifting and manipulating her so she's straddling me. It's not sexual, though I do love having her like this, too.

It's a practical position, especially when one of my arms slides along her lower back, pinning her against me, while the other brushes her hair back behind her shoulders while I wait for her to answer.

"I haven't gotten the ick yet," she whispers.

"Okay . . . ," I drawl.

"I still like you," she says, and it feels like a confession. My thumb brushes over her skin.

"And I still like you," I inform her.

"But you're normal."

"I think that's the first time you've ever described me like that. Normal," I say, trying to get a smile on her face. It's a success when she lets out a small laugh.

"Don't get used to it."

"I could get used to a lot of things when it comes to you." Her body tightens, and she buries her face in my neck, hiding away from my words and the emotions they create. I allow it when she starts to speak into the skin there.

"Tonight is date seven."

"Hmm," I say, letting her have this, running my fingers through her hair gently, her body relaxing further into me.

"I never make it past seven, Theo."

There it is.

Tonight is when we're tested. When she finds out if I'm going to be the first to make it further, if I'm passing her ick factor.

But doesn't she see?

We're on date one hundred. Two hundred. I've been seeing her every day for almost a year and she hasn't gotten the ick that I know of. We've been engaged for almost three months and she's still here. She's been sleeping in my bed for weeks and we're still solid.

We're well past seven.

"Katrina, don't you—" I start before my phone rings. My brow furrows as I glare at the device on the other bed and how Katrina's body tenses and then starts to move, attempting to extricate herself from my hold.

"You should take that."

"Katrina—"

"I have to take a shower and start getting ready." She steps back farther, but I grab her hand as I stand, her eyes meeting mine.

Fear.

Fear is in her eyes. But why? What is she so fucking terrified of, and why does this arbitrary date have to change anything?

"I want to finish this conversation. Right after your shower." It shouldn't stay in the air between us. Even though it's an obnoxious company party, I want her to enjoy tonight. I want to enjoy tonight with her.

"I have to get ready," she whispers, bending to the bed and lifting my phone as if to show me the time. "I have to unpack."

"We're talking about this soon."

"Sure," she says, her smile small and fake, twisting a knife in my gut. "Later." She walks off as I tap the screen to answer the call, but even as she does, I can hear what she didn't say out loud.

. . . *or never.*

FORTY-EIGHT

KAT

"I hate to rush you, but we really do have to head down. Judy will murder me if we're late," Theo says from the bedroom of the hotel room while I'm sitting on the closed toilet in the bathroom, finishing the buckle of my shoe.

It turns out I wasn't bullshitting when I told him I couldn't have some grand conversation about our nonexistent relationship after his call because I needed to get ready. Between my shower, where I shaved every square inch of my body, double cleansed my hair, and did a hair mask, painting my nails while I did a face mask, and blowing out and setting my thick hair in rollers before meticulously painting on my face, I've been in this bathroom for what feels like an eternity.

I definitely didn't do everything and more with the intent of not leaving this bathroom. Nope. Absolutely not.

But I won't deny having *the talk* with Theo is making my stomach hurt so much, I've barely been able to sip on the iced coffee he brought in for me about an hour ago. A plastic cup sits on the vanity, filled with a watered-down latte and no ice.

I don't want to hear about how it will be good when I finally get the ick, how it will make things easier, how we agreed to be temporary. How once he gets the job and things settle, we'll be going back to how things were. I don't want to be reminded of how Theo has no time for a relationship, that his job will always come first and the past few months didn't change that.

No, I just want to enjoy this last night before the ick happens. I'd much rather live in my delusional world, thank you very much.

"I'm almost done!" I shout then start toward the bedroom, fumbling with one of the long teardrop earrings Abbie lent me as I walk into the room. Finally, it's in, and I snap it shut before standing straight and turning toward him, wiping my hands down the front of my dress.

God. He looks good. So fucking good in an impeccably-tailored black tuxedo, his hair slicked back, his face shaved clean, his hands in his pockets.

He looks perfect. And without even looking, I know instinctively we look perfect together, a power couple in every sense of the word.

I'm wearing the floor-length dress I bought with Savannah, black with no sleeves, just impossibly thin straps dotted with black crystals. There's nearly no back, and instead, the fabric dips and drapes to just above where my spine ends. The top isn't anything special, and although the slightly-scooped neckline is meant to be almost modest, with my curves, it all looks decadent. It skims tightly along my hips and thighs before flaring out to the floor with a slit that reaches up to my mid-thigh. It's simple and sexy, the female equivalent to a tux, in a way.

The ultimate little black dress.

My hair is in big, loose curls, one side pinned back with a hair clip adorned with black crystals of different sizes. With winged liner and a red lip, it's all giving very much old Hollywood glamour, and I fucking love it.

Standing a few feet from Theo, I wait for him, watching his eyes roam every inch of my outfit, my hair, my makeup, the high stiletto shoes with a peep toe, red nails peeking through.

An eternity passes, and soon, I start to feel self-conscious.

"Is this . . . Is this okay?" I ask, fighting the urge to bite my lip because even though my lips are stained red (an alleged "kiss-proof" find from Abbie, my resident makeup guru), I don't trust that kind of shit not to smudge or transfer to my teeth.

He doesn't speak still, instead staying leaned against the wall, ankles crossed at his shiny wing-tip shoes, hands in his pockets, continuing to take me in.

Fuck. It's too much.

"I . . . I have another dress. It's more . . . covered. I can go change —" I step to reach for the backup dress I brought, but his growling voice stops me.

"If you take a single thing off, Katrina, we're never leaving this fucking hotel room. Not for the gala, not for dinner, not for fucking breakfast tomorrow." His lips quirk a bit. "I'll call room service for sustenance, but that's it."

Sustenance. Because . . .

He hears the words I don't say.

"Sustenance because I'll fuck you for twelve hours straight, minimal breaks."

Oh, I think.

"Oh," I say out loud. "That would require a bit of sustenance." My eyes are wide, and I feel them go wider as he smiles and shakes his head. My heart beats out of my chest as he takes his hands from his pockets, as he pushes off the wall and takes the few steps to me, winding one arm around my back and tugging me close until I'm up against him with an *oof.*

Then he tips his head down, preparing to press his lips to mine.

"Theo! My makeup!"

"Don't give a shit about your makeup," he says, his voice a low rumble against my chest. A bra is impossible in this dress, and suddenly, I'm thankful for the annoying padding in bras, because I feel my nipples go hard with his words.

Even more so when one hand trails to my jaw, cupping my face and tilting it up, the other trailing down to my ass.

And then he kisses me. Hard and long and full of so much emotion, so many words I would both kill for him to say out loud to me and am much too terrified to hear, and I want to cry.

I don't, of course, because getting winged liner right on the first try is a stroke of pure luck and there's no way in hell I'd get a second application right.

Finally, he breaks the kiss, both of us panting as he presses his forehead to mine, looking down at me. His thumb swipes gently over my cheek.

"God, you're fucking beautiful," he whispers, but it's as if it's a confession to himself, not something for me to hear.

I don't respond.

I can't really, not with thick emotion clogging my throat.

"We have to talk after all of this shit," he says, and the nausea returns. "I have to get your head right."

"Theo—"

"But let's just enjoy ourselves tonight. Once everything is clear, we're going to have that talk. And Katrina, I'm not going to let you talk me into some fucked shit."

I don't know what that means, but it feels ominous.

It starts to click with his next words, though, and something warm and golden starts to slide through me.

"I'm gonna make it to eight, Katrina. And nine and ten and one hundred." He presses his lips to mine once more, gentle and sweet and filled with something I don't want to look at too closely in case I'm wrong.

When I check my lips in the reflective wall of the elevator, I'm both stunned and impressed to know that Abbie's lipstick is, in fact, kiss proof.

FORTY-NINE

KAT

Although Theo has been making this event seem like it's akin to getting his fingernails ripped out one by one, I have a blast, forgetting about my ick and the engagement and Warren and Melody and everything in between.

I came last year, but was much too new at the company to really know anyone, much less enjoy myself. It's a fundraiser Judy, once again, has organized on behalf of Catalyst Records, benefiting marginalized artists. The proceeds create grants to work on their music and to cut a demo. The file is then their property, with no attachment to Catalyst, and they're free to use it to send to labels and agents. They are encouraged, of course, to submit to Catalyst, but it's not a requirement.

The room is packed with the who's who of the industry—agents and artists and producers mingle and laugh and dance. Theo wanders about schmoozing and chatting, but I don't follow him around this time. His sister came over to me within minutes of our arrival, screamed about my dress (her dress was also gorgeous—a deep midnight blue with silver sparkles that looked like stars), and told her brother, "I'm stealing your girl. We're gonna go dance!"

I froze, reaching toward Theo, ready to make my excuses. This is a work event, after all. But he grabbed my hand, pulled me in close, pressed a kiss to my lips, and whispered in my ear, "Go. Go have fun and dance with my sister. I'll keep an eye on you."

And he has. Every time I look up, even though he's always in a different spot around the room, his eyes are on me, keeping track of where I am at all times, winking and smiling small if we meet eyes before going back to his conversation.

The whole night has been beyond fun, but now I'm exhausted and in dire need of a sip of water and a bathroom break. "I'll be right back!" I shout to Savannah after a while. "I need a break!" She gives me the requisite *do you want me to come?* look, but she's happy, dancing with friends and cute boys who aren't named Warren Michaels, so I shake my head and tell her to stay.

I'm endlessly grateful I did, too, when the sound of angry voices hits my ears as I wander, trying to find a bathroom that doesn't have a huge line.

"I can't believe you, out there fucking kissing her!" a woman's voice shouts.

"What the fuck am I supposed to do, Mel?" a man asks, exasperated.

"Not kiss her in front of me!" the familiar voice shrieks, and I press my back to the wall in the shadowed corner like some kind of expert movie spy.

It's Melody and Warren, arguing in a corner far enough from the party, they definitely think they're alone. Part of me thinks I should leave because if they catch me eavesdropping, I don't know what would happen, but I don't think it would be good.

But I also know Warren is planning something to fuck with my man, and I'm convinced Melody knows something about it. So I take the risk and stay and listen, praying to the revenge gods give me something—anything—as I quietly fumble with my phone to start recording just in case.

And the revenge gods don't disappoint.

"You just need to hang the fuck on. The vote is in two weeks, and once that's done, we're home free. Catalyst will be in my control come October, and Jeff will be retired. Then we can be together." His voice is syrupy sweet now, but it's coated in lies.

It seems Melody doesn't have a fraction of my ability to read people's words and intentions because her anger slows, turning whiny.

"That's all I want, baby. To be together." There is the wet sound of kisses that actually makes me nauseous, and again, I think about walking off to save myself from having to bleach my brain, but it stops, and Melody's complaining starts again.

"I just don't understand how this is all going to work," she says. "It seems too complicated."

Warren groans and sighs, and I can't see him, but I can picture the irritated glare he gives her.

"I told you. Your father and I have stock in Travis's label." Travis, the owner of Blacknote. "Once I get the president position, I'm sending any promising artists their way and vetoing them from being signed to Catalyst. They're already stocked with a great lineup, thanks to me sending them all of the artists Theo keeps finding. Once Catalyst starts to tank, Blacknote will acquire it at nearly no cost, including all of their existing big-name artists. Our stock is going to skyrocket, and Travis has a spot for me on the board. I'll get the VP position and I'll be president once he retires."

"It just seems so . . . confusing," she says, a pout laced within the words.

"Everything is confusing for you, baby," Warren says, and Melody giggles before there are more wet sounds. Not a single part of me can understand a man speaking so poorly about you to your face, giggling, and then making out with him. "I just . . . Why not just work for Catalyst? They're a good label. They have Cassandra," she asks long moments later.

There's another exhausted sigh before he begrudgingly explains.

Clearly, the revenge gods are on my side today.

"Because Jeff Banks, Theo Carter, and his high and mighty father fucked it all beyond repair. The contracts they have in place give their artists way too much fucking power. Blacknote makes 500% more off every dollar an artist brings in. If they get acquired, Blacknote can renegotiate those contracts with better terms."

My stomach churns with understanding.

There it is.

There's his big plan for when he takes over, why he wants Catalyst so badly. He wants the artists who are loyal to Jeff, Theo, and Catalyst, but doesn't like the terms they're signed for.

My mind goes to the times Theo has had to remind some of the board members of how the artists are to retain control of their art, how they deserve the large cuts they receive that are much bigger than industry standard because they create the music.

Those board members would be happy to go along with Warren's plan, I'm sure, if he promised them a slice of Blacknote.

"What if you don't get president? Then what happens? Do you have to keep pretending you're in love with stupid fucking Savannah Carter? I'm tired of being your dirty secret."

"Oh, don't worry. I have everything I need to send Carter packing. No one's going to want to vote for him." I need to find Theo. We need to plan. We need a way to use this information to get Warren out of Catalyst once and for all to save the business.

The reality is, there's a chance his plan could work. If he didn't have such a big ego and wasn't so cocky, he could have gotten the president position, could have won Catalyst, and everything would be fucked.

Except Theo chose me as his partner in chaos.

Fortunately for us, Warren has no idea what kind of woman he's fucking with or the man I'd give everything to protect.

"Now, enough questions. Remind me why I should go to you when this is all said and done, when I can have any piece of pussy I want," Warren says. I expect to hear a gasp and a slap, but instead, there's another little girlish giggle before the sound of a zipper fills the halls, and I decide that's my cue.

I tiptoe away to find Theo, my boss, my love, my coconspirator, so we can begin to plan.

One last scheme is needed before we're through.

FIFTY

THEO

"Come on," Katrina says, grabbing my hand and dragging me toward the exit of the room where the party is taking place. It's starting to wind down, most of the attendees off getting drunk and dancing instead of mingling. I was scanning the room for her, ready to make our quiet escape, but this is unexpected.

"What?" I ask.

"Come on!" Her eyes are wild, her smile wide as she continues to pull on my arm.

"What's going on?" I ask, tugging and stopping her, pulling her close. When she's like this, I have no idea what to expect, but at least the smile on her face tells me it's not that she's hurt or angry.

"I found out his plan," she says low under her breath, just loud enough for me to hear over the music.

"What?" She doesn't answer this time, instead walking with a mission toward Jeff and Judy.

"Hey, guys, we're headed out," she announces. There's still a chaotic sparkle in her eyes, and the smile on her lips is genuine, but it's not because she's talking to the Banks.

"Oh, of course! It's getting late. You and Sav were having a blast, cutting a rug! You must be exhausted!" Judy says, bending to give Katrina a kiss on each cheek.

"I'm sure Theodore has other ideas," Jeff teases with a deep laugh. "That dress has been turning heads all night."

"Jeffrey!" Judy exclaims, slapping her husband on the chest. Katrina just smiles wider and laughs.

"See you guys later," she says.

"Dinner next Sunday? We have to wedding plan!" Judy asks. Katrina hesitates, her smile faltering for the first time since she came to me and dragged me off. I know why, and I fucking hate it.

Once she tells me what has her all wound up and after I fuck her into submission, we have to have our talk once and for all.

"We'll be there," I say, pressing a kiss to Judy's cheek and shaking Jeff's hand.

Final goodbyes are exchanged, and Katrina practically drags me off, Jeff's laugh following behind us as she does.

"What's going on, Katrina?" I ask once we're in the ear-numbing quiet outside of the event space. She doesn't answer until we're at the elevator bank. A red-tipped finger presses the up button, and she looks both ways down the hallway, checking for listening ears, I suppose.

"I heard Melody and Warren in a hall. They were arguing. She was bitching because he was here with Savannah—" she says in a whisper.

"Yeah, well, he's dating her—" She shakes her head.

"No. Well, yes. I was right, Theo. I was right. He's cheating on her with Melody. They have some . . . grand plan."

My stomach heaves as I picture my sweet sister, her eyes wide and happy as she gazed up at Warren today, totally in love.

"What do you mean?" We step into the excruciatingly slow elevator, and I hit the button for our floor at the very top of the hotel. Once the door closes, secluding us, she starts talking excitedly, no longer whispering.

"I've got a plan. We have to frame him. We have to—"

She's smiling wide, her eyes wild, but she's jumping from topic to topic as if I have already been clued in to whatever she's excited about.

I grab hold of her shoulders, pushing her against the wall of the elevator and trying to get her to calm down, to speak clearly.

"Kat, I see you're excited, but—"

"Fuck yes, I'm excited!" she says, and I think if I wasn't holding her, she'd jump and clap or dance or something so very Katrina, it would make me smile. "We've got him, Theo! He thinks he's got it in the bag, but he doesn't. We won. We—"

It's clear she's not slowing any time soon, so I use my new but reliable tactic for calming Katrina down, pressing my lips to hers and kissing her. Instantly she quiets, her eyes drifting shut, her hands moving to the back of my neck, and I can't help but smile into the kiss. When it breaks, I press my forehead to hers and whisper against her lips:

"Honey, I need you to slow down and explain, okay? I'm happy you're excited, but you've got to tell me what's going on before I can get on your level." A subdued version of her laugh pings off the metal walls of the elevator before she speaks, finally making sense.

"I was looking for a bathroom without a line and wandered way out of the way, and I heard Melody and Warren fighting. She was mad he kissed your sister in front of her. They're together, Theo." My stomach churns, and I hate knowing my sister is going to get hurt at the end of all this. "But he explained his plan to her, why he wants Catalyst. He's going to tank it and let Blacknote acquire it, because he has stock in them, and Travis has made all these big promises to him. He admitted he's been sending your artists there. I heard him say it."

"But why not just . . . ," I start, wondering why the fuck he wouldn't just run Catalyst, an incredibly successful company, but then . . . "The artists' percentages."

"Exactly," she whispers.

"Fuck." I step away from her, running my hand through my hair, pacing in the small elevator, but she's still smiling, still excited. Her heels click as she walks over to me, putting her hands on my chest, that wide smile brightening up my life despite these dire circumstances.

"Don't you get it? Theo, we did it. We did it!" I shake my head because it's her who doesn't get it.

"He's going to ruin the company, Katrina. My father's legacy."

"No, he's not. He thinks he is, and we can let him think that, but now, we have a plan. We know how to tear him down. He gave us everything we need. Now we just need to prove it to everyone else. Don't you see it?"

Slowly, I push the panic aside to see the pieces then watch them fall into place, and I get it.

She's right.

We can work with this. We have two weeks to put a plan in place, and from the look of Katrina, she already has an idea for how to do it.

Catalyst is going to be mine.

Or, at the very least, it's not going to be Warren's, which, when I push my ego to the side, is more important than me running it.

The elevator finally dings at the top and suddenly, I'm feeling the same chaotic, joyful energy she is. I grab her hand, tugging her out as we head toward the hotel room, eager to work this feeling out from under my skin. I open the door to our room, holding it open for her.

She enters and turns to face me, starting to walk backward, that same wild smile on her lips as her hands move to the big clip in her hair, messing with it for a few moments before tossing it on the spare bed.

"So what first? Should we call someone? Or should we brainstorm our revenge? I've got an idea, but I know your genius little brain has something better." She's talking a million miles a minute, clearly hyped on adrenaline and joy and excitement. I walk over to her, standing in front of her, and smile wide.

"How about first, we help you get out a bit of those good vibes and excess energy?"

"What?" she asks, her nose scrunching in confusion as she sits on the edge of the tall bed. I step closer until I'm between her legs, and I tangle my fingers in the hair behind her head and tip it back before I press my lips to hers.

"Warren and all of his bullshit will be there tomorrow. He'll be there six hours after I make you moan my name and fill you with my cum at least twice." Her eyes go impossibly big, and I fight the laugh brewing in my chest.

"Six *hours*?!" I shrug.

"We can take a break halfway through, but I don't want to talk about Warren during that time." I tug her up until she's standing in front of me again.

"You're insane," she murmurs.

"Insane about you. Now come," I say, grabbing her hand and forcing her to stand.

"Turn," I instruct, and she does, facing the mirror on the wall opposite the foot of the bed. Now her eyes are crazed but in a completely different way—with excitement and lust and need.

My fingers find the zip of the dress, a short one considering how much of her back is bare, then drift up to her shoulders to find and tug one thin, crystal-studded strap to the side, then the other. The entire dress falls to the ground and pools at her feet. Looking over her shoulder at her in the mirror, I see her mouth is open a bit, her bare chest rising and falling with each already labored breath.

She's standing in just a small pair of lace underwear and her heels, her long hair draped down her back, her miles of brown skin on display, the nipples on her full breasts peaked.

Not for the first time, I'm reminded that I'm the luckiest man on earth.

Running one hand over her stomach, up to cup her breast, I use the other to brush her hair to the side, pressing my lips to the pulse on her neck. I leave my lips there when I speak against her skin.

"Look at this, at us. How fucking perfect we look together." I'd been thinking it all night, how we fit perfectly at this event, a power couple out for vengeance, but it's not just tonight. It's always. We fit at the office, her constantly keeping me on my toes and making sure everything runs smoothly. We fit perfectly at home, with the way she slid into my life there like she was always meant to live there with me, bringing joy and sunshine to my empty halls.

Her breath catches in her throat as she watches, her eyes never leaving the mirror. Her gaze shifts to my hand as I tug her nipple then release it, sliding back down her soft belly, dipping into the waistband of the underwear until I'm cupping her.

Without even dipping in, I know she's wet, feel it against my hand.

"This? I'm keeping this, Katrina. I'm keeping you."

"Theo—" she whispers, hesitance in the single word, so I cut her off, letting a finger slide inside of her. She gasps as her wet allows me in easily, already so fucking ready for me.

Always ready for me.

Mine, my mind whispers.

Mixed in with the joy and excitement in her eyes has been fear. I know what it is, of course—fear that this will end badly, that I want to stick to our original plan of being temporary, that she'll get hurt. It's my job to assuage it, and I'm starting now.

Pulling my finger out, I drag the wet digit up and circle her clit, her knees buckling, her leaning into me as they do, a low moan dragging from her.

"Theo," she says again, but it's a beg, not the warning of before. It makes me smile at her skin. I press my lips to her neck, sucking there as I slide my fingers back down once more, this time pushing two fingers in.

"You keep thinking this is going to end, so fucking scared something's going to happen, but you don't get it, honey. We're it." I press my lips to hers again, remove my fingers before sliding them in, crooking them as I do, and her breath leaves her chest in a shaky exhale. "You and me. I'll fight for it if I have to, but me and you, we're it."

She opens her mouth to argue, but I steal the words from her, moving the arm wrapped around her waist up to her breast, cupping and tugging at the nipple as my hand works in her panties faster, fucking her with my fingers as she tightens around them. I groan into her neck, and her pussy clamps harder. Her breathing is rapid, the rise and fall of her chest pushing her tit into my hand as I continue to play with her nipple, but our eyes stay locked on one another.

She knows what this is.

A claiming.

This is me telling her what we are and how this is forever.

"Watch me worship you," I say as her eyes start to drift shut. She's close to the edge, the first of many orgasms I plan to give her tonight. They snap back open, moving to where my hand is playing with her clit. "It's all I want to do. All I've ever wanted to do, I think," I muse, thinking back on all the times I jacked off thinking of my pretty little assistant and the guilt I'd feel after.

"Theo—" Again, she tries to argue, but I press my lips to the spot she loves below her ear, and she moans. Her hand tries to reach back, to touch me, to return the favor and even the scales, but I shake my head.

"Let me have this, Kat. This one is just for you," I whisper, and her hand drops before shifting to rest on top of mine in her underwear.

I groan as she helps me, as we take her higher and higher together, her hand telling me when to go faster, when to go deeper. I hold her as her knees buckle a second time, as her little pants become full moans, but she doesn't close her eyes again.

"That's it, kitten, purr for me."

That does it. Her small hand presses mine, pushing my fingers deep, forcing the heel of my hand to grind into her clit as her body goes lax. My arm is on her waist, holding her up as she convulses, moaning my name as she does.

God, she's fucking gorgeous.

Once she catches her breath, I slide my hand out, moving it up to her mouth.

"Clean them," I command, eyes locked to hers that flare with heat. In the mirror, I watch her lean forward just a bit, her tongue swirling around then as she cleans herself off me. My cock is painfully hard as I watch, and we look absolutely decadent like this. Her completely naked sans a pair of tiny panties, heels, and me completely dressed in a full tuxedo. When she moans around them, I finally remove them and step back.

"On your hands and knees on the bed, face the mirror," I say as I start to remove my tux jacket. I should hang it or keep it somewhere safe, but I've no patience for that, instead simply tossing it in a corner.

"What?" she asks, still dazed form her orgasm.

"You're watching everything tonight, Katrina."

"Watching . . . ," she starts before her words trail off and her eyes go hazy. I smile at her before tipping my chin at the bed. She doesn't ask again, instead eagerly crawling on, leaving on her shoes like she knows I like.

"Panties can come off," I say, working on the buttons of my shirt next. She does as I ask, removing her panties and then positioning at the edge of the bed.

"You know what I used to think about before you were mine?" Her eyes go hooded at my low, deceptively casual tone. I step to where her face is, thrilled to note my cock lines up perfectly with her mouth like this. I put my hand to it and use the other to brush her hair back and over her shoulders as she tips her chin up to look at me. I don't wait for her to speak before continuing.

"Long before you were mine, back when it was so totally fucked to even think about you that way, I'd think about hiding you below my desk during a boring as fuck meeting, having you suck my cock while someone droned on and on about who fucking cared on the phone. No one but me would know you were down there, sucking me off like a good little girl." She moans, and I rub the head of my cock along her lips, her tongue coming out to lick the precum there.

Then she opens without me having to say, taking the head into her mouth, her eyes locked on me as she rolls her tongue along the tip.

"Other times." I lean forward, sliding my cock in a bit then back out. "I'd picture you on your chair, legs spread, entertaining me while I worked." Another mewl leaves her throat, obscured by my cock in her mouth.

"Get me wet before I fuck you." One of her hands leaves the bed to grab my balls as she starts to move her mouth along my shaft, and I moan, watching her.

I could watch her like this all fucking day.

But I'd much rather be inside of her, so I slide myself out and then climb on the bed behind her. I press my lips to the bottom of her spine gently and then move to my knees, positioning behind her, notching the head of my cock before starting my slow, slow slide inside. She moans, low and loud, her eyes drifting shut as she does.

"Uh, uh. Eyes open, Kat. Eyes on me while I fill you." She moans again but opens her eyes, and it makes me smile. Even like this, filled with me, already on the edge of orgasm, she rolls her eyes at me.

I hope, of all things, that never changes. That she always gives me shit, always finds me irritating.

It makes me hard.

Both of my hands move to her full hips, holding her as I slide back out slowly. I lock eyes on hers in the mirror before I slam in hard. We both moan at the feel, and I move one hand to her hair, twining it around my fist and tugging hard so her head goes back, so I get a better view at my girl taking me,

"God, you feel so fucking good." I groan through gritted teeth.

"Please, fuck," she murmurs as she starts to move her hips back, meeting my thrusts, fucking herself on me. I let her, my hand moving from her hip as I bend a bit to reach her clit then start to rub there, my mouth close to her ear.

"You're mine, Katrina. This pussy? It's mine. Your pleasure? All fucking mine. Your body? Mine. The sooner you get this and realize that's not changing, the better."

"Theo—" she starts, but I don't let her finish.

This is an ambush. This is me staking my claim, showing and telling her exactly how I feel with no room for misinterpretation.

My hand trails up her belly, pressing against her chest and using it to pull her up until her back is against my chest, that arm wrapping around her belly. I continue to make short, shallow thrusts into her, and her head starts to dip, eyes breaking contact in the mirror. My hand in her hair moves, cupping her neck and jaw, tipping it up and forcing her to watch us.

It's fucking beautiful, her breasts swaying with each movement, her soft curves against my hard lines, her dark hair a mess all over her shoulder and my hand. Her eyes are wide, pupils dilated, locked on mine.

"Look at us, Katrina. Feel this and watch it and try and tell me there's a better fit than this. Tell me anything on earth feels better than when I fill you."

She moans loud, and her pussy tightens around me. I nip at her ear, the hand on her throat moving down her stomach and to her clit, circling the swollen spot until her hips buck into me. I groan into her back at the feel but stop altogether then.

My hand is on her clit, my cock buried deep, my eyes locked on her, completely unmoving.

I have her attention now.

"You can't tell me, Katrina. You can't. You can tell yourself this is going to end until you pass out, but when you wake up, I'll still be here, waiting for you. Because you're mine. And I take care of what's mine, be it your body or your mind. We gotta get your mind straight, but right now, you can watch me control your body."

Finally, she tightens on my cock planted deep, moaning loud.

"Goddammit, Theo, then do it! Take care of my body!" I smile, nipping at her neck, but I start to move again if only because I know I don't have long myself.

"Watch," I whisper, nipping her ear. "Watch me make you come. Watch the control I have on your body. Every part of you has given into me, knows your mine to your bones, except for your beautiful mind. We'll get you there, though."

She doesn't argue.

Instead, her entire body goes tight, her mouth dropping open as she tightens on me, a silent scream leaving her lips as my hand works her clit, as she comes apart in my arms. I follow her over the edge, her orgasm pulling me down with her, and I grunt her name as I fill her.

FIFTY-ONE

KAT

"This is real, you know," Theo whispers in the dark of the hotel room as we lie naked in the bed together, long minutes after we've come down, and my previous loose and languid body freezes.

"What?"

"This?" His hand swipes down my naked hip and then gestures between us. "It's real. It's not fake."

"I don't—" I start. But he keeps talking, and my heart pounds heavily with each syllable.

"I wonder if it ever was, you know?" he asks in a whisper. "Or did we play pretend so well because we were always real? Were we just too scared, too stupid, too stubborn to see it, to admit it?"

In any other situation, I'd argue that I'm not stubborn, proving his point perfectly, but not tonight. Right now, I can't say a single word at all, much less argue his point. "You know, up until recently, I didn't do anything I didn't think out fully. Nothing caught me off guard, because I was always prepared, had always done the math and figured out how things would go before I took that first step." He pauses then brushes my hair back and smiles at me. It stops my heart. "I don't like being caught off guard."

"That's how I know my ick factor is all jacked up," I whisper into the dark. "That should have given me the ick. I love spontaneity." Theo rolls his eyes but continues, ignoring me.

"I hired you because you did the same, you know. Anticipated my questions, paused before answering, and gave me a perfectly-curated answer. Not lies, not precise manipulations, not telling me what I wanted to hear, but you'd take your answer and craft your honest response in a way you thought would land well with me."

I open my mouth to argue, but he stops me.

"Not in a manipulative way, but in a thoughtful way. In a way that now, I realize, was you anticipating what I needed, what I wanted, even then. You've always done that. Even from the very beginning. It's just . . . changed."

"Changed?"

"Now you do it for everything. It used to be just for work stuff. Now you worry about me outside of work. You fight to keep me safe, to keep me from getting hurt, to make sure I'm happy." I lick my lips but I don't argue.

He's not wrong. I do that, anticipate his wants and needs and make them happen so his day goes smoothly. It wasn't until recently I realized he did the same though.

"You do it for me too, you know," I whisper.

"I know. Because I love you."

The world stops spinning.

My blood stops pumping, and my heart stops beating.

I stop breathing.

But Theo doesn't stop at all, his fingers still running through my hair over and over before he continues speaking as if he didn't tilt my world on its axis.

"I think I've loved you since you first walked into my office, that little purple skirt and suit jacket. You were a . . . breath of fresh air. You didn't care who I was. Fuck, you made fun of me in your interview, asking if I ever smiled."

I did.

I did ask that.

I made a stupid joke about how I might not have a fancy degree, but I can make a mean cup of coffee, and he huffed out a laugh but his face stayed neutral. As someone who has always valued my ability to make others laugh, to better their day by making fun of myself, his lack of an actual laugh was . . . unexpected.

I had tipped my head a little at him, my brow furrowing, and asked, "Do you smile?"

"What?"

"Do you smile? Like, do you know how? Or is there some kind of medical condition stopping it I should be aware of, or . . . ?" My words trailed off, and he glared at me.

It, like everything I do in life, was a test.

If this man couldn't handle my humor, couldn't handle my needling, this position wouldn't be a good fit for me. Like everything in life, I got icks from jobs, and I might as well learn at the start if this wasn't going to work.

His dark blue eyes were stunning in their fierceness as he looked at me like he was reading my internal code, dissecting it, and then writing a master's thesis on what he saw there.

It felt like I was naked.

"I smile at things that are worthwhile. A self-deprecating joke about a woman who is clearly intelligent and personable does not deserve the effort of a smile or a true laugh. So yes, I do know how to smile, but I won't encourage you to talk poorly about yourself to make others comfortable."

I felt shocked, blown away by his frankness and the way he cut right through all of my bullshit to my true intention.

"Now, when can you start?" he asked, closing the folder with my information and folding his hands together on top of it, once more throwing me off kilter.

That was the beginning of . . . well, everything.

Looking back, I think that's why I value every single smile he's ever given me, cataloging them like the precious things they are. Most people give theirs freely, smiling politely at strangers or at people they don't like, but not Theo. He only gives you a smile if you earn it.

It's a gift.

"That was rude," I whisper. "I was at an interview and I made fun of you."

"It was you. You showed me you from the very start, Katrina." He moves, rolling over me, pinning me in place, his eyes burning into mine.

"I think that's been your issue all along. You hide the parts of you you think people won't like, the chaos and the mess and the brat, and when you start to show little pieces of you, you're scared people will prove you right. Or you find some other reason to write them off, to say they give you the ick."

I could argue that I don't do that, but what's the point? I'm naked in front of him, literally and figuratively, and he sees right through me.

"Sometimes, they don't like it, what I show them of myself," I admit painfully.

"But I do. The more you show me, the more I love you, Kat." His hand goes to my cheek, his thumb strumming on the skin there. "But you never hid the parts I think you hide from everyone else, did you? You never hid your toughness, your take-no-shit attitude. You never hid how you're fierce and loyal and protective."

I read between the lines. "But I did hide?" He nods.

"You hid your heart from me. You hid your softness. You hid the part of you I want to protect most of all. And if you let me, Katrina, I'll do it forever, protect your soft spot. I'll do it until you're so tired of me, and then I'll work to keep protecting it, because I know that just means somehow, I got deeper and you're scared again."

My heart is pounding, tears burning behind my eyes when I finally speak again, the words creeping past the ache in my throat as I do.

"I'm scared," I whisper into the dark.

"That's okay," Theo replies.

I wonder if that's why I love him, why I've fallen for him against all odds. He doesn't tell me there's nothing to be scared of, doesn't say I'm being silly. He doesn't even try to comfort me or ask me to clarify. He just tells me it's okay, that my feelings are valid. He lets me trust my gut, lets me feel anything I'm feeling, then helps me work around it, not through it, when I'm ready.

"I've never done this. Been with a man." I pause then smile. "Well, I have, but not like this. Not in a way where I'm completely open to him. Vulnerable."

"Do you believe in spirits?" he asks strangely, pushing my hair behind my ear. He does it just to touch me, I know.

"Spirits?" I ask with a smile. It feels good, a break from the heavy. "Like ghosts?"

"Yeah. Ghosts. Or just people sticking around a bit, messing with things." I think about it for a moment before answering, and he smiles as if I'm proving a point.

"Yeah, I think I do. There's too much coincidental evidence pointing to them being a thing," she says, and I nod.

"I think all those months ago, it was my father speaking."

"What?" I ask through a stunned laugh.

"I told Jeff I was engaged, and I had no idea why the fuck I would do that. It made no sense. There were so many other options and that's what I landed on?"

"Are you telling me the ghost of your father haunts Catalyst Records and possessed you to tell his best friend you had a fiancée you definitely did not have because he thought it would push you to me?" I can't help but laugh as I say it, and he chuckles but shrugs.

"Maybe. It kind of makes sense in a convoluted way. Maybe even my father knew I'd crumble without you and you'd help me out of any crazy situation I got myself into."

"God, you're insane."

"And you love me," he says, his voice low and soft and silly, and god, it's beautiful really. Being with him like this.

"But what if . . ." I feel the smile melt off my face.

"What? What is it?"

I'm tempted to say nothing. To tell him I'm fine and put on a smile and move along, but that's not us. That's not how Theo and I are.

"What if it happens?" I whisper my biggest fear into the dark. "What if this goes great but we hit nine or ten or fifteen and I get the ick?"

"Then we talk about it. Then we work through it. There is no such thing as perfection, Katrina. We are never going to be perfect. Humans are flawed. Couples are flawed. The difference is if you're willing to work for it." He cages me in place, doing a push-up and pressing his lips to mine quickly. "And I'll work to the bone on this, on us, if it means I get to kiss you whenever I want, if I get to see your face when you're sleeping in my bed, if I get to hear your laugh in my home. If I get to love you, I'll do what I have to do to keep you, Katrina." My chin quivers with emotion.

"You're going to make me cry."

"Can't have that, now can we?" he asks with a widening grin. "Guess I just have to make you come instead." A shiver runs through me, my body already shifting emotions, before my stomach grumbles.

"Ugh, I'm starving. I think I was promised twelve hours of bliss, but I was also promised sustenance," I say with a smile. "I forgot to pack snacks. We'll have to wait for food to come before we can get into round two."

Theo rolls his eyes and stands, presumably to grab the room service folder or his phone to order some kind of late-night delivery, but instead, he digs through his large leather overnight bag. He tosses something at me and it hits me in the head, followed by another.

"What the—"

Pretzels.

Another item flies across the room, this time hitting me right in the boob. Theo laughs as I pick it up, inspecting it.

A mango chili lollipop.

"You packed me snacks?" I ask with a small smile.

"I'd crumble without you, Katrina. Have to make sure you're well-nourished so that doesn't happen."

I stare at him as he smiles at me, clearly proud of himself. I roll my eyes, even if they're burning a bit with the desire once again to cry.

Instead, I give him a snarky smile and say, "Yeah, I guess I'll let you keep me. So long as there's snacks involved."

He bursts out laughing before tackling me to the bed, and I have to wait another half hour before I get my sustenance.

I'm totally okay with it.

FIFTY-TWO

KAT

We smile and chat and mingle through the breakfast the next morning. Theo uses the opportunity to schmooze the people who are hungover and over life, but as soon as we get in the car, we start to plan.

"How do we tell Savannah?" he asks when we're about halfway home, his voice low and serious.

I know it's eating at him most, his sister being tied up with Warren. "She's never going to believe me, but also, she needs to know. I already feel bad about letting it get too deep and not telling her our thoughts."

"She wouldn't have wanted to hear it, not without having proof."

"Even with the recording, I'm worried she won't believe us and that it will backfire. I'm worried she'll cut me off." Looking over at him, I see his jaw is tight, and stress is clear on his face. I reach over and squeeze his hand.

"I'll handle Savannah, okay?"

"You'll handle her?" I nod.

"I'll assemble the crew."

His face drops a bit, and he starts to shake his head. "Katrina, I don't know. Savannah doesn't know any of your—"

"You're a man, so you don't get it. But every woman needs a crew of girls who have her back no matter what. Who have gone through what she has and who will do what we have to, to make her feel better, to get hers back." His face shifts again, and I fight the laugh bubbling in my chest at his conflicted expression.

"Absolutely not. I know you and your friends have a strange sense of right and wrong, but—"

I lose the fight, and even though I'm laughing at him, he starts to smile.

"When we get back, call Sav and tell her to come over. You go do whatever you have to do, and I'll talk to her, and by the time my girls get here, she'll be ready for them." He opens his mouth again as he hits a red light, but I stop him, putting my hand on his cheek. "You know I'll take care of your sister, honey. Trust me." Long moments pass as he stares into my eyes, reading me, scraping me clean of all of my masks before he touches his mouth to mine.

"I'll call Savannah."

"It was me," Savannah says, her voice low.

"What?"

It's long past when Savannah came to Theo's, looking confused and guarded. Long past when I sat her down and told her everything —about the president position, my original gut feeling about Warren, Theo and my engagement and the relationship that came from it, and my ick. I entrusted her with all of my secrets—our secrets—before finally telling her about Warren and what I heard.

I had thought it would take some convincing or proof, but instantly, she started crying, as if she had known all along but didn't want to admit it. My heart broke for her.

"It was me who told Warren you two were at the office." My brows furrow, but Abbie speaks before I do.

"The day of the snowstorm?" Abbie asks, brushing Savannah's hair back and behind her shoulders. She nods tearfully and sniffs before explaining.

"I have Theo's location on my phone. Warren was at my place during the storm and asked where he was. I thought he was just being thoughtful because they're friends and work together. I checked and told him he was still at the office. He asked again later in the night, and I remember sometime in the early morning, he was looking at my phone. Right after, he told me he was going into the office early for a meeting."

Well, at least that explains how he knew he'd find us there.

"I'm sorry, Savannah," I say for what feels like the millionth time.

"It doesn't help, but honestly, we've all been there," Cami says. Right after her first cry after the girls showed up, we all went around, explaining just how good of company she was in, telling Savannah about all of the times we've had our hearts broken.

"At least you weren't being framed for embezzlement," Liv says with a half-hearted smile, reminding her of the time her douche of an ex did just that.

"I just . . . I don't understand," Savannah says between hiccups. "Why did he have to drag me into it?"

"Because he's a piece of shit, honey," Abbie says, standing to grab a bottle of water and sitting on the arm of the couch as she hands it to her.

Silence comes through the room as she takes a sip and then catches her breath. Finally, she looks up at me with big, puffy eyes and gives me a small smile.

"At least you and Theo got together. One good thing happened from all of this." I share the small smile, feeling guilty for having even a tiny spark of joy while she's hurting.

"I'm really sorry I didn't say anything earlier, Savannah. I didn't —" She shakes her head, cutting me off.

"No. I wouldn't have listened, and we would have gotten off on the wrong foot. Theo tried once, and I didn't talk to him for a week. He had the wool pulled so far over my eyes." She shakes her head and sighs. "God, I'm so stupid."

"No, you're not," Cami says, reaching for her hand. "You were in love with him since you were a kid. When that happens, you have rose-colored glasses on. It's natural. And he's a manipulative fuck."

"He's really good at convincing people he's a good guy, Sav. Just look at the board. They all buy his bullshit."

"Not you and Theo," she says.

"Honestly? I had to work really hard to convince Theo he was as bad as we all know he is. He also gave Warren the benefit of the doubt. But like you, once he saw him clearly, he came to my side."

She shakes her head. "He had the company to save. How am I supposed to get over this? I feel . . . like he took something from me. I know that's melodramatic, but . . ."

"No, it makes sense. He did, Savannah. He took your trust and your love, and he threw it out. He manipulated you. You're allowed to feel however you want. And you have to do what you need to to get over him. We're here to help."

"I don't know what I need," she says with a sad shrug. "I'm just . . . sad."

A beat of silence passes before Cami speaks. "You need to get back at him," she says, surprising all of us. We look at her, taken aback. "What? Isn't that what we do? One of us gets fucked over, we all fuck them over?"

"Don't get mad, get even," Olivia says with a smile.

"Oh my god, yes. That's it! You need revenge!" Abbie says, clapping her hands and standing, walking over to her bag.

"Revenge?" Sav asks.

"I mean . . . ," I start. "It's kind of our specialty." I don't know if this is the best idea, but suddenly, a small smile grows on Savannah's face. For the first since she got here really.

"What kind of revenge?"

"Glitter!" Abbie says with a shout, holding a pen in the air and a notebook in her hand.

We're approaching the point of no return, but the thought of Warren Michaels covered in glitter is kind of appealing.

"The answer does not always have to be glitter, Abbie," Cami says. Abbie gives her a look.

"Glitter makes everything better."

"Then why would you want to glitter anyone as revenge?" Cami asks, raising a brow at her in a challenge.

"It's better for me, not for them. Duh."

"I'm so confused," Savannah says, her eyes ping-ponging from Cami to Abbie as they argue. "But also intrigued."

There's no going back now.

"So, we're kind of really good at getting revenge on assholes. It's our calling. When Abbie's asshole ex dumped her, we put glitter in the vents of his car, changed his coffee orders, and re-tailored all of his clothes so they were a bit too small."

"And I fucked his boss!" she says with a wide smile. Savannah's eyes go wide.

"Yeah, that too. Don't worry, she married him, too. Then Cami had these mean girls at her work. We got their car towed and made it look like their credit cards were declined, because they were bitchy rich girls."

"And I fucked one of their dads," she says.

"Hey! We agreed not to talk about that!" Olivia says, putting her hands over her ears, and Cami sticks her tongue out before turning to Savannah and smiling.

"Liv is my partner's, Zach's, daughter. At the time, I thought she was part of the group of mean girls, but then eventually, she helped me fuck with them."

"Wow," Savannah says.

"Ooh, me next!" Liv yells. "My ex left me at the altar, and I tried to kill him a few times. Not intentionally, of course," she adds when Savannah's eyes go wide with concern. "Like, I thought he was just a big pussy and afraid of bees, so I tried to order a beehive to his house, but it turns out he was afraid of them because he was deathly allergic. Oops." Savannah snorts out a laugh.

"He had an FBI agent watching him, because he was embezzling, and the FBI agent stopped her."

"And I fucked him!" she says then laughs maniacally.

"Jesus, Liv, calm down. You're going to scare her off," Cami warns.

"No, no, I'm into this," Savannah says. "But . . . I don't have to fuck anyone, right?"

"No," I say. "No, Savannah. You don't have to fuck anyone, I promise."

"Can we brainstorm what to do to Warren? Kat and Theo are already fucking him out of a job, apparently, but I want to do something too."

"It's what we do. We're the revenge girls," I say with a smile, because if I can't talk them out of it, why not join in on the fun?

"We're like, the Revengers. You know, the Avengers, but revenge?" Abbie proclaims with a laugh.

"Revengers, assemble!" Liv yells gleefully, throwing a fist in the air.

"Oh, my fucking god, Revengers!" Abbie claps excitedly.

"Absolutely not," Cami says.

"No, this is amazing. We're the Revengers! Bad ass bitches out to get revenge on all of the worst people," Abbie proposes. Cami groans, tipping her head back and throwing her arm over her face, knowing this is a lost cause.

"Revengers is kind of a flex," Savannah says with a growing smile.

"Jesus Christ, please stop, you're just encouraging them." Cami groans, and Liv turns to Abbie.

"We should get rings! Like the Avengers."

"No, I think that's actually Captain Planet with the rings."

"Well, whatever. I want pretty rings."

"Oh, yeah, we totally need some kind of membership ring," Abbie says, nodding. "Maybe I can design them and have Damien buy them. Can mine be pink?"

"Totally, but I want purple. Cami, what color do you want?" Liv asks.

"I want you all to shut up."

"You know," Savannah starts, leaning toward me. "Your friends are kind of scary, but in a fun way."

"We get that a lot," I say.

And then we get to planning.

FIFTY-THREE

KAT

Monday morning, I wake up in Theo's bed before the sun, a little hungover and a lot more hopeful after the previous weekend.

The world feels a bit brighter: Theo and I are trying things for real and I'm throwing my concern about my ick into a box and locking it up tight, the girls and I crafted an extensive plan for how to make Warren miserable before the vote, a small comfort to Savannah who cried and laughed in equal amounts yesterday, and Theo and I have finalized the perfect plan to ensure not only that Warren won't get the chance to run Catalyst, but that he won't be working for the company much longer.

But although the world feels brighter, the bed feels colder, Theo nowhere to be found, despite it being barely past 5 am. Stretching, I roll out of bed, tend to my bathroom needs, and brush my teeth before walking through his penthouse until I find him sitting on the couch, ending a call in the living room.

Leaning in his doorway, I watch as he puts his phone down with a sigh, seemingly content with whatever business he already completed this early in the morning, before he turns and looks at me. His eyes rake over me, taking me in wearing just a tee of his and a pair of panties, before he smiles, opening his arms, indicating I should come sit with him.

He doesn't have to ask me twice, and I move quickly, straddling him and burying my face into his neck, sighing as I do. Something about being wrapped up in Theo's strong arms always makes me feel like I'm safe and I'm *home*.

Part of me wonders if all those boys and men I decided gave me the ick, if I just knew from the very beginning I didn't feel this all-consuming sense of *home* with them. If I convinced myself it would happen later, and when it didn't, I cut my losses early.

"Where were you?" I ask, my voice whiny even to my own ears. I can feel him smiling against the top of my head. I'm learning quickly that Theo likes me clingy and whiny. He gets off on me needing to be with him.

"Miss me?" he asks, his chest rumbling.

"Yes, actually. It was cold and lonely."

"Hmmm," he replies, more a feeling than a noise. "I'm sorry, kitten. I woke up and couldn't fall back to sleep, too much on my mind. I decided to make a few calls, see if I could get anything rolling."

"Any success?"

"Called three different PIs with different specialties. Two answered."

"And . . ."

"One is digging into the financials of Warren to figure out how deep he is and get a log of income that might be a tip-off, like large sums of money deposited into his account, anything that would indicate him getting a kickback for referring artists to Blacknote. Same for Ray Harmon. He's also digging into any shell companies that are in their control to determine if they have stock interest in Blacknote." I pull my head back to look at him.

"It's barely 5:30, Theo."

"PIs hold strange hours, and if you're offering good money, it doesn't matter what time you call, someone will answer."

"Wow," I whisper and again, Theo smiles at me.

I don't think I've ever seen him smile as much as in the past forty-eight hours, and a part of me knows it's me finally removing our seven-date restriction, finally pulling my walls down and letting him in.

"The second PI is keeping an eye on his physical whereabouts—meetings, conversations, anything we can't see in the company phone logs."

"I don't envy that guy," I say. "I bet he's going to find something weird as fuck." Theo laughs, but my head is back in his neck, his hand brushing my hair down my back. We're quiet for long beats, just sitting in comfortable silence before I speak.

"Are you nervous for today? You're going to have to look at him, play the game for two weeks."

"No," he replies concisely. I can't help but laugh. "We've got a good plan. We have a time crunch to finish what we need, but I'm confident we'll get there. I have a feeling he has a grand plan, something he thinks is going to fuck us over, but what we have is going to get him fired, so it doesn't really matter. We're saving Catalyst one way or another." I don't like how that sounds, how he phrases it.

"You're going to get the president position, you know," I tell him. "There's no doubt in my mind." He lets out a noncommittal noise, and I lean back to better look at him, putting hand to his cheek. "Theo—"

"Jeff was right all those months ago." His words are low, his gaze far off, like he's in another world, another time. I pause, confused, but he tightens his arm on my back until I'm forced to lie chest to chest as he holds me there, letting me listen to his words through my ear over his heart and, what I think to him is most important, not looking at his face.

"I had no life. And more, I wasn't *looking* for one. Catalyst was what I lived and breathed." I cut in, feeling it necessary to clarify and stick up for him.

"There's nothing wrong with that, you know. Lots of people—"

"I could have missed out on this," he says in a whisper, the band of his arm on my waist tightening. "Missed out on you. On us." I can't argue with that, obviously. Another long beat passes in silence before he speaks again, his words filling me with golden warmth. "I'd do it all again. Lie about being engaged and call up Cassie Dawson and make a scheme with you. I'd get stuck in Warren's closet with you and get snowed in and fuck you on his desk." I laugh, and I feel his short rumble of a laugh too.

"I didn't think that part was up for question," I say, and his hand runs down my hair, down my back.

"If it meant we ended up right here, together and happy, I'd do it again. It was worth it for this, even if at the end of it all, I don't get the company." I fight the knot in my throat at his words, the rush of anxiety they bring, before I open my mouth to argue, to reassure. I don't get the chance, though. "But I'm going to get the company, Katrina. I'm going to destroy Warren Michaels's life and then I'll have fucking won, once and for all. Beat him, got the company, got the girl." This breaks the moment and I scoff out a laugh, finally pulling back to look at him. He's smiling at me, looking down, already dressed for the day while I'm still in my pajamas.

"You know, for a man who started all these shenanigans determined to only make *himself* look better and spotlight his own accomplishments, adamantly *refusing* to let me live out my little revenge plot, you're now out for blood." His face goes hard.

"A life lesson," he says. "I should always listen to my gorgeous, intuitive, wildly smart assistant." His hand that's been grazing up and down my back moves lower at my side, dipping under the tee and cupping my ass.

"I think you should listen to her now, show her exactly just how much you appreciate her," I suggest with a smile, tipping my hip to grind my center on where he's already getting hard. His smile grows wide and wicked.

"We have to make it quick," he says, his other hand dipping

below the shirt as well. "We've got revenge to execute." My hands cross, tugging the shirt over my head.

"Yes, Mr. Carter."

And with a growl, I'm on my back and he's showing me *exactly* how much he appreciates my wit, intuition, and, of course, my body.

FIFTY-FOUR

KAT

"Hey, Theo, Katrina," Jeff says as we walk into the office on the day of the vote. Theo's fingers reach out, twining with mine as we walk to where he's standing outside of his office, a kind smile on his lips.

"What's up?" Theo asks.

"You nervous for today?"

"No, not really," Theo lies. "Can't really change anything now. It's out of my hands." Jeff claps Theo's shoulder, shaking it.

"No matter what, I'm proud of you, Theodore. Your dad would be proud of you, too." I twitch my nose, trying not to give in to the emotion. Theo nods his head. "Sunday. Judy wants you two over for dinner, yeah?"

"We'd love that," I say with a smile. It quickly fades as Warren walks in the front door and then over to where we're all standing.

"Morning, Jeff, Theo," he says, ignoring me completely. I roll my eyes. "Big day, yeah?"

I want to punch him in the face. So badly. Just once.

"You've got a little something," Theo says, breaking me from my daydreaming moment and pointing to his cheek. "Right there."

Then I see it.

All over Warren are tiny specks of fine powder glitter. It looks like he got most of it, but it's glitter. Without burning whatever came in contact with it, you'll be finding it until you die if you've been glitter-bombed.

I smile wide. We weren't sure if it would work, glitter in Warren's vents, considering it's past needing the heat on, but it was unseasonably hot this morning, so he must have turned the air conditioning on. . . God, I wish I could take a photo. Savannah would love this.

"Glitter?" I ask, tipping my head at him. "Didn't take you for the arts and crafts type." His nostrils flare and his jaw clenches, and I fight the laugh bubbling in my chest.

"Some bitch put glitter in the vents of my car," he grumbles, and I tip my head to the side in faux confusion.

"Some bitch? Strange, aren't you dating Savannah?" Jeff's head snaps back. Even though none of this matters, our plan too solid and concrete, it's still another great shot, a hit to his confidence. "Oh, shoot, that's right. You guys broke up last week. Tough break, buddy." Warren glares at me. His jaw goes tight, and I fight the urge to laugh. It probably wouldn't be great for the cause. Instead, I look to Jeff, whose brow is furrowed in confusion.

"Something happen between you and Savannah?" Jeff asks.

"Oh, you know, it's just a misunderstanding. I have to do the whole send her flowers and chocolates thing and she'll get over it."

Get over you cheating on her and only dating her to have an in with her guardian? *I don't think it will be that easy,* I want to say, but I don't. Before anyone can respond, Jeff's phone rings in his office.

"Gotta go get that. See you all later. Meeting's at one." Then, he walks into his office and closes the door behind himself.

"See you at one," Warren says with a cocky grin.

"Yes, you will," Theo says, then leads us to his office, where he closes the door behind us, pins me to it, and kisses me until I forget all about Warren and his bullshit.

After our morning kiss, I barely see Theo or get any work done, nerves eating at me.

I don't even snack.

"Hey," he says when it's time for us both to head into the board-room, grabbing my hand and tugging me into him. The assistants all attend this annual meeting as well, which is perfect since I'd rather die than miss this.

"Hey," I whisper against his lips.

"You good?" I smile.

"Aren't I supposed to ask you that?"

"I've got this in the bag. How are you?"

"Nervous," I admit.

"Nothing to be nervous about, kitten," he says confidently, sending a shiver down my spine. He only ever calls me that when we're alone, usually when he's inside me, and he knows it, too. He feels the shiver and smiles. "Later."

"Tease," I murmur.

"How about I show you what a tease I can be tonight?" I roll my eyes and slap his chest, starting to pull away. His fingers circle my wrist and he keeps me in place with an arm around my waist.

"Hey," he says. "No matter what happens, no matter what Warren says, you keep your chin up. You stay strong."

"What?"

"No matter what happens, don't worry. We've got this, Katrina."

"You're scaring me, Theo."

"No time to be scared. Just promise me, no matter what happens, you keep your cool." Looking into his eyes, I try to read between the lines, to see his secrets, but I can't see anything. Nothing at all.

Except for love. Adoration. Excitement.

So I nod.

"Okay, Theo." He smiles at me, pressing his lips to mine once more before stepping back and twining his fingers with mine.

"Okay. Let's do this thing."

Theo squeezes my hand as we walk in, leading me toward a chair lining the wall before he sits at the table not too far from me. Jess welcomes everyone to the annual meeting, says a few words about businesses, and then announces the vote will commence.

"We're going to give both Warren and Theodore a chance to speak before we vote," Jeff says. "Would one of you like to go first?" Warren stands instantly, a shit-eating grin on his face.

"I would," he says.

"Great. Give your final remarks to the board." He nods, fixing his suit jacket before his face gets excited. Excited and mean.

"You know, I could spend this reminding you of my many, many achievements for this company," Warren starts, and I fight a scoff but not the eye roll. I notice then that Theo is turned slightly toward me, and he's smiling at me like he finds me entertaining.

"But we all know the amazing things I've done to help grow Catalyst. Instead, this morning, I need to bring something to your attention. I hate to bring this up on such an important day, but I find it imperative to tell you all before the vote that Theodore Carter is lying to all of you." Murmurs fill the room, and before he even speaks another word, I know what he's going to say.

Somehow, Warren Michaels knows about Theo and me. About the true nature of how our relationship started.

But how?

It doesn't take long for him to reveal himself.

"I recently hired a private investigator to look into Katrina Delgado, and what I found was . . . shocking, to say the least." I look at Theo, and I'm shocked to see he's sitting back in his chair, a small smile on his lips, his arms crossed on his chest. He turns his head to me, just a fraction of a shift, and winks at me.

He *winks* at me.

Somehow, he knew this was coming.

That's why he warned me not to do anything. Suddenly, I don't care that all eyes are on me. I remember his words and straighten my shoulders and tip my chin up defiantly.

I won't let this man see me shaken.

"It turns out, in her free time, Katrina Delgado works for a business called The Ex Files. It's a small business based in Ocean View where a matchmaker vets men for red flags—kind of sexist if you ask me since she doesn't vet the women similarly, but that's beside the point." I roll my eyes, because of course he would be offended by that.

Because he would never get past the written questionnaire, let's be honest.

"That's how she and Carter started. He needed a fiancée, and he hired her to be his."

Confused murmurs fill the room, and Warren stands, beginning to pace the boardroom like some kind of processor at a college giving a lecture. God, he's such a douche.

"You see, months ago, Jeff Banks told Theodore that he wouldn't back him in getting the president position because he had no one in his life. He lives such a sad, lonely existence, doing nothing but focusing on Catalyst." I make the wise decision to glimpse at Jeff despite the anxiety and anger brewing in my belly and see his jaw gets tight.

Interesting.

"She's essentially prostituting herself to Carter to trick all of you and Jeff into thinking he's a real family man," Warren says with a nasty smile.

That's the line that breaks Theo's cool, perfect timing since Warren is right behind him.

"What the fuck did you just say?" he asks, his voice low and menacing, and even I am terrified. I've never seen him like this, angry and ready to blow. His fingers are curled into a fist.

"I'm just saying, she's selling herself—" Theo pulls back his fist, and somehow in time, I'm able to stand, rush over, and grab his wrist.

"Theo! No. No." Theo drops his arm and turns slightly toward me. "No. He is so not fucking worth it, Theo. Just look at him, honey. He's desperate. Don't ruin this." Then I lean in a bit, my lips at his ear. "Remember, we have better revenge than this bullshit. He's scrambling. Who cares if he calls us out? Who cares what he says about me?"

He turns to me fully, his hand moving to my jaw, his forehead coming to rest on mine, and for a split second, I think about all the people in this room, watching us, intruding on our private moment. But it disappears when I see the concern and indignance in his eyes.

For me. He's angry and worried because someone is talking shit about me.

"I care," he murmurs. I smile.

"I know. And that's hot, boss man, but unnecessary." He nods, his forehead shifting along mine before he lets me go. He grabs my hand and once more walks me over to where I was sitting before returning to his chair.

Eyes are on us. Burning, taking us in, dissecting this interaction and trying to fit it into the new information they just got from Warren.

"Sorry, continue," Theo says with a wave of his hand at Warren, and I fight a laugh.

Jeff, though, doesn't.

I look at him, and he smiles, winking at me.

Well, that's not what I was expecting.

"So, uh, yeah," Warren says, thrown off his trail. "I, uh, just wanted to bring this to all of your attention before the vote is enacted. Let you know the kind of man who wants to run this company." People are whispering, and I watch as Warren walks back to his seat and sits with a smug look.

Even now, he thinks he won. He thinks he did something big. Before Jeff can speak or hand the stage to Theo, he takes it.

"Before I talk to you all about the president position, I'd like to speak on what Warren just brought up," Theo starts, and I feel like I might be sick as I watch him stand, straighten his suit, and then wink at me.

God. He's so fucking handsome.

And in that moment, I know we'll be okay. It's a strange time for the realization, but it hits all the same.

I'm not going to get the ick. We're solid. I'm so madly in love with this man, and, if I'm finally being honest with myself, I have been for some time.

I smile at him, and I think, somehow, he knows the epiphany I just had.

"A few months ago in this room, I found out Jeff was retiring. It blew me away. Then I was told it would be either myself or Warren getting the position of president, and again, I'd be lying if I said it didn't shock me. I always thought this business would one day be in my hands. It's my father's legacy. Many of you were around when my father started this company with Jeff, saw me come in here as I grew up, watching him work.

"When I spoke to Jeff after the announcement, he expressed some concern with how my work-life balance looked. While I was unhappy with his insinuations"—he smiles at Jeff, who, to my surprise, smiles back—"I now can see he wasn't necessarily wrong. What was wrong, was me losing my mind and telling him I not only had a woman in my life, but I was engaged." He smiles and a few members of the board chuckle as he shakes his head self-deprecatingly. "Not sure what I was thinking, but I said it all the same. That same day, I called a friend whose wife owned a matchmaking service for some help. A few days later, I found myself at a table, sitting across from my gorgeous assistant and finding out on her downtime, she worked there." He smiles at me, wide and handsome, and god.

He's in his zone.

"Long story short, she convinced me she was the best choice to be my fake fiancée since we had already spent so much time together and we knew each other so well. I'm so damn glad she did. Over the next couple of weeks, we began to realize we were always meant to be here, to be together, and I'm grateful for the push Jeff gave me. At the end of the day, I might not have the position at the company my father built, but I did find the love of my life."

There are a few *awws* and a very loud scoff from Warren, but I ignore that because Theo's eyes are on me as he speaks, as if this whole conversation is just for my ears.

The love of my life.

There it is.

This is us. Him and me, together. A team. No matter how the rest of today goes, we have that.

"More than a few of you have come up to us over the past few weeks to tell us that, looking back, it was obvious we were together. So I fell in love with Katrina Delgado during the time we were pretending to be engaged, and now we're real, but I'm not actually sure we ever weren't real. It's always been us." He shrugs.

"You can let that choice I made a few months ago impact your decision on whether you want to place me at the head of Catalyst Records, and that's your right. But I want you to ask yourself if it wasn't for that, would you have decided I was the best option? Do you think your relationship status should decide if you get a job? Whitney, you're single. Does that make you more or less qualified to be on this board?" She looks taken aback, but he skips to the next member.

"And you, Jim. Your daughter is going into law school. Should her not being married or having a steady social life since she's, you know, going to school to be a lawyer have an impact on what kind of law firms she gets to work at? I appreciate Jeff's mentorship, and I know he came from a place of love and compassion, but my personal life has nothing to do with Catalyst Records. The only thing I do agree with there is that you shouldn't let my relationship with Jeff or the fact that my father was one of the founders of this place decide if I should get this job. You should vote on my merit—my track record for caring for the people at this company, for finding talent that will continue to grow Catalyst, and my love for this business."

When I look around the room, I see heads are nodding and people are smiling.

"Now that that's over," Theo says with a wide smile, his eyes moving from Warren to Jeff then, finally, to mine. "I have an announcement of my own."

"Well, might as well throw the entire agenda out the window at this point," Jeff mumbles, and I laugh out loud.

"I promise this will be worth it." Jeff nods. "I have a second item for the board to vote on today if we can all agree on it." A murmur runs through the room. It's unheard of for anything to be brought up for a vote by someone other than the president.

"Can we ask what it is?" Jeff inquires, and even though somewhere in my gut, I know Jeff trusts Theo with his whole being, his face shows concern and even panic.

"Warren Michaels has been selling confidential information from Catalyst Records to Blacknote for kickbacks and plans to make Catalyst go under if he gets the president position so his and Ray Harmon's stock in Blacknote will increase. I would like to vote to remove him from the board and from Catalyst Records."

With that, the room fills with noise.

FIFTY-FIVE

KAT

"This is bullshit," Warren says with a strained laugh. "He's been trying to accuse me of this for years. He's mad about a mix-up from college, and he's never gotten over it."

"You know, you're right, Warren. I have had a feeling for quite some time that you were taking information and artists I was bringing to meetings and sending them to Blacknote, creating a bidding war or simply stealing artists right out from under us. You lure them with better-looking contracts, but tie them to Blacknote for extraordinary lengths of time and with terms that will fuck them in the long run. It's why you're looking to make Catalyst go under, isn't it?" Theo stands, walking around the large table until he's behind Warren, putting his hands on the back of his chair and looking over the board members as he explains.

"You see, Warren's plan is to continue to send the talents with real potential over to Blacknote and to, as quickly as he can, tank the stock and name of Catalyst Records. Once we're on the border of bankruptcy, Blacknote is going to purchase the business at a steal. Once he does that, he can alter all of the existing contracts to better suit their bottom line, like reducing royalty percentages and increasing term length. Artists would have to agree to these changes or risk losing the original rights to their music."

It's interesting to look around the table and see mostly wide, astonished eyes. It seems that, unlike Warren thought and Theo feared, most of the members of the board agree that would not be great. Ray Harmon seems panicked, knowing he's being dragged down, and Rick O'Connor, the board member Warren is closest to other than Ray, looks like he doesn't think it's a bad idea.

But the rest?

Theo was right: Warren doesn't have them on his side the way he thinks he does. I wonder if he ever did or if this is the nail in his coffin.

"Everyone, I think we all need to really sit and think about this. This is an incredibly dangerous lie to throw out there—"

"It's not a lie," I say, suddenly feeling brave. All eyes shift to me, and I almost second-guess that braveness, but I keep going.

"Shut up, you bitch. What the fuck do you know?"

"I would greatly appreciate it if you didn't speak to my woman like that ever again, Michaels," Theo says, danger in the words. I roll my lips into my mouth and fight off a smile. "We have all the proof we need to pin all of the leaked clients on you."

"Proof? Of what? You can't prove anything."

"I think I'll let my gorgeous fiancée explain," Theo says with a wide smile.

"She's just a fucking assistant! She can't be trusted to know anything. This is—"

I'm already pulling my phone up, though, and pressing play on a "demo." We made it the day after the gala, the girls and I a little drunk on mimosas and emotions, and it took about forty takes before Abbie could get through the song without laughing, but we did it.

And now her "debut single" is playing in the room.

"That's the artist Theo brought to the table last week," Jeff says, suddenly understanding. "Blacknote just signed her."

"Yeah, well, unfortunately, that contract isn't going to be very valid. Thankfully, her husband was the one who drafted it, so it should be easy to get her out of." I hit pause on the song and smile sweetly. "That? That's my best friend, Abigail Martinez. And that song she's singing is an AI-created sound bite. Weird that Blacknote would sign a woman with an entire social media platform made of bot accounts and only one demo, but I guess when you're reckless and think you're bulletproof, trying to ruin someone's career for your own benefit, you don't really do the research, do you, Warren?"

His face is going red, and I think if I wasn't in a room full of witnesses, he might try and hurt me.

"The song, by the way, was one the computer and I wrote about you," I say with a laugh. "I thought it was a bit poetic, don't you think? Writing a song about revenge, about an asshat of a man who thinks his shit doesn't stink, who thinks no one deserves anything even close to what he does, and then using it to orchestrate your own demise?" I smile dreamily. "After all of the artists you stole from Theo, I figured it was great payback."

"On the bright side, I did find a way to get back all of those artists that Warren handed to Blacknote," Theo says, and my brow furrows because I haven't heard this part yet. I was under the impression those were all lost causes. Theo catches my eyes and gives me a devilish smile.

"I've been talking with the board of Blacknote, and they've agreed to step into negotiations for us to acquire them . . . and their entire catalog." A gasp goes through the room, and I watch the color drain from Warren's face.

"I-I . . . You're lying. That makes no sense, Carter. This is all pandering to get the president position."

"Oh, I think we can probably all agree the vote is not going to happen today. Right, everyone?" he asks, and everyone nods and agrees. "But I'm happy to explain more about this deal I've been working on. You see, you're not the only one who can afford a PI, Warren," Theo says. "Turns out, they're hemorrhaging money and they need someone to take them on. They were incredibly thankful when I started to dig through their financials to try and figure out where everything has been going, since they've taken on so many lucrative artists." My eyes move to Warren, and his bravado is gone. I look to Ray, and his face is as white as can be. "Any idea why that might be, Warren? Ray?"

"I don't know anything about that company."

"Oh, strange. Because here"—I start to hand out financial documents with payout numbers—"are transactions that occurred from the main account of Blacknote, though there was no code for accounts payable attached. Funny, it seems most of these can be attached to something one of you purchased and came into brag about or when we somehow lost a client to them."

Theo looks to me, smiles and winks, and slowly, I feel my lips turn up with a smile as I shake my head at him.

"You and Ray Harmon were receiving kickbacks when you sent Travis a client. Unfortunately, Travis didn't have anyone else in on this information, so he was basically stealing from the company. As of nine this morning, Steven Schaefer is the interim president while we work through the acquisition."

"I don't . . . This is . . ." Slowly, Warren starts to walk toward the door to leave.

Is he really going to try and run?

Fortunately, it seems Jeff has the same idea and is already on his phone.

"Hi, Jess, can you send security up here? We have a situation where we'll need to detain Warren Michaels. Could you also call the local police? I think we have some criminal charges we'll need to file, and he'll need a professional escort from the building."

With that, I look at my man.

His eyes are already on me, his smile wide.

All I can do is smile back.

We fucking did it.

FIFTY-SIX

THEO

There's a lot of commotion for long hours after my revelations in the boardroom. Warren and Ray Harmon both tried to leave, but the building security made sure they couldn't until the police came, at which point they were arrested on suspicion of corporate espionage. With everything the PI found for me, plus the financial documents from Blacknote and the recording, it's not going to be hard to charge them with it.

Then there was a lot of conversation with the board regarding the merger and acquisition of Blacknote and a call with Steven. At some point, I looked over at the corner where Katrina was sitting, making sure she took copious notes for me, and she had a mini bag of pretzels she was munching on, reminding me we needed to order in a late lunch.

And now, it's nearly five o'clock, but although many of the employees and board members are leaving for the day, I know mine isn't over yet.

"Theodore, Katrina, would you mind coming into my office, please? I think there's a long overdue conversation we need to have."

Katrina looks at me with wide eyes I'm sure I return before we have a silent conversation, and I nod, grabbing her hand.

"Yes, I agree."

We make our way to Jeff's office, closing the door behind us, and Katrina and I sit in chairs across from his desk. It feels kind of like being at the principal's office, and I'm anxious until Katrina's hand in mine squeezes tight. I look to her, and she gives me a small smile, and I know then, we can do this if we're together.

Finally, Jeff sits across from us, folds his hands, and looks at us expectantly.

"Jeff, look, I'm so sorry. We—" I start.

"Mr. Banks, it's not—" Katrina tries, but we both stop speaking when Jeff smiles and crosses his arms on his chest, sitting back in his chair.

"You know you're a shit liar, right?" That stops us in our tracks.

"What?" I ask.

"You're a shit liar, Theodore Carter. Your father was, too, you know. Couldn't tell a lie to save his life. I used to call him Teddy Washington. He fucking hated that." I wait for him to explain, but he doesn't.

"I'm sorry, Jeff. I really don't understand what you're saying." He smiles again and leans forward.

"Do you really think that you could come to my house for dinner, your assistant wearing your mother's engagement ring, and I wouldn't question it?"

"I mean . . . I—"

He cuts my sentence off by reaching into a drawer on his desk, shifting things around, and finding a piece of folded paper. I'm not sure what it is, but Katrina must because her hand squeezes mine and she whispers, "Oh fuck," under her breath.

"I'm assuming you wrote this?" he asks her, raising an eyebrow. When I look at my girl, her eyes are wide, locked on the paper I now see is covered in her handwriting.

It comes back to me.

It's our history. Read it and memorize it later.

She told me not to bring it into the house, but I don't remember what I did or didn't do with it. I never even thought of that paper after that night.

"Judy found it. We had a good laugh over it, reading your relationship history." When I look at Katrina, she *glares* at me.

"I told you to leave it in the car!" she shouts, unable to stop the urge to fight with me, and even though this entire situation is beyond fucked, I can't help but smile.

"Jeff, I'm really so sorry. I know it was wrong, and you fully have the right to be angry with us—"

"Angry?" I stop speaking altogether. "Why would I be angry?" I turn to look at Katrina, who has a similarly confused face on.

"Well, I lied to try and trick you into backing me for president." Jeff waves a hand at me.

"You two had been dancing around one another for *months*. So when you showed up at my house with her on your arm, telling me you're engaged, she's wearing your mother's ring, and you look like you're about to vomit, I knew I needed to see how it went. Thought if anyone could pull your head out of your ass, make you see there's more to life than work, it would be this firecracker here," he says, tipping his head toward Katrina. She smiles, but I continue to sit in stunned silence.

"Now, I'll admit, Warren had the wool pulled over me. I thought he was an ass, but I really didn't want to believe he was being as malicious as you kept trying to tell me. And for that, I'm sorry. I should have listened to you before it came to this. I hope you forgive me with time."

Still, I don't move, don't breathe. Katrina squeezes my hand tight once more.

"So that being said, I'll be holding a vote sometime in the next week or so, once all of this insanity dies down." He pauses and somehow, I know it's for dramatic effect. It's very much his way, after all. "I'll be voting this time. And I'll be voting for you, son." My mouth drops open in shock. There were a lot of things I expected from this conversation, but this was never one of them.

"I don't . . . ," I start. "I don't understand."

"I never doubted you'd get the votes, Theodore. I just wanted to make it so that when you were in charge, no one on that board could question if you *deserved* that job. I knew if you were in that place, you'd work to the bone to prove yourself to them. Bonus, I got to tell you you had no life, and it gave you a jumpstart to *make one*. I didn't foresee the fake relationship thing, but I'll admit, it was entertaining."

"Are you saying you only told me you wanted me to have a social life so you'd have an excuse not to vote?"

"Well, I guess when you put it that way, yeah."

"Why wouldn't you just *say* you didn't want to vote because you didn't want to influence it?"

"Well, I kind of did at that meeting, you know." I glare at him because he knows *exactly* what I mean. Finally, he sighs. "You know, grief and guilt are funny, fickle things. I miss your dad every day, and when I look at you, I see him. Even way back then, I didn't want to disappoint your father. I guess a part of me never wants to disappoint you either." Suddenly, there's a lump in my throat, painful and aching, too big to speak around, and my fingers hold tight to Katrina's hand.

"I get it, Jeff. I know Theo does too. I know you and I both always believed in him, but I think, in a way, this entire experience helped him to believe in himself, too. Though, I will request next time you want to teach him a life lesson, can we make it a bit simpler? Let's not put the entire company into jeopardy, yeah?" This makes Jeff laugh out loud, his head tipping back and the sound filling the room.

"You really do like to bust people's chops, don't you?"

"Mostly men with too much influence and not enough ego," she says with a sweet smile. I shake my head and look to the ceiling, but Jeff just laughs again.

"I like you, Katrina," he says to her then turns to me. "Don't let that one slip away, you hear me?"

"Don't plan to, Jeff," I vow, looking at Katrina and smiling, and she blushes.

"Alright, well, it's been a long day. Why don't you get her home? Katrina, I don't think you've eaten anything but a few snacks today," Jeff says, making me laugh out loud as I stand.

"Trust me, it's an ongoing thing," I reply. Hugs are exchanged, and we head for the door.

Katrina walks out in front of me, but I pause when Jeff speaks lower, his words just for me.

"Oh, and Theodore?" My shoulders go tight at the tease in Jeff's voice.

I thought I had made it out clear, but . . . "We've all done it. But please, for the love of god, try and be a bit more discreet. And definitely *not on someone else's desk*. Even if he is an ass."

"Jesus fuck," I say but don't stop to try and stick up for myself, argue, deny, or ask how he knows. Honestly, I don't even want to know. Instead, I walk out, headed toward my office and my girl.

And as I do, Jeff's booming laugh follows behind me.

FIFTY-SEVEN

KAT

"You did it!" I say once the office door is closed behind us. I'm effervescent with joy and excitement. He smiles, his eyes tired, but he still pulls me into him, burying his face into my neck.

"We did it," he says there, his words vibrating and tickling my skin.

"I can't believe you didn't tell me about buying Blacknote!" I yell, finally alone to scold him.

"I wanted the drama," he says with a smile, and I shake my head. "You were amazing."

"I know," I acknowledge. He laughs and then kisses me for a long while before he pulls back. I put my hand between us, needing to get this done before I lose the courage. "I should give this back," I say, fumbling for the ring he slid on my finger what feels like another lifetime ago.

I can't before his hand moves to grab mine, stopping me.

"Leave it on, Kat. My ring does not leave your finger, except for when I put a new one beneath it." I read between the lines of his pretty words but shake my head all the same.

"I can't, Theo. We're not . . ."

"We are. We are, Katrina. You know that. I know that." I stare at him, feeling that constriction in my chest, the panic of this. "This is real. We're real. We're not going back to how things were."

"Theo . . ."

"Called your landlord this morning. If you grab your things by the end of the week, you get back your security deposit." That makes my head snap back.

"What?"

"If you pack everything up by Sunday, you get your security deposit back. If you take much longer than that, he's going to charge you for the month. Once that happens, I'm not sure if I can argue with you getting your deposit back, but he did agree to cancel your lease whenever you're ready."

"I . . . What?"

"We already agreed you wouldn't have to worry about incidentals, as he's going to start slowly redoing each apartment, win-win. He can charge more with all the changes."

"I . . . I'm sorry. Where am I supposed to take all of my stuff if I'm not living there?" I ask, blinking at him. He stares back.

"Well, our place. Unless . . ." He pauses. "Unless you want to just get rid of all of your shit. I figure your furniture isn't sentimental, but you'd want your clothes and your photos. Your shoes."

"Obviously, I want my shoes, Theo," I say with an eye roll.

"Of course," he says with a smile, still holding me.

"I need you to explain this to me like I'm five. What's the plan?"

"You're moving in with me. For real." I shake my head and smile like he's the insane man he absolutely is.

"No, I'm not."

"You absolutely are."

"Theo, this is . . ."

"Do you want to go back to how things were?" he asks suddenly, surprising me.

"What?"

"Do you want to go back to how things were? You, my assistant, you sleeping in your own bed. Us not being . . . us?"

"Well . . ." I pause and answer honestly. "Well, no."

"Me neither. So you're moving in with me. Half of your shit is already at my place."

"But . . . all of my stuff is clutter. You're neat and organized and . . . minimalist."

"Your stuff isn't clutter. It's life. Bring your life into my place, Kat. It's been lonely and dead for so long." My heart pulses. "I love you," he whispers against my lips. "I want this for real. Forever. I want to date for real. I want to let Judy plan some chaotic wedding, but I'm telling you now, I want a simple ceremony. Just us and our closest people. I know your girls have to be there, and your parents. My sister would riot if she wasn't there, same with Jeff and Judy, but that's it. The reception can be wild and crazy and chaos."

"You . . . You want to get married."

"Of course. I'd crumble without you, Katrina." A tear drops with his words, and as is his way, he doesn't swipe it away, telling me not to cry. He lets it fall, lets it slip to the corner of my mouth then kisses me, tasting it on my lips. It lasts long, him kissing me, putting everything he feels for me into it.

When he breaks it finally, he rests his head against mine.

"So what do you say?"

I smile then shift my hands behind his head, biting my lip as I try to do my task without looking before I smile at him, showing him my right hand where his mother's ring now sits, leaving my left ring finger empty.

"I won't take your ring off, but I want a proper proposal, Theodore Carter. Saying 'here' in my shitty apartment parking garage and giving me a ring is not what I'm going to tell our kids one day." When he sees it, he smiles wide.

"Are you ever going to stop busting my balls and making life difficult?" I shake my head.

"Never."

"Good."

He waits a full ten months until tulip season to put his mother's ring back on my finger properly.

Hey, reader!!

In this last section of the epilogue and the wrapping up of the Season of Revenge series, there is a mention of pregnancy (not Kat and Theo, but another couple from a past book). If you are struggling with infertility, miscarriage, or if for *any* reason you don't enjoy reading about that topic, you can skip the last few passages and know that Kat, Theo, and the Revengers have their own happily ever after.

You are loved, you are important, and you are seen.

Love,
Morgan

EPILOGUE

Cami

"Hey," I say, stepping into the living area of our hotel room, where Zach is sitting, legs spread, the neck of a bottle of beer held loosely in his fingers.

"You ready?" he asks.

"Yeah, but I don't have to be there for another twenty minutes or so."

"Hmm," he says, a lazy smile growing on his lips as I walk closer to him. "What should we do to pass the time?" He leans forward, placing his beer on the coffee table. He looks *good*. His hair has gone a bit gray at the temples, somehow making him ten times hotter, and with a white button-down and a yellow tie to match my dress, I can't resist him.

But *finally*, my chance is here, and I refuse to miss it. I step between his legs, and his hands move right to my skin, sliding up and down in a way that's supposed to look comforting but is anything but.

"Wanna play Barbies?" I ask, and his brow furrows. I fight to make my face stay neutral. I've been saving this one for almost a week, waiting for the perfect moment.

"What?"

I lose the battle halfway through the punchline, and my smile breaks through. "You can be Ken, and I can be the box you come in."

A beat passes, and I watch it process in his mind before his head tips back, and he barks out a laugh.

"Jesus, fuck, you're a piece of work," he says, tugging on my knees until I fall onto the couch, straddling him. His hand moves up my back, gripping my hair to guide my face to his.

"No, no! Zach, no, I'm serious! I'm not redoing my makeup!" His lips touch mine, and without my permission, my body slackens, the fight leaving me.

"Zach," I whisper.

"A quickie," he says, his lips trailing down my neck.

"We can't be late."

"I'll be quick," he assures me.

"Really, Zach, I'm serious," I whine as his lips move down my throat. "We can't do this." My fingers move to the buttons of his shirt, and I feel more than hear the deep rumble of his laugh.

"Of course not." His hand moves to the straps of my dress, pushing them down until my breasts are hit with cool air.

"Quick," I whisper.

"Quick," he agrees.

Olivia

"Olivia Valenti, stay out of it," my husband says as we drive to the hotel.

"What?! I was just saying!"

"You're never *just saying*, Liv," he scolds, exhaustion in his words.

"I could be. You don't know."

"Not a soul knows you as well as I know you."

I hate that he's right.

"I'm just saying, she could probably use someone in her corner. She just had her heart broken, and David is a fucking *asshole*. He deserves a little glitter in his life." Andre groans.

"You're retired, Olivia."

"A Revenger never retires."

"Jesus fucking Christ."

"Would it really hurt that much if we just snuck into his house and—" The car jerks as Andre slams on the brakes on the side of the deserted road. I roll my lips into my mouth, biting down as I watch him undo his seatbelt, open his door, slam it shut, and walk around the front of the car, admiring just how good his ass looks in those suit pants. Sure, he wears suits to work most days, but there's something about seeing it on a random Saturday that feels . . . *decadent*.

Especially when he does it all broody and annoyed with me.

He stops at my door, jerking it open then leaning in to undo my seatbelt, and pulls me from the seat, pressing me up against the side of his SUV.

"You know, we don't need to make photo ops for paparazzi anymore, Andre."

"God, I can't stand you."

"You're a bad liar," I whisper back.

"I'm not getting a call from the local police again, telling me you're breaking into a man's car to put glitter in his vents."

"Oh, stop it. Warren deserved it *most of all*, and once we told them what was happening, they became our lookouts!" Andre shakes his head, exasperated with me as usual.

"You do revenge, you let me in on it. If I say no, it's a no, Olivia. *I'm* your lookout while you execute." I stand there, taking in my handsome husband before I lift a hand, holding it to his cheek.

"God, you really love me, don't you?"

"More than anything."

Abbie

"No, no, over there," I say, pointing to the window with the most light, watching my husband's muscles flex underneath his button-down shirt.

"Are you fucking with me?" he asks, looking over his shoulder at me, and I shake my head.

"A little to the left." For the record, I'm so totally fucking with him. I don't care where the chaise lounge is. I doubt Savannah will even take photos of Kat on it—it's not her style. Now, if it were *my* wedding? I would have a photo shoot on this damn sofa, lots of pink roses, and maybe some tulle and marabou feathers (faux, of course) and ... Well, it doesn't matter.

It's not my wedding.

I just want to watch him move this thing a few more times.

He stands and glares at me, reading my face, and I know I'm totally caught. The smile spreads on my lips, and he walks to me, shaking his head.

"You know I'll do whatever you ask, but if I spend all this time moving furniture, I'm missing out on the downtime you have before your girls show up." My belly flutters with his words.

"Downtime? Now what, Mr. Martinez, could you possibly do with *downtime.*"

He steps closer to me, his hand tugging on the silky blush dressing gown I have on, revealing skin and lace beneath. "Jesus fuck." He groans, his hand moving to my belly, sliding up and up and up, only stopping when his palm is resting against my throat, where I know my pulse is beating crazy.

"I could think of a few things," he says before kissing me breathless. When he finally breaks the kiss, he looks at me, raising a thick brow in question.

"The furniture can stay," I murmur, and his deep laugh fills the room.

"I love you, Abigail," he whispers against my lips before he shows me just how much on that pretty white chaise lounge.

Kat

"I'm here! I'm here!" Cami says, walking into the bridal suite and waving something in the air.

My something blue.

I don't miss how her lipstick is a bit smeared or how the back of her dress isn't fully zipped.

"God, did you really have to fuck my dad before you came here?" Liv asks with a roll of her eyes. Cami glares at her then smiles.

"Actually, yes. Weddings do things to me." A beat passes.

"Oh, god, I think I'm going to be sick," Olivia says, covering her face. I was watching the exchange in the mirror at the vanity, but now I turn to look at them, at my friends.

Abbie is in a gorgeous pink baby doll dress that floats to just above her knees, puffy sleeves dotted in sparkling gems, her long blonde hair perfectly curled. She looks like a real-life Barbie.

Savannah is in a dark-purple-and-blue-patterned maxi dress, comfy for photos I told her she didn't *have* to take for us, but she insisted on it.

Cami is in a buttery yellow dress that floats to her shins, the thick straps at the top ending in pretty bows.

Finally, Liv is in a gorgeous, loose pale-green dress that makes her dark hair and green eyes pop.

Except, her face looks a bit green too.

"Oh, shit." She groans then runs off to the bathroom, where we hear retching. All four of us exchange confused glances except for

Cami, who is staring at the bathroom with a glare, her arms crossed on her chest.

"What's going on?" I ask, though, in my gut, I know. Cami continues to stand, staring, and no one speaks until Liv comes back in after brushing her teeth, a small, guilty smile on her lips.

"When are you going to stop playing this game?" Cami asks, tapping her toe on the tile floor.

"What game?" Liv looks somewhere beyond Cami, but definitely not *at* her.

"Don't play dumb. It isn't becoming on you."

"Cami—"

"You're pregnant," Cam says. Abbie gasps, instantly covering her mouth and tearing up. When I look back at Cami, who is staring at Liv still, her face is soft and gentle. I look back to Liv, whose eyes have started watering.

"We wanted to wait until I was 12 weeks," she says. "And for Kat's big day to be over."

"Oh, my god," Cami whispers, and that's when the tears start. I start fanning my face, trying to stop it, but I know it's no use as I watch Cami take three steps and pull Olivia, her partner's daughter, for all intents and purposes *her* daughter, into her arms. Liv instantly starts sobbing and I hear Abbie start to cry too, but I can't bear to break my eyes from the scene in front of me.

It's beautiful. It's healing. It's . . . my people.

My people at their absolute most happy on the happiest day of my life.

Long, long minutes later, Savannah, the newest addition to our little crew, sniffs, clears her throat, and speaks.

"I hate to be the one who breaks things up, but we've got like, ten minutes until the car arrives to take us to the ceremony." We all jump back and giggle and start waving at our faces to dry them down. Abbie comes up to me and starts dabbing at me.

"See, I told you it would be cry-proof."

"Oh, is that what this was? A good little test to see if I would cry through my makeup?" I ask. Liv smiles and laughs.

"Exactly. You're welcome. At least you know when Theo makes you sob in front of everyone, you'll look pretty."

That's also new, Theo letting my girls call him Theo as well. Upon the first dinner party with everyone, Cami stopped mid-sentence, looked at him, and said, "I'm sorry. I can't do it. I can't call you Theodore. It's stupid." The table went silent before I burst into loud laughter. Everyone followed and when it died out, he spoke.

"Theo is fine," he said.

And that was that.

"Okay, okay, we've gotta rush this, I guess. So here's your new," Abbie says, walking over with a small box.

"Abbie . . ."

"I'm not listening to that," she says. "Every bride needs the good luck." I roll my eyes but take the box anyway. "And honestly, it's selfish because I really wanted one." Furrowing my brow, I open the box and instantly start laughing.

"Shut the fuck up," I say then look up at Abbie, who is showing me her hand, a pink version of the small, girly signet ring in the box before me, a gem encrusted R in the center. Then I look at the girls, each with one of their own.

Orange for Cami, purple for Liv, red for Savannah, teal for me.

"She talked me into it," Cami says, staring at the ring on her right ring finger. "But honestly, it's too funny to hate on."

"Shut *up*. Normally, I'd throw a fit over you spending money on us like—"

"Damien bought them."

"Of course he did. Normally, I'd throw a fit over *Damien* spending money on us, but I'll let this fly. They're perfect, Abs. Thank you."

"Love you, babe. I'm so happy for you. I'm so glad our scheming and revenge somehow found us all our someones."

"If you make me cry, I'm going to be late, and I'm not being late for this," I whisper through a frog in my throat.

"I've got blue," Cami says, bumping Abbie out of the way with her hip and handing me a tiny scrap of blue lace.

"What the—"

"It's your garter." I bust out laughing but bend over and slide it over my foot to my thigh.

"You would. Thank you, Cam. Love you."

"I got borrowed," Liv says. When I look at her, I almost start bawling again, just thinking about her being pregnant. "No! No more of that shit. I can't handle it." That makes me laugh instead of cry, which is a win. "This is a bracelet my dad gave me to wear to *my* wedding as my new. Now, it's your borrow." She reaches over and puts it on me, a simple, pretty diamond tennis bracelet, but perfect in its simplicity and its meaning. I put my hand to it as she steps back.

"Love you, Liv."

"Okay, me last!" Savannah says, clearly excited. "First—" She reaches behind her for a bag, then pulls out a box and a bag. "Theo begged me to bring you these." I laugh out loud, taking in the box of *Gansitos* and a bag of pretzels. "He said in case you needed some nourishment, he doesn't want you passing out at the altar." I blink, fighting back tears once more because even now, he finds ways to take care of me. I accept the treats, putting them to the side as she then grabs and reaches into a tiny drawstring bag. "These are technically Teddy's, but our mom gave them to him for, well, you, one day."

"What?" I ask, confused, but Savannah jiggles the bag into her hand and shakes her head.

"Judy had a box, a bunch of jewelry my mom bought for Teddy and me. I've gotten a bunch of things, a necklace for my sixteenth birthday and pearl studs when I graduated high school, but all he got were these." She opens her hand, and I look for just a moment before I break.

"Oh, my god," I say, choking on a sob when I see the two stud earrings. I grab one, looking closer at what seems like rubies and emeralds cut and set to look like two tiny red tulips. "How could she know?"

"I don't know, but it's like she always did, Kat. My mom and your *abuela* were somehow in cahoots, I just know it," she says. I continue staring at her for a long beat before she speaks again, the words choked through unshed tears. "I'm so happy you're going to be my sister." I don't reply.

I can't.

Instead, I pull her in tight for a hug that she instantly returns.

I hold Savannah like that for what feels like an eternity, both of us fighting and failing at our attempt not to cry before a sniffly Abbie speaks.

"I hate to break it up, but we gotta go," she whispers. I step back and fan my face, looking around at my girls.

My best friends in the entire world.

"Let's go get me married," I say.

Theo

Her eyes are already watering as she blinks at the piece of paper she's holding in one hand, her other in mine, and I squeeze tight. She takes a deep breath before those big brown eyes with gold specks throughout that I noticed on my assistant, not because we spent so much time together, but because I was madly in love with her even then, meet mine.

"I spent my entire life hyper-fixating on things and getting bored. I would see people for who they are, seeing the worst in them, the things they hide from the light. I was so scared I'd miss something and I would regret it, that I shut everyone out. I thought I was doomed to be alone, to never make it past seven, to watch friends find their forevers from the sideline." She takes one more deep, shaky breath before she looks at me again.

"Thank God you're a total idiot who made up the world's worst lie to try and get a job, huh?" I bust out laughing, as do our dozen or so witnesses. "That lie that you told in panic was the absolute best thing that ever happened to me, and I'll forever be grateful you told it. Because I have you, the man who helped me heal when I didn't know I was broken, who showed me love is about so much more than tolerating someone's every quirk, and who always makes sure I have snacks nearby." Another round of laughs bursts out.

"I can't wait to be Mrs. Carter. I love you so much, Theo."

She takes one last deep breath before nodding then moving to her tiptoes and pressing a surprise kiss to my lips.

"Now, now, you're supposed to wait for me to give you the all clear before you do that," the officiant says, and we all laugh.

"Sorry," she whispers, a blush blooming on her cheeks.

"Now, you, Theodore. Would you like to read your vows?" I nod, pull the perfectly folded paper out of my suit, and look at it.

It has everything I feel for Katrina and more written there in a neat 10-point Times New Roman.

I take a deep breath.

And then I rip it in half.

And again and again until the paper is just white confetti around our feet.

Kat seems a mix of annoyed and amused when I look at her.

Typical, really.

I smile at her, grabbing one hand and putting my other to her cheek.

Like always, the calm I feel encompasses me.

And then it's just us.

It's just Katrina and me standing in uncomfortable clothes and I'm talking to my best friend.

My only friend, as she likes to tell me.

"There were a lot things on that paper, but there's really only one I need to tell you. Something you already know, of course, because you know everything about me. You know what I ignore and what scares me. You know what I need and how to give it to me. You know when to let me stew and when to kick me in the ass, when to tell me to suck it up and get working. You know me, Katrina. And I know I would crumble without you." I say it, the thing she told me regularly anytime I threatened to fire her, the statement we both always knew was true, but it took me a bit longer to realize it meant in everything.

Her eyes water and her full lips, stained a cherry red that I know won't come off when we kiss, thanks to Abigail Martinez being in charge of her makeup, purse as she tries not to cry, but she fails.

I watch the single tear fall, watch her smile and mouth, "I love you," back to me when I mouth it first while the officiant rambles on about who knows what.

All that there is in this field where I realized I was in love with her is me and her and a million tulips.

"You may now kiss the bride," the officiant says finally, and I smile at my *bride* when she reaches up and touches her left ear before settling her arms on my shoulders.

"I love you, Mr. Carter," she whispers.

"And I love *you,* Mrs. Carter," I say back, and I feel her shiver as I press my lips to hers, as the small group of our closest friends and family cheer around us. As we do, a strong breeze whips around us, lifting Katrina's hair and veil, and I know, just like the first time we were here, just like when I proposed for real in these fields, my mother is here and she approves.

When the officiant announces us as Mr. and Mrs. Carter, we turn to everyone, lifting our joined hands. Kat looks around, smiling, catching the eyes of her girls and her parents and my family, but I look at her.

That's the photo that sits in my office until I get the honor of voting our daughter into the position of president of Catalyst Records thirty-four years later.

At the start of all of this, Katrina told me I deserved revenge on Warren, and I guess I did.

After all, the best revenge is falling in love.

ABOUT THE AUTHOR

Morgan is a born and raised Jersey girl, living there with her two sons and daughter, and mechanic husband. She's addicted to iced espresso, barbeque chips, and Starburst jellybeans. She usually has headphones on, listening to some spicy audiobook or Taylor Swift. There is rarely an in between.

Writing has been her calling for as long as she can remember. There's a framed 'page one' of a book she wrote at seven hanging in her childhood home to prove the point. Her entire life she's crafted stories in her mind, begging to be released but it wasn't until recently she finally gave them the reigns.

I'm so grateful you've agreed to take this journey with me.

Stay up to date via TikTok and Instagram

Stay up to date with future stories, get sneak peeks and bonus chapters by joining the Reader Group on Facebook!

WANT THE CHANCE TO WIN KINDLE STICKERS AND SIGNED COPIES?

Leave an honest review on Amazon or Goodreads and send the link to reviewteam@authormorganelizabeth.com and you'll be entered to win a signed copy of one of Morgan Elizabeth's books and a pack of bookish stickers!

Each email is an entry (you can send one email with your Goodreads review and another with your Kindle review for two entries per book) and two winners will be chosen at the beginning of each month!

ACKNOWLEDGMENTS

There's something to be said about having good fucking people in your corner, and while I like to think I'm the kind of person who makes sure everyone now I love and appreciate knows it, I've grown to absolutely love writing acknowledgments in my books. (Though I fully always panic that I forgot people and I know I totally do every time: if I do, please just know it's the ADHD and not that I don't love you.)

This book was not easy, not by a long shot. It made me cry more time than I'd like to admit, and I truly believe it helped me grown as an author and as a person. Dramatic? Maybe. Real? Absolutely.

But I know without a shadow of a doubt I would not have made it here without my people, the people who have held my hand and brought me water and made sure I paced myself and urged me to take care of myself in order to help me cross the finish line and I want all of *you* to know who they are and just how fucking amazing they are.

First and foremost, as always, thank you Alex. Thank you for bringing me lunch and taking care of the kids and letting me just cry when I really needed to. Thank you for always believing in me, especially when I simply can't believe in myself. Thank you for being my Theo, for bringing me snacks and making sure I never have a single thing to worry about except for what I want to focus on. I could never in a million years do any of this without you, despite what you think.

Next, Ryan, Owen, and Ella. You'll never see this, (and if you do, please pretend you haven't, truly, it's for the best) but I hope you know how freaking lucky I am to be your mom, how everything I do is for you guys, and how I can't wait to see what kind of people you grow up to be.

Madi, who designs my covers and my swag and has truly becoming one of my emotional support humans: I love you so fucking much. Sometimes people fall into your life that you feel like were always supposed to be there, and for me, that is absolutely you. Thank you for listening to me vent and helping me figure out what a story I missing and for sitting on calls and bullying me to write.

Regan, who, without, I truly know to my bones there would be no book. Thank you for making sure everything that needs to get done gets done for keeping me on track, and for giving me way more grace when I just *don't* do what I was supposed to. I'm so grateful I found you because I truly couldn't function without you. Oh, and thanks for letting me trauma dump to you all the time and letting me send you videos of Noah Kahan and his crazy eyes.

Ashleigh and Emily mostly for providing comedic relief and for making me laugh when I need it most of all. Ashleigh, you terrify me in the best way and thanks for always reading us bedtime stories, and Emily, I think you are so devilishly cunty.

Norma, for taking my disasters and editing them into something people can possibly, maybe read, and for taking my, 'hey I'm sending you 3/4 of this book, still writing the final 1/4 and I'm behind schedule' emails and just running with them.

Taj, who will send me 18510 texts and when I don't respond to any of them, never gets mad. Thank you for holding my hand through all of the stuff much to scary and intimidating for me, for accepting and understanding that I fall off the face of the earth sometimes, and for being the best agent and friend ever.

Isabella, thank you for being willing to work with me, to tell me more about our life and your childhood and how we could incorporate it into Kat's story. Thank you for being so amazing and understanding, even when I'm a total moron.

Sylvia, thank you for your kindness and graciousness and willingness to talk to me and guide me in the right direction for working towards writing with more sensitivity.

To my amazing sensitivity readers, Kimberly and Karime, thank you so much for being willing to work with me and help me learn.

To Lo, who is always an amazing ear and an even more amazing friend, even when I miss all of her calls and all of her texts.

To my ARC readers, the people who are always chomping at the bit to get whatever I throw their way and help me welcome it into this world with sparkles and confetti cannons. I'm so grateful for all of you.

And finally, thank you to you, my sweet, sweet, dear reader. You who have been with me on this wild and crazy Season of Revenge journey, who have rooted for me and encouraged me to try new things and given me grace. Thank you for reading my work, for loving my work, and sharing my work. You've changed my life in ways I could never explain, and for that, I am forever grateful.

ALSO BY MORGAN ELIZABETH

The Springbrook Hills Series

The Distraction

The Protector

The Substitution

The Connection

The Playlist

Season of Revenge Series:

Tis the Season for Revenge

Cruel Summer

The Fall of Bradley Reed

Ick Factor

Big Nick Energy

The Ocean View Series

The Ex Files

Walking Red Flag

Bittersweet

The Mastermind Duet

Ivory Tower

Diamond Fortress